Political Thought in Canada

Contemporary Perspectives

COMPILED AND EDITED BY
STEPHEN BROOKS

IRWIN PUBLISHING
Toronto Canada

Canadian Cataloguing in Publication Data

Main entry under title:
Political thought in Canada : contemporary perspectives

ISBN 0-7725-1500-X

1. Political science - Canada-20th century - Addresses, essays, lectures. 2. Canada - Politics and government - 1963- Addresses, essays, lectures. I. Brooks, Stephen, 1956-

JC/253.P64 1984 320.971 C84-098789-7

1 2 3 4 5 6 89 88 87 86 85 84

Printed in Canada by Les Editions Marquis Ltée
Typeset/Alpha Graphics Ltd.

Published by
Irwin Publishing Inc.
4386 Sheppard Avenue East
Toronto Ontario
M1S 3B6

Contents

Contributors

JANET AJZENSTAT lectures in the Department of Political Science at McMaster University, and has written a Ph. D. thesis on liberalism and Lord Durham.

GREGORY BAUM is the author of numerous books, including *Catholics and Canadian Socialism* and *Ethics and Economics: Canada's Catholic Bishops on the Economic Crisis*. Baum teaches at St. Michael's College in Toronto.

THOMAS R. BERGER, formerly a justice in the Supreme Court of British Columbia, now teaches in the Faculty of Law at the University of British Columbia. His published work includes *Fragile Freedoms*.

STEPHEN BROOKS lectures in the Department of Political Science at Carleton University, and is the author of articles on Canadian politics and public administration.

BARRY COOPER teaches in the Department of Political Science at the University of Calgary. His writings include work on the political thought of George Grant.

ALAIN G. GAGNON is the author of numerous books and articles on politics in Quebec, and has recently edited a reader in Quebec politics entitled *Quebec: State and Society*. He lectures in the Department of Political Science at Carleton University.

RAINER KNOPFF teaches in the Department of Political Science at the University of Calgary. He has written a number of articles on liberal democracy in Canada.

DENIS MONIÈRE is the author of *Ideologies in Quebec: The Historical Development*. He teaches in the Department of Political Science at the University of Montreal.

RALPH NELSON teaches in the Department of Political Science at the University of Windsor. He is a co-author of *Canadian Confederation: A Decision-Making Analysis*, and *Introduction to Canadian Politics and Government*.

NORMAN PENNER is the author of *The Canadian Left: A Critical Analysis*. He teaches in the Department of Political Science at Glendon College.

JENNIFER SMITH teaches in the Department of Political Science at Dalhousie University. She is a foremost student of the Confederation period.

Preface

This collection of original essays offers contemporary perspectives on important aspects of political thought in Canada. The examination of political thought is approached from several angles, including the relationship between religion and politics, democratic theory, French-Canadian nationalism, the role of intellectuals as definers of and participants in the ideological discourse of society, and the reconsideration of historical evidence in understanding current controversies. In putting together *Political Thought in Canada* our intention has been to produce a book which is suitable both as a supplemental text for survey courses in Canadian politics and history, and as a main reader for more specialized courses on the political traditions of French and English Canada.

Obviously, not all of the interests of students of Canadian political thought can be covered in a collection of moderate size. One is compelled to choose. In justifying the selection of topics and the organization of this volume I maintain simply that the issues addressed are prominent in the study of political thought in Canada. Other choices were possible, and much remains to be done in exploring our binational political tradition.

A number of debts were incurred in the development of this book, and it is with pleasure that I acknowledge them. First, I should like to thank Kenneth D. McRae, a foremost student of Canadian political thought, whose teaching stimulated my own interest in this field. The editorial assistance of Norma Pettit and the early involvement of Gladys Neale, both of Irwin Publishing, are greatly appreciated. For financial support which made this book possible, I should like to thank the Social Sciences and Humanities Research Council.

Finally, I would like to thank Christine Brooks for her patience and active participation in this project.

Stephen Brooks
Ottawa, April 1984

Political Thought in Canada

Introduction

STEPHEN BROOKS

The study of political thought in Canada appears handicapped by the traditional reticence of Canadian politicians in matters that transcend the prosaic accommodation of competing interests. Consideration of the "grand issues" of politics is uncommon, or at any rate seldom is carried on at a level that makes explicit the ideological presuppositions which underlie various positions. The extension of state enterprise in Canada illustrates this point. Government participation in the economy through direct production and investment activity has occasioned only the most superficial debate about the proper role of the state. Both advocates and critics are likely to argue the matter in terms of jurisdictional rights, regional and group interests, and efficiency considerations. In the end the extension of state enterprise is frequently ascribed to Canadian "pragmatism"; less an explanation than the start of a more profound inquiry.

Various theories have been advanced to explain the *apparent* ideological consensus which characterizes Canadian politics. One such explanation is the fragment theory, as developed by Louis Hartz and applied to Canada by, most notably, Kenneth McRae and Gad Horowitz.[1] Briefly, the fragment theory argues that ideologies develop as a result of their competitive interaction. Where this dialectic is absent (or, at any rate, profoundly attenuated), as, presumably, in the case of New World societies founded by European emigrants who represent only a part of the ideological spectrum left behind in the Old World, the subsequent development of political thought occurs within the confines of the original value system. The isolation of a part of the ideological spectrum from the rivals it faced in the Old World has, according to Hartz, traditionalizing consequences.

> For when a part of a European nation is detached from the whole of it, and hurled outward onto new soil, it loses the stimulus toward change that the whole provides. It lapses into a kind of immobility.[2]

While considerably more complex than this summary would suggest, at bottom the fragment theory is distinguished by two main arguments: i) ideologies evolve as a result of their interaction; and ii) the development of political thought in fragment societies like English or French Canada is determined at the origin, viz. by the political values of the New World society's founders. Canada is considered to be a two-fragment polity, comprising an English Canadian society of predominantly liberal origins (though the significance of "imperfections", that is, non-liberal elements in the early value system of British North America has been a source of considerable disagreement), and a French-Canadian society inspired by the feudal values of pre-Revolution France. This latter characterization seems especially problematic, and it is one of the major failings of the Hartzian approach that it does not provide an adequate understanding of the "Quiet Revolution" and politics in contemporary Quebec.

Whereas the Hartzian fragment theory assigns primacy of place to the independent working of ideas in the development of a nation's political tradition, what might loosely be described as the political economy approach starts from such structural factors as commercial and communications networks, and class configurations, in explaining the development of political ideas in French and English Canada. This paradigm embraces metropolitanism, with its implication of cultural dependency of the hinterland upon the metropolis, Beardsian explanations of political thought as interest justification, and neo-Marxist understandings of political values as products of class experience. The rationale for grouping these different approaches under a single class of explanation has to do with two features they share: i) political ideas are considered to be dependent upon structural conditions, though the structures identified as deterministic may range from patterns of commerce and communication to the system of production and consequent class formation of the society; and ii) the ability of one party, whether the metropolis, the ruling elite, or the dominant class, to impose its system of political values upon the broader society is assumed. On this latter point, consensual politics (understood here as non-class politics) may be produced by the success of some dominant segment of the society in getting its own ideology accepted as the conventional wisdom.

Both Hartzian approaches (and I would include within this category the valuable revision of David Bell[3]) and political economy understandings are able to explain the phenomenon of consensus politics. Indeed the Hartzian fragment theory, like the nation/non-nation model of Bell and the formative events theory of S.M. Lipset,[4] is *primarily* an explanation for the remarkable attenuation in the New World of those ideological divisions which are common in Europe. The advocates of the Hartzian approach argue that value consensus is genuine, and a product of formative influences at the nation's founding. However, for those writing in the political economy tradition the consensus is only apparent. Below this level lie structural contradictions which, eventually, must find resolution through a politics of conflict.

The theme of consensus versus conflict, the organizing principle of this brief survey, is at the centre of disagreements between competing paradigms for understanding political thought in Canada. On balance, those interpretations which attach primary significance to such factors as the "cultural baggage" brought to Canada by immigrants (whether the founding population or subsequent waves of immigration), or formative experiences (especially the Loyalist experience in the English Canadian political tradition and the Conquest in the case of French Canada) subscribe to a consensual view of Canadian political thought. Of course it is possible to start from these considerations and arrive at non-consensual conclusions about the political traditions of French and English Canada. In the case of English Canada this may be accomplished through an understanding of Loyalism as ideological conservatism. This does not require a denial of the predominance of liberalism, but rather that conservatism be acknowledged as a legitimate and significant part of the English-Canadian political tradition. This is essentially the thesis advanced by Christian and Campbell in their attempt to argue that the three major national political parties, the Liberals, the Conservatives, and the CCF-NDP, have, historically, been the carriers of liberalism, conservatism, and socialism, respectively, in Canadian politics.[5]

Similarly, one can acknowledge the critical importance of the Conquest for the subsequent development of the French Canadian political tradition, while not accepting a consensual interpretation of that tradition. If the Conquest is understood to have resulted in socio-economic decapitation, removing from *Nouvelle France* that commercial class which in the normal course of events would have dominated the economic and political life of the nation, the dominant role the Roman Catholic Church came to occupy in French Canada does not then appear a natural consequence of features of French-Canadian society which pre-date the Conquest (an interpretation which Michel Brunet has labelled the "romantic school"[6]). Instead, the strength of non-liberal values well into the twentieth century is understood as a product of arrested modernization. With increasing industrialization and consequent changes in class formation, structural conflicts within this society could no longer be contained. These burst into the open with the Quiet Revolution, though the stressful discontinuity between the "official" ideology of conservatism and the modern features of Quebec's socio-economic system was evident much earlier.[7]

The question of whether consensus or conflict is more apt as an ordering principle in the study of political thought in French and English Canada depends in part upon the scope of the analysis. Hartzian fragment theory is a comparative approach which enables one to understand the political tradition of a New World society in terms of the Old World from which it arose. Viewed against the backdrop of European ideological discourse, the history of political ideas in the United States, French Canada, or English Canada is certainly less broad. Consequently, value consensus emerges as the distinguishing feature of these New World political traditions, though the caveat "compared to..." must accompany this assessment. Cross-national surveys of party competition and class-based political behaviour generally remark upon the comparatively low level of ideological conflict in the Canadian polity.[8]

However, when the analytical lens is narrowed to encompass only Canada, ideological division (with ideology understood as the consciousness produced by social conditions, necessarily partial, and expressed as a justificatory system of values) is more readily apparent, though students of Canadian politics may be more accustomed to understanding this conflict in terms of regionalism or ethnolinguistic cleavage. C.B. Macpherson's *Democracy in Alberta* (1953) remains the classic work on the conjunction of class, regionalism and the ideology of protest in Canada. Unlike S.M. Lipset who, in *Agrarian Socialism* (1968), develops an explanation for the rise to power of the Cooperative Commonwealth Federation (CCF) in Saskatchewan which rests upon the combination of ethnographic and religious features of the population with the exigencies of Saskatchewan's peculiarly dependent one-crop economy, Macpherson is uncompromising in arguing the critical significance of class, emphasizing the "relatively homogeneous class composition" of Alberta and its "quasi-colonial" relationship to eastern Canada. Indeed the subject of agrarian protest in English Canada, as also in the United States, has proven fertile ground in the treatment of ideological conflict within the English-Canadian political tradition.

Lipset's *Agrarian Socialism* represented the first major contribution by this American sociologist to the ongoing debate on the nature and causes of differences between the American and English-Canadian political tradition. This pan-American comparative approach informs, either explicitly or implicitly, much of both the academic and the popular literature on the political values of English Canada.[9] The significance of the Loyalist migration and, more generally, the theme of revolution versus counterrevolution are central to this approach. The academic literature in this genre is ably summarized by Lipset in his article, "Radicalism in North America"[10]: an article that is remarkable for the author's abandonment of the premise that the political value systems of the two societies differ in important ways. Instead, Lipset concludes that institutional factors, particularly in respect of constitutional differences and electoral systems, are most crucial to an understanding of the apparently greater success of social democratic parties in Canada as compared to the United States.

The primacy of institutions as determinants of the political traditions of French and English Canada represents an approach which is both promising and problematic. Consider first the argued effect of federal structures in terms of orienting political discourse around non-class issues, a structural bias described by Porter in *The Vertical Mosaic* (1965). The disadvantageous impact of the national electoral system on class-based political parties represents a second widely acknowledged example of institutions operating as dampers on ideological debate. Why is the left (understood as the view that class inequality should be the most salient basis for political division and that, therefore, politics should be polarized around the issue of class conflict) so weak in Canada? The impact of the national electoral system alone is an inadequate explanation, as the case of the United Kingdom makes clear. But when the effect of federalized structures for conflict resolution and, perhaps more important, for the very recognition of what constitutes a politically relevant conflict is added to the bias of the electoral system, a more persuasive thesis emerges in explanation of the comparatively low level of ideological polarization characteristic of Canadian politics. And when the bias of these institutions is supplemented by their conscious manipulation by political elites with a vested interest in the suppression of the class cleavage, the argument becomes more convincing. Jenson and Brodie's recent book, *Crisis, Challenge and Change: Party and Class in Canada* (1981), represents the best effort to date in support of this thesis. Their challenge to the conventional wisdom on the allegedly functional operation of brokerage party politics extends the critique advanced by Gad Horowitz in his article entitled, "Toward the Democratic Class Struggle" (1966). Horowitz wrote:

> No one can convince me that the ordinary Manitoban feels his antipathy toward the Quebecois more deeply than he feels economically and socially disadvantaged by his non-elite status. He is class-conscious, all right, and powerfully so; but he has to live with a political system which makes his ethnic identifications directly relevant to politics and his class identifications irrelevant to politics.[11]

Institutions are not neutral containers: they act to structure political life along particular lines. The self-evident nature of this proposition is indisputable, but its implications for the quality of political discourse in Canada are not always appreciated. For example, proposals for Senate reform in Canada have at stake the inter-governmental or inter-regional balance of power and therefore do not address the more fundamental question of what shall be the basis for political division in Canada. These proposals are presumptuous in failing to consider the possibility that a cleavage other than region or perhaps ethnolinguistic community ought to structure public policy-making. On the other hand, proposals for thoroughgoing reform of the national electoral system, along the lines of some system of proportional representation, are more likely to involve a fundamental criticism of the way in which the current order structures political discourse in election campaigns. The advocates of proportional representation prefer to see elections fought around issues which cut across regional and ethnolinguistic lines, a condition which would favour the class polarization of Canadian politics. No doubt this is one reason for the greater popularity with Canada's political elites of proposals for Senate reform.

If consideration of the role of institutions in shaping the political tradition is insightful, its problematic side is also apparent. Presumably, political institutions have origins which can be identified with some degree of confidence. In the case of the United States, the tripartite system of checks and balances which came to be enshrined in the Constitution of 1787 was to some degree a product of the founders' familiarity with Montesquieu's ideas of countervailing power and their revulsion to any concentrated political authority after the pre-revolutionary experience. Institutions of government have antecedent sources. These may appear to be, simply, perceptions regarding the shortcomings of other institutions. And so, on one level, it is quite defensible to argue that Confederation was proposed as a way out of the deadlock of double majority in the legislature of the United Canadas. However, one must still address the question of why particular choices were made when other institutional arrangements were possible. Based upon their decision-making analysis of the Confederation Debates, White et al. remark upon "the almost complete absence of any recourse to more than elementary theory in developing a basic constitutional document". They conclude that the Canadian founders were operating within a broad ideological consensus on such matters as the basis of sovereignty, responsible government and the appropriate character of representative institutions.[12] In view of the ideologically unreflective quality of the founders' deliberations, in marked contrast to the fathers of the American republic, one is inclined to speculate upon the importance of major conflict and reaction in giving rise to articulate expressions of political thought. The gradualism of Canada's constitutional evolution has not provided occasion for profound reflection upon the fundamental political principles which undergird the polity.

However, the relationship between Canada's two great language communities has proven more productive in generating reflection on the relations between groups of citizens, and between these groups and the state. This is especially true in the case of French Canada. Evidence of this is found in the voluminous writings of French-Canadian nationalists. The historical concern of French Canada with its rights, *comme un peuple*, has not been matched by a similar preoccupation in English Canada. Given the numerical superiority of the English-speaking community since the mid-nineteenth century, English Canada's preference for majoritarian theories of democracy is not surprising. Historically, concessions to the group principle have been products of perceived political expediency rather than intellectual conviction.

The purpose of this survey of selected themes and approaches has been to convey an impression of the unsettled theoretical backdrop against which the essays in this volume appear. Clearly, there is no conventional paradigm for the study of political thought in Canada, nor even agreement regarding the proper subject of such an inquiry. The subsequent chapters in this collection do not represent an attempt to defend any particular position. Eclectic in subject and approach, they should be read for the *aperçus* they provide into the political traditions of French and English Canada.

Religion and Politics

In his essay entitled, "Religious Freedom and Party Government: The Galt-White Debate of 1876," Rainer Knopff addresses the nineteenth-century controversy between liberalism and theocracy. While his immediate subject is the 1876 debate between Alexander Galt and Thomas White over the appropriate response to ultramontane proposals of a "Catholic Party" in Quebec, Knopff prefaces the debate with a discussion of the longstanding conflict between liberals and ultramontanes regarding the separation of church and state. The debate itself, carried out in speeches and a number of pamphlets, brought into sharp focus the conflict between the liberal view that the polity ought to be a religiously neutral sphere and the Church's argument that the liberals violated their own principle of separate spheres when they presumed to determine what was the proper realm of theology and what lay outside. The denial of a religiously neutral sphere where the population could divide on nonsectarian issues constituted, in Galt's view, a threat to the civil liberties of all citizens. This position was squarely within the Lockian tradition regarding toleration, viz. a tolerant regime cannot tolerate the intolerant. At the same time, the defenders of the ultramontane position were correct in their argument that the liberal doctrine of separation between church and state effectively involved the subordination of the former to the latter.

With the decline in the political significance of religious affiliation during this last century, the likelihood of a confessional issue becoming an important basis for political division must strike contemporary Canadians as remote. Unaccustomed to the churches playing an active role in the politics of the nation, the forthright views expressed in the January/1983 statement of the Canadian bishops, "Ethical Reflections on the Economic Crisis," came as a surprise to most Canadians and occasioned controversy on both the substance of the bishops' critique and the appropriateness of such an intervention. But as Gregory Baum observes in his essay, this fundamental critique of the economic policies of Canadian governments, a critique inaccurately labelled "Marxist" by some politicians and economists, was predictable from the leftward position toward which the Catholic Church has been evolving over time.

In "Beginnings of a Canadian Catholic Social Theory" Baum examines a number of pastoral documents produced by the Canadian bishops over the last decade, in support of his argument that the Roman Catholic Church has developed a socio-political critique which is substantially similar to that advanced by members of the New Political Economy in Canada. Far from the corporatism that once distinguished Catholic social theory, the Church's currently evolving position is informed by a conflictual image of society and a recognition that social structures may be the agents of oppression. Baum observes that the bishops' New Year's message was intended to provoke consideration of alternative futures, and thereby create an awareness of the extent to which conventional policy prescriptions are trapped within parameters defined by the interests of the dominant groups in society. The development of a church which is socially and politically *engagé* is not limited to the Roman Catholic Church in Canada. There has been ecumenical cooperation among several of the churches on questions of social justice, both in Canada and globally.

Democratic Values

As one of Canada's most articulate spokesmen for liberal-democratic values, Thomas R. Berger, formerly of the Supreme Court of British Columbia, addresses questions raised by Janet

Ajzenstat and Jennifer Smith in two subsequent essays. It is Berger's view that the Charter of Rights and Freedoms and the Rights of the Aboriginal Peoples of Canada sections of the *Constitution Act*, 1982, testify to the "distinctive" Canadian contribution to the theory and practice of liberal democracy. He considers the recognition of group rights (language and aboriginal) a tolerant approach which distinguishes Canada from the more deliberate assimilation/integration policy followed in the great liberal democracy to the south of us. Moreover, he suggests that the Canadian approach to human rights and freedoms represents a model more likely to be emulated by other nations than that of the United States.

Like Smith, Berger traces the relationship between political values and the institutions which give them expression. At the same time, his position in support of the constitutional entrenchment of group rights anticipates an issue raised by Ajzenstat, viz. the problematic accommodation of the principle of nationalities in a liberal democracy which values the principles of universalism and achievement. Berger's optimistic suggestion that Canada may be a proving ground, at the forefront of world developments in the treatment of human rights and freedoms, resembles Pierre Trudeau's vision of Canadian liberal democracy. The combination of an American-style charter of individual rights and liberties with constitutional recognition of certain group rights is fundamental to this view. But as Ajzenstat will observe, it remains an open question whether the latter will not result in serious vitiation of the former.

While liberal-democratic values predominate in Canadian society, they have been challenged in the twentieth century by the advocates of social democracy. Social democracy is about equality in treatment and equality of conditions. It is distinguished from liberal democracy by its identification with disadvantaged and exploited groups in society, and while it calls for radical reform it accepts the ground rules of parliamentarianism and competes for popular support on the same basis as ideologies of the privileged. In his essay entitled, "The Development of Social Democracy in Canada," Norman Penner identifies the CCF-NDP as the primary carrier of social-democratic values in

Canada, but he acknowledges the role of liberal reformism in undermining the popular support that this social-democratic party might otherwise have achieved.

The ideas of J.S. Woodsworth, a founder of the CCF and for decades the principal socialist spokesman in Canada, figure prominently in Penner's analysis. The moral fervour of Woodsworth is expressed in the final paragraph of the CCF's founding document, the *Regina Manifesto*:

> No CCF Government will rest content until it has eradicated capitalism and put into operation the full programme of socialized planning which will lead to the establishment in Canada of the Co-operative Commonwealth.

In fact, Penner traces the contemporary divisions in the NDP back to this early period, and to Woodsworth's failure to understand the national question in Quebec and his highly centralist prescriptions for Canadian federalism.

The transition from the uncompromising socialism of the *Regina Manifesto* (1933) to the muted reformism of the *Winnipeg Declaration* (1956) reflected the CCF's recognition of the apparent futility of a straightforward class appeal, and a shift in party orientation from its western farmer/eastern intellectual origins to closer ties with organized labour. But despite this shift, and notwithstanding several provincial successes, social democracy as represented by the CCF-NDP has never seriously threatened the dominance of liberal-democratic values. Penner follows David Lewis in arguing that this failure can be ascribed to three factors: i) liberal reformism, especially as practised by the Liberal governments of Mackenzie King; ii) opposition to the CCF from the Communist Party, notwithstanding the broad similarity in their concrete legislative goals during the 1930s and 1940s; and iii) the failure of the CCF-NDP to accommodate ideologically the national demands of Quebec.

As an analytical concept, the term democracy has declined in usefulness during this century. For this reason Ralph Nelson's essay, "Variations on the Democratic Theme," represents an important contribution to the clarification of the issues involved in the Canadian context. Nelson describes the development of democratic thought in English Canada since the Second World War, identifying the internal and external factors that have contributed to this development. Democracy as a system for arriving at legitimate and authoritative decisions versus democracy as comprising certain ends; democracy as a political system versus democracy as a social system; pluralist, Marxist, and consociational variants: these are the major considerations which order Nelson's survey of developments in democratic theory in English Canada over the past several decades.

In his choice of scholarly writings as the evidential basis for his analysis, Nelson alerts one to the significance of intellectuals as both barometers and participants in the development of political thought. This is done in an even more direct way for French Canada, in Alain G. Gagnon's later examination of Quebec's social science intelligentsia during the period 1960-80. Nelson's decision involves an implicit acknowledgement of the impoverished state of reflective thought among English Canada's political practitioners; a state of affairs which, with certain notable exceptions, has gone unchanged since it was remarked upon by such European commentators as Goldwin Smith, André Siegfried, and J.A. Hobson.

French Canada

> ...the content of nationalist ideology has varied over time, but...there is a line of continuity which runs through these various forms of nationalism. Since the English Conquest, the Québécois have used different means and strategies in putting up fierce resistance to assimilation. They have carried on a relentless struggle to reconquer the political power that was lost with the military defeat of 1760. (DENIS MONIÈRE: editor's translation)

While clearly the fundamental constant in the political tradition of French Canada, the concept of nationalism has undergone important changes over the past two centuries, both in terms of its substance and its carriers. Denis Monière's provocative essay,

"Currents of Nationalism in Quebec," presents an interpretation of the historical development of this concept whereby nationalism is understood as the ideological product of underlying class relationships. Indeed, Monière's identification of the major phases and causes in the development of Quebec nationalism is broadly similar to that of Marcel Rioux.[13] Monière rejects unequivocally interpretations of nationalism which stress deep-seated cultural traits of the French-Canadian population. Part of the value of his own understanding lies in the emphasis Monière places upon the relationship between English and French Canada in the determination of the content of nationalism in Quebec.

Monière's analysis of historical currents of nationalism in Quebec is complemented by Alain Gagnon's contemporary focus (1960-80). In the first section of his study Gagnon examines the class position and functional role of Quebec's social science intellectuals. In his own words, "Thus, we will inquire into the social significance of intellectual practice". The second part of his analysis describes specific instances of *engagement* (social involvement) by Quebec intellectuals, through such forums as trade unions, technocratic planning via *animation sociale*, the journal *Parti Pris*, and the *Centre de formation populaire*. At the same time as he discusses the practical and theoretical significance of participation by Quebec's social science intellectuals, Gagnon performs the valuable service of acquainting the English reader with the literature on this subject produced by Quebec intellectuals.

Gagnon observes that the *engagement* of Quebec social scientists during the contemporary period continues a tradition whereby the educated elite, whether journalists, politicians, ecclesiastics, or academics, has always played an active role in the definition of Quebec society and in the conduct of its politics. In this sense he is developing a theme which Nelson introduced, viz. the significance of intellectuals as both barometers and participants in the evolution of political thought. However, the case of Quebec is differentiated from that of English Canada by the *engagement* dimension. With few exceptions, and the League for Social Reconstruction is certainly the major one, the social involvement of English-Canadian intellectuals has been much less significant than that of their French-Canadian counterparts, in terms of both practical and theoretical consequences.

The changing circumstances of Quebec's social science intellectual class are described by Gagnon as having passed through three stages: a period of institutionalization and maturation in the social sciences prior to the Quiet Revolution (1960); followed by a period of consolidation and increasing significance (valorization in Gagnon's terms) during the state expansion of the 1960s; and finally a period of crisis in which adverse economic conditions and a particularly acute fiscal crisis of the state have contributed to a decline in the influence of the social science intellectuals. Agents of modernization and ideological change, this group has been unable to translate its success at the ideological level into a dominant social position.

Historical Evidence and Contemporary Insights

While all of the essays in this volume use historical evidence in support of their arguments, the three selections in this final section are notable for their use of the historical record to refute conventionally held views. Barry Cooper draws upon a wide variety of literary and historical material in arguing that political thought in western Canada is mistakenly viewed through concepts developed out of the experience of the East. In her reconsideration of Lord Durham, Janet Ajzenstat sets out to do two things: i) to take issue with the prevailing interpretation of Lord Durham's proposals for assimilation of the French Canadians, an interpretation which reflects poorly on either Durham's political astuteness or cultural tolerance (or both); and ii) to demonstrate the contemporary relevance of Durham's liberalism. Finally, Jennifer Smith's essay on federalism and Confederation suggests that current proposals for reform of such regionally representative national institutions as the Senate should be judged in terms of their implications for basic principles of Canadian government. An awareness of these implications, which Smith finds in the Confederation Debates, is, she suggests, often missing from contemporary proposals for more effective representation of Canada's regions in our national institutions of government.

Cooper's analysis of political consciousness in western Canada demonstrates how the study of what is conventionally conceived of as regional political culture can be executed as an inquiry into a distinct stream of Canadian political thought. He argues that the myths and symbols central to an understanding of political thought in what was once Upper Canada (Loyalism, exile, and so on) are inappropriate for an understanding of the Canadian West. As his review of the West's literary tradition seeks to demonstrate, their application reflects a sort of cultural imperialism. Similarly, Cooper follows W.L. Morton in arguing that eastern Canadian historiography imposes alien interpretations upon the history of the West. He concurs in Morton's view that, "The difference between prairie and other Canadian politics is the result of an initial bias, which, by cumulative historical process...has resulted in traditions and attitudes even more distinctive than the original bias". Because the political realm has been appropriated by eastern Canadian concerns and symbols, the concept of western alienation is seen to be more profound than a disaffection with Liberal government policies. Cooper suggests that it is properly understood as a "political phenomenon whose basis can be found in the initial bias that Morton detected, political subordination", and therefore is at the heart of what is distinctive in western Canada's political consciousness.

The conflict between liberalism and nationalism is central to Janet Ajzenstat's reconsideration of Lord Durham's famous *Report*. Ajzenstat contends that the notorious proposal for assimilation of the French-Canadian population is not evidence of an illiberal streak in Durham's thinking, but the very proof of his uncompromising commitment to the liberal principles of universality and achievement, as against particularism and ascription of any sort. Consequently, there is no discontinuity between the Durham who proposes assimilation and the Durham who advocates responsible government. Ajzenstat argues that the inability of English-Canadian historians to perceive this is due to their failure to address the *Report in toto*, and place it in the context of the liberal tradition of which Durham was both a product and an illustrious spokesman. Durham's liberalism, descended from Hobbes and Locke, runs afoul of the contemporary pluralist variant which considers indifference to national groups tantamount to illiberal intolerance. But as Ajzenstat writes: "Discrimination on the basis of race, origin, colour or creed—to use the famous liberal formulation—was regarded as the very definition of intolerance and injustice.... To identify the individual in law with the community of his birth was formerly thought reprehensible and may now seem commendable". The relevance of this insight for contemporary public policy in Canada is clear.

Like Ajzenstat, Jennifer Smith turns to a particularly prominent documentary source in the history of British North America, in this case the Confederation Debates. Smith examines the relationship between political thought and the institutions of government, focusing upon the contrast between *intrastate* federalism (where conflicts between regions are resolved within the institutions of the national government) and *interstate* federalism (represented by the current system of federal/provincial relations, with territorial interests poorly accommodated by the national parliamentary system). She writes: "(The) debate on interstate versus intrastate federalism is in part a debate on parliamentary versus republican government". The Fathers of Confederation were aware of this dimension of the federalism question, but Smith suggests that contemporary advocates of intrastate federalism (particularly those who propose a reformed Senate) often fail to consider the consequences of change for other principles of Canadian government. She argues that while congressionalist reform of Canada's Parliament would provide for instrastate federalism and, therefore, accommodation of regional interests at the centre, it also has consequences for the balance of political power within the state apparatus at the national level. Certainly the principle of unity of action, basic to a British parliamentary system of government, would be imperilled by congressionalist reform. Smith is critical of reform proposals which leave unexamined the political thought presuppositions that underpin new institutional arrangements.

NOTES

[1] See Louis Hartz' theoretical introduction (Chapters 1 and 2) in *The Founding of New Societies* (New York, Harcourt Brace & World, 1964), and Chapter 7 by Kenneth McRae, "The Structure of Canadian History," in the same book; Gad Horowitz's two essays, "Conservatism, Liberalism, and Socialism in Canada: an Interpretation," *Canadian Journal of Economics and Political Science* (1966), and, "Notes on 'Conservatism, Liberalism and Socialism'," *Canadian Journal of Political Science* (1978); and S.F. Wise, "Liberal Consensus or Ideological Battleground: Some Reflections on the Hartz Thesis," *Historical Papers* (Canadian Historical Association, 1974).

[2] Hartz, *The Founding of New Societies*, p. 3.

[3] See David Bell, "The Loyalist Tradition in Canada," *Journal of Canadian Studies* (1970); and David Bell and Lorne Tepperman, *The Roots of Disunity* (Toronto, McClelland and Stewart, 1979).

[4] The best statements of the formative events theory are contained in Lipset's books, *The First New Nation* (New York, Basic Books, 1963), and *Revolution and Counterrevolution* (New York, Anchor Books, 1970).

[5] W. Christian and C. Campbell, *Political Parties and Ideologies in Canada*, 2nd edition (Toronto, McGraw-Hill Ryerson, 1982).

[6] Michel Brunet, "The British Conquest: Canadian Social Scientists and the Fate of the *Canadiens,*" *Canadian Historical Review* (1959).

[7] See Pierre Elliott Trudeau, "Quebec on the Eve of the Asbestos Strike," in Ramsay Cook (ed.), *French Canadian Nationalism* (Toronto, Macmillan, 1969).

[8] The classic work in this genre is Robert Alford, *Party and Society* (Chicago, Rand McNally, 1963).

[9] On the popular side, see Pierre Berton's recent book entitled, *Why We Act Like Canadians* (Toronto, McClelland and Stewart, 1982).

[10] Lipset, "Radicalism in North America," *Transactions of the Royal Society of Canada* (1976).

[11] Horowitz, "Toward the Democratic Class Struggle," In R. Schultz et al., *The Canadian Political Process*, 3rd edition (Toronto, Holt, Rinehart and Winston, 1979), p. 223.

[12] W.L. White et al., *Canadian Confederation: A Decision-Making Analysis* (Ottawa, Carleton University, 1979).

[13] See Marcel Rioux, "The Development of Ideologies in Quebec," translated from the French by Gerald Gold in *Communities and Culture in French Canada* (Toronto, Holt, Rinehart and Winston, 1973).

Religion and Politics

Religious Freedom and Party Government: The Galt-White Debate of 1876

RAINER KNOPFF

Party government as we know it in the West involves the historically novel willingness of political factions to admit their partisanship, even when in power, and to endure voluntarily, if painfully, the rule of opposing parties.[1] This is not possible when party division concerns the question of how best to achieve human perfection. This question gives rise to what Tocqueville called "Great Parties", which claim to possess objective truth about the highest things, and which thus deny both partiality (or partisanship) and the legitimacy of political opposition.[2] The peaceful and voluntary (though never quiet) alternation in office of avowed "partisans", which characterizes our own time, requires the limitation of public debate to the lower level questions of how best to secure individual rights and liberties, and a determination to banish the higher questions to the private sphere.[3] In brief, liberalism, particularly the liberal principle of religious freedom, is the precondition of our form of party government. It is not surprising, therefore, that in Canada, as elsewhere, the struggle to establish party government involved the dispute—itself a dispute of Great Party proportions—between the forces of liberalism and theocracy. This essay analyzes an episode in this controversy: the 1876 debate between Alexander Galt and Thomas White about the proper response to the ultramontane-inspired "Catholic Party" in Quebec.

I

The Galt-White debate took place in the context of an escalating battle between liberalism and Catholic ultramontanism. This battle dated back to the early years of the nineteenth century, when the growth in Quebec of a French-Canadian lay elite came to challenge the traditional power and influence of the Church.[4] Prior to 1791, the Quebec Act had created a coalition of interests between the colonial government, the seigneurs, and the clergy, in which the latter group played a pivotal role.[5] By providing a representative assembly, however, the Constitution of 1791 enabled the newly emerging *petite bourgeoisie* to contend for political influence.[6] Effectively excluded from the commercial pursuits dominated by the English merchants, this group turned to the professions, which it practised among the landed peasantry from whom it was drawn.[7] Given their natural influence with the peasantry, whose political importance was ensured by the fact of near universal suffrage, these professionals found a convenient outlet for their talents and frustrations in the assembly when depression threatened their financial security.[8] There they were able to secure the power and influence they coveted, and there they fought a "nationalist" battle, on behalf of the agrarian classes to which they were so closely tied, against their lay rivals: the capitalist (and English) section of the bourgeoisie.[9] The latter, having fought so long for the "rights of British subjects", including a representative assembly, were ironically compelled to retreat to the "irresponsible" executive to defend themselves. In constitutional terms, the struggle thus took on the colour of a battle for and against the democratic principle of responsible government.

The political power of this lay elite was no less alarming to the Church than it was to the English merchants, for despite its rejection of bourgeois commercialism it manifested the traditional bourgeois anti-clericalism.[10] Indeed, the doctrine of popular sovereignty, which the French middle class appropriated for its democratic constitutional struggle, was itself seen to be heretical from the theocratic view that all power comes from God. The propagation of popular sovereignty was therefore a decisive symptom of anti-clericalism in the eyes of the ultramontane clergy.[11]

Needless to say, when this democratic struggle culminated in 1837 with the defeat of the Patriotes, as they had come to be known, the Church took full advantage of the opportunity to reassert its authority. This it did by using the uncertainty created by the rebellion to secure the good graces of both the colonial authority and the people. To the former it attempted to demonstrate the necessity of an independent Church as a moderating influence on the people, and hence as the chief bulwark against further unrest. For the latter it sought to fill the gap left by a lay leadership that was disorganized, to some extent in exile, and suffering the natural popular disrepute that comes with failure. Faced with the success of the Church's strategy, and the fact that its own struggle against the English merchants was doomed in the context of the political union of the two Canadas that followed in 1841, the French *petite bourgeoisie* could continue to exercise some measure of influence within its society only in alliance with the Church. Under the leadership of Lafontaine, the majority of this class abandoned its radicalism to strike just such an alliance.

A minority refused to accept this strategy, however, and continued to uphold the radicalism of the pre-1837 period; indeed, under the pressure of events (especially after 1848) it became even more radical, particularly in its anti-clericalism. This group of liberals became known as the Rouges, and by comparison their erstwhile reformist colleagues became the Bleus. The latter, in conjunction with the Tories and moderate reformers of Upper Canada, soon formed the Liberal-Conservative party, thereafter to become simply the Conservative party.[12] Alexander Galt, one of the protagonists in our debate, eventually became a leading figure in this party and one of the chief architects of Confederation. During the early 1850's, however, his closest political associations were with the Rouges, largely because of his agreement with them on the religious question.[13]

The essence of the Rouge-ultramontane controversy was already evident in the clerical reaction to the doctrine of popular sovereignty propagated by the Patriotes, and manifested dramatically in the rebellion. This reaction was most clearly set out in Bishop Lartigue's famous *mandement* of 1837, and consisted of the claim that popular sovereignty was a heresy. Reformers such as Papineau refused to accept this as a proper theological assessment. They insisted that in pronouncing on the doctrine of popular sovereignty the clergy had left the realm of theology and had trespassed on the independent political realm. Insofar as this criticism implied a separation of church and state, it simply confirmed the clergy in its suspicion of heresy.[14] After all, how could a layman presume to decide the theological question of the extent and boundary of religion? To the hierarchy, then, it was the liberals, not the Church, who were overstepping their proper sphere.

This reciprocal accusation of confounding politics and religion was to become a hallmark of the controversy between Rouge and ultramontane, a controversy that began in earnest in about 1848, when the upheavals in Europe and the grant of responsible government at home once again placed the doctrine of popular sovereignty at centre stage.[15] This doctrine (or the "principle of nationalities" as it was often called) was then leading in Europe to the campaign to unify Italy, a project that involved the destruction of the Pope's temporal power. In both Europe and Quebec this attack on the Papal power brought into sharp relief the disagreement between liberals, who thought that political power flowed from the consent of the governed, and theocrats, who insisted that it came from God.[16] From the latter perspective, the Church, as the earthly representative of God, had the right to supervise state action in most circumstances, and the complete unification of the two spheres in the Papal states was merely the logical conclusion of such reasoning.[17] It was the basic premise of that reasoning that the liberals called into question.

In Quebec, the issue pitted the ultramontane clergy against the Rouges in the *Institut Canadien* who, through their paper, *L'Avenir*, were supporting the Italian insurgents. The fact that the liberal charge of illegitimate clerical interference in politics was now levelled at the Pope himself made the issue all the more serious in the eyes of the ultramontanes, and they wasted no time in coming to the Pope's defence. Once again, that defence consisted in attacking the liberal premise, namely the separation of church and state.

When the Rouges complained of clerical interference in the political domain, they were not thinking merely of abstract theoretical attacks on the doctrine of popular sovereignty. Those attacks implied the right of the church to intervene directly and actively in political life, and the clergy had not hesitated to undertake such intervention. Ever since the Rouges had entered electoral politics, the influence of the priest in his pulpit had been used against them.[18] This pulpit politics was further encouraged by the *Syllabus of Errors* of 1864, which, together with the *Declaration of Papal Infallibility* in 1870, constituted the battle cry of Pope Pius IX against the secular and revolutionary liberalism of Europe. The fact that the early Rouges had patterned themselves on European and American models ensured that Canada would have its own version of this struggle, and the Church braced herself firmly against the political aspirations of the liberals, arguing that heretical enemies of religion had no business manning the levers of power. It is true that by the early 1870s French-Canadian liberalism had openly abandoned its Rouge origins, and had tried to dissociate itself from European radicalism; moderation became the new watchword and secularism was disavowed. By this time, however, the damage had been done, and any party that dared to call itself Liberal was seen by the Church to be the old Rouge serpent in a new disguise, wilier and more dangerous than ever.[19]

In 1871, this electoral opposition to the Liberal party was formalized by a number of Catholic laymen—not, however, without the support of influential members of the hierarchy—in a document entitled the "Catholic Programme". Published in the leading ultramontane newspapers as a guide to Catholic voters in the upcoming elections, the "Programme" argued the close connection of politics and religion, and the consequent necessity of choosing candidates for their religious as well as their secular qualifications.[20]

Basing themselves on a recent pastoral of Bishop Laflèche, the authors of the "Programme" maintained that because a great many civil laws were unavoidably related to religion, the political representatives of a Catholic people had the duty of representing not only the temporal, but also the spiritual and religious interests of their constituents. The doctrine of the separation of church and state was therefore "an absurd and impious idea, especially in a constitutional regime that, attributing all power of legislation to parliament, puts in the hands of those who compose it a double-edged sword of terrible proportions".[21] Hence, it was necessary that the representatives of the Catholic population subscribe fully to the doctrines of the Church in religion, politics, and economics, and that this should be the primary criterion for choosing a candidate.

In the particular political circumstances of the time, the "Programme" contended, these principles led to the support of the Conservative party, which, besides being the best defender of social authority, was the only party that offered serious guarantees to religious interests. The authors hastened to add that they did not understand by the Conservative party a group bound together only by interest and ambition, but "a group of men sincerely professing the same principles of religion and nationality", namely, "an inviolable attachment to Catholic doctrine, and an absolute devotion to the national interests of Lower Canada".[22] Thus, although the Conservative party was generally speaking worthy of support, this support must always be subordinate to religious interests. In choosing a candidate, therefore, the Catholic voter should bear in mind the following rules:

> (1) If the contest is between two Conservatives, it goes without saying that we shall support the one who accepts the programme we have just outlined.
>
> (2) If on the contrary it is between a Conservative of any shade whatever and an adept of the Liberal school, our active sympathies will be given to the former.
>
> (3) If the only candidates who come forward in a constituency are both Liberals or oppositionists, we must choose the one who will accept our conditions.
>
> (4) Finally, in the event that the contest is between a Conservative who rejects our programme and an opportunist who accepts it, the position would be more delicate. To vote for the latter

> would be to imperil the Conservative Party, which we wish to see powerful. What decision should we make between these two dangers? In this case we would advise Catholic electors to refrain from voting.[23]

These rules constituted the blueprint for a Catholic party in Quebec; their effect was to intensify active electoral opposition to the Liberal party by ultramontanes, both lay and clerical.

II

It was against the background of these theocratic developments in Quebec that Galt and White engaged in their controversy in 1876. As one of the leading Fathers of Confederation, Galt had been responsible for securing the educational guarantees of Section 93 of the *British North America Act*, which allow the federal government to intervene to protect the rights of separate schools in the provinces. For Galt this had been primarily a matter of protecting the Protestant minority in Quebec, of which he was the chief spokesman.[24] In the same vein, he had sought to secure Protestant electoral influence by inserting into the Act provisions preventing the gerrymandering of certain constituencies in which English Protestants predominated. Alive, as ever, to the precarious position of the Protestant minority, Galt was concerned by the Church-sponsored campaign to alter the population balance of these entrenched constituencies, a tactic that threatened to destroy the protection these constituencies offered.[25] This, combined with the increasingly theocratic outlook of the hierarchy, posed the threat of a Church-dominated legislature trampling on Protestant rights. In such circumstances, Galt thought, the only remedy would be the federal veto. But, given the political climate, even this might prove to be ineffective. For "if...nothing be heard but adulatory paeans to the hierarchy, to obtain their political support and influence, how can we expect to receive attention when we appeal to a government at Ottawa, almost all of whose supporters from Quebec owe their seats to the clergy?"[26] It was against this background that Galt felt impelled to take up the pen against the alliance between his own party and the clergy. He was obviously not as certain as was John A. Macdonald that those intransigent ultramontanes, Pope Pius IX and Montreal's Bishop Bourget, would soon be replaced by younger and more moderate men.[27]

The immediate occasion for the first of Galt's two tracts—*Civil Liberty in Lower Canada*[28]—was the public controversy caused by a speech given by the Honourable Lucius Seth Huntington, in December 1875, during a by-election in Argenteuil, Quebec. Huntington, the postmaster-general in Alexander Mackenzie's Liberal government, was in the riding on behalf of the Liberal candidate, and was to give a speech outlining and defending government policy. Speaking first at the political meeting, however, was the Conservative candidate, Thomas White, a Protestant and a free mason, who used his allotted time to complain of the tactics being used against him; namely, that he was denounced as an anti-Catholic free mason in Catholic parts of the constituency, and a priest-ridden lackey of the hierarchy in the Protestant sectors.[29] In short, he deplored the appeal to religious, rather than to purely political divisions in the election.

Once the subject had been raised, Huntington felt constrained to say something about the religiously based opposition characteristically faced by his own party in Quebec, and, in addition to his prepared remarks, mounted an attack on the alliance, consecrated by the Catholic "Programme", between the ultramontanes and the Conservatives, particularly the Protestant Conservatives. Indeed, he went so far as to advocate a break in existing party alignments, suggesting an alliance of all Protestants with the Liberals, against the ultramontanes.

This speech gave rise to an extensive parliamentary debate questioning the political propriety, especially for a minister of the Crown, of attacking the Catholic Church and advocating a political alignment based primarily on religious divisions. Even Huntington's Liberal colleagues found it difficult to defend him, and the Conservatives to a man (including the staunchest Orangeman) berated him for attempting to sow the seeds of religious dissension among masons and ultramontanes who, having agreed to keep their religious differences out of politics, found common ground on the purely political tenets of Conservatism.[30]

It was at this point that the veteran Conservative, Galt, now out of Parliament and thus not bound by party discipline, showed his Rouge origins by supporting the Liberal Huntington. Undertaking to defend Huntington's proposed political realignment, Galt sought to identify a profound change in the attitude of the hierarchy to political matters since the *Syllabus of Errors* and the *Declaration of Papal Infallibility*. Before this change, he argued, the support given by the Catholic Church to the Conservative party in Quebec represented no danger; after the change, it did.

Under the old view, according to Galt, the clergy used to be "conscientious and scrupulous in the discharge of their duties, and tolerant of the claims of others".[31] "The peaceful, loyal, modest, intelligent priest who, in almost patriarchal spirit, had directed the consciences of a simple peasantry," had, before the promulgation of the Vatican decrees, put forth "no pretension of interference in civil matters...beyond the legitimate influence which no one desires to deny to the clergy of all persuasions, in their character of citizens."[32] This older view declared the

> equality of creeds; of Liberty of thought and deed; the entire separation of Church from State was solemnly entered on the Statute Book; the Roman Catholic Church reposed on the guarantees granted by the British Crown; it was not aggressive, it meddled not with political strife, it pretended to no superior rights over other Churches, and though it was as a rule favourable to the Conservative party, it never presumed to dictate to the leaders of that party, their political course.[33]

The consequence of this old view, in other words, was an independence or freedom of thought among the Catholic laity on political matters. The new attitude of the hierarchy, by contrast, was characterized by the denial of this freedom and the attempt to extinguish it. This new attitude was based on the notion that "the regulation of faith and morals", which is the proper business of religion, was "to be extended to embrace the whole field of human thought and action", including political thought and action; which is to say that the hierarchy claimed the right "to control and direct the scope of political action and public law within the province of Quebec, treating it as their own peculiar domain, and regarding us [the English Protestants] as strangers and aliens holding no status of our own, but simply tolerated in their midst".[34]

The tendency of this new view, to the extent that it was accepted by the Catholic population, would have been to eradicate any political differences among Catholics. By denying the distinction between the political and the religious spheres, and by thus extending the principle of hierarchical authority to all matters, the Church would have brought all Catholics into the same political fold. As we have seen, this eradication of the political differences among Catholics took the form of constraining them to vote for the Conservative party, which naturally gained a great political advantage thereby.

As Galt saw it, this political advantage led Protestant Conservatives to turn a blind eye to the illegitimate excursions of the clergy from the sacristy. In doing so, however, they were supporting and strengthening an increasingly intolerant clergy and helping it to gain control of political life in Quebec. Without the support that the Protestants gave to the political pretensions of the Church, some Catholics might have found the courage to maintain their political independence. But, said Galt,

> The contest must appear to them hopeless when they find arrayed against them all the religious forces of their own Church, and the influence of those who ought to sympathize with their desire to be free from ecclesiastical tyranny.[35]

By thus helping the Church to gain complete political control of the Catholic population, the Protestants were placing their own future in danger, for the intolerance manifested by the Church must ultimately extend to Protestantism. Having made use of the Protestant minority to help crush dissent within its own camp, the hierarchy would then have used the political weight of the newly consolidated Catholic majority against its former allies. The result would have been a religious civil war.[36]

The solution to this problem, as Galt saw it, was for all Protestants to resist the mistaken attitude of the Church that her sphere of competence and authority extended to political matters. This, however, would have required a temporary alliance of Protestant Conservatives with Liberals of all religious persuasions against the ultramontanes.

III

Galt's tract quickly achieved as much notoriety as had Huntington's original speech, and was subjected to similar criticisms. These criticisms were most articulately presented by Thomas White himself in a pamphlet entitled *The Protestant Minority in Quebec in its Political Relations with the Roman Catholic Majority*. White, it will be recalled, had occasioned Huntington's remarks by complaining that he was being branded either as priest-ridden or anti-Catholic by his opponents, depending on the composition of the audience. To White, Huntington's attack on the Conservative-ultramontane alliance was simply another example of this tactic. It was little more "than a clever attempt, in an intensely Protestant, and hitherto Conservative constituency, to secure an electoral triumph by rousing the Protestant sentiment of the people against one, against whom the Catholic sentiment had already been so successfully raised in another place".[37] According to White, Huntington was appealing to religious, rather than to purely political motives. In calling for Protestants, *qua* Protestants, to align themselves against the Conservatives, he was calling for a party division along strictly religious lines, and Galt, in supporting him, was doing precisely the same thing. Indeed, the fact that this part of Huntington's speech was given such prominence to the exclusion of his purely political remarks, together with the fact that such a prominent Conservative as Galt had publicly supported it, indicated to White "that a new departure in politics had been resolved upon, and that a new ground of division, a purely religious one, [was] to be urged upon the people of the province of Quebec".[38] But was not such a party division on religious lines precisely what

Huntington and Galt ostensibly wished to avoid? Would it not have brought on the religious war they were so concerned to prevent? In brief, White's criticism of Galt was that the latter's advice was self-defeating, if not self-contradictory; for if followed, it would have led to precisely what it sought to avoid.

Agreeing with Galt that the eradication of any political differences among Catholics would be dangerous, White nevertheless argued that there was little prospect of that occurring. True, the Liberals were weak, and the Church often sided with the Conservatives against them, but that had been true for at least twenty-five years, during much of which Galt himself had benefited without complaint from this alliance. During this period, political differences among Catholics had persisted and now Galt, who was apparently so concerned to maintain them, was proposing a policy that would have annihilated them altogether. This was so, White argued, because there was no longer a significant difference of *religious* opinion among the Catholic population. All Catholics, he maintained, including liberal Catholics, had come to admit the authority of the Church in matters of faith and morals, a view that Galt characterized as "the extreme view enunciated at Rome". There had, indeed, been a time when there was "a Catholic minority which could, by its public utterances, be described as that section of the Roman Catholic party who do not accept the extreme view enunciated at Rome'," [39] but Galt had not then (although others had) urged an alliance of the Protestants with this Catholic minority. That time had passed, however, and the Catholic population was now at one. Indeed, in Quebec all political parties, including the Liberal party, had accepted the Catholic doctrines on these points. Therefore, said White,

> when you describe the liberals of the Province with whom you now invite Protestant Conservative alliance, as that section of the Roman Catholic party who do not accept the extreme views enunciated at Rome, you simply declare them to be non-Catholics according to the rule which...they have claimed as binding.[40]

and,

> there can be little doubt that badly as that minority were beaten at the polls at the last election, they would have stood a fair chance of being literally swept out of Parliamentary existence, had one so intimate with them as you are, on the eve of the battle, called for Protestant union in their behalf on the ground that they were a "section of the Roman Catholic party who do not accept the extreme views enunciated at Rome". At the time they expressly repudiated such a position, and a Protestant manifesto, issued in their favour and based upon the supposed necessity of protecting them from their own church, must have proved a fatal blow to them.[41]

In short, by making the primary political issue a *religious* one, on which Catholics were all united, Galt's proposal would have overwhelmed and submerged the very *political* differences between Catholics that he wished to protect and maintain. On this religious issue there would have emerged two religious parties—one Protestant and one Catholic—precisely what Galt was trying to avoid. And, as Galt himself would have concluded had he accepted the foregoing argument, the position of Protestants as a religious minority "certainly cannot be benefited by any attempt at political organization based on religious opinions such as you suggest".[42]

During the Parliamentary debate on Huntington's speech, Masson, Conservative Member for Terrebonne, had similarly argued that the proposed realignment would be a purely religious one, and would result in civil strife. He maintained that Catholics were not priest-ridden, but insisted that even if they decided to subject themselves totally to their clergy in *political* matters, that would be their *religious* opinion and nobody else's business.

> ...it is not the business of any man who does not profess our creed, no more than it is any of our business to interfere with your opinions, or the opinions of those who profess a different creed from ours; and the way in which they form those opinions, so long as our brethren of different creeds...do not...follow [the] guidance [of their clergy], it is their own lookout. So long as they wish to follow the guidance of another class of men, it is, again, their lookout.[43]

Indeed, unless such a policy of minding one's own business were followed there would be no peace in the country.

> ...if we wish peace and harmony to exist among the different creeds that divide this country, we must make up our minds to attend to our own business. When difficulties arise among Protestants, let it be well understood among Catholics that we are not to interfere with them unless the discussion affects us, and Catholics humbly require that when things relating exclusively to their creed are debated, Protestants shall not interfere so long as there is nothing in our opinions or actions that can be detrimental to the Protestant population of this country. Thereby there will be tranquility in this country; but so long as there is interference like that of the hon. gentleman with matters that he does not understand, there will be discord.[44]

IV

Both the arguments for and against political realignment, then, appear to have been based on the desire to prevent the emergence of parties based on a religious split. Both, moreover, wished to avoid the formation of such parties for precisely the same reason: to avoid civil strife, if not civil war. Both positions subscribed to what we have described as the liberal view that religious freedom was the only effective guarantee of religious peace, and hence peaceful party competition; the difference lay in what they considered to be legitimate religious opinion.

The arguments of Masson and White, for example, were clearly based on the assumption that the ultramontane belief that politics must be subjected to clerical oversight was a purely theological belief, and that freedom of religion must, therefore, be extended to it as much as to any other religious belief. White was very clear on this.

> You [Galt] refer to and quote the Pastoral letter of Monseigneur Bourget as a reason for the "disruption of our former party alliances"....But there is this to be said, that it is simply a strong illustration of the fundamental differences between the two sys-

> tems of religious faith. Roman Catholicism denies to its membership the right of private judgement. Protestantism on the contrary is based upon that right as its leading and distinctive characteristic. Bishop Bourget is dealing with a class, who being Catholic, yet deny the absolute authority of the Church in matters of faith and morals, and these he condemns. That condemnation to Protestants would be simply intolerable; but it is neither intended to, nor does it, apply to us.[45]

As the last sentence of this quotation reveals, White did not consider the value of freedom to be so absolute that one must extend it even to those who would destroy freedom. One *could* tolerate Catholic intolerance, however, because it was intended to apply to Catholics only, as an article of their faith, and anyone could escape its strictures simply by renouncing that faith. On the same point, Masson had this to say:

> I will appeal to the Protestants of Lower Canada to tell us whether this is not the case. It is nothing to you who influences our opinions, and it is nothing to you whence we take our instructions so far as these instructions result in the liberal and tolerant policy which every French Canadian and every Catholic in the Province of Quebec is ready to give to all our fellow-countrymen to whatever creed or nationality they may belong.[46]

If the position of the Protestant minority had been in danger it would have been another matter, but, according to White, there was no evidence of this. Indeed, he went to great pains to show that

> No request made by Protestants has ever been refused. A mere handful in the legislature, although nearly three times as many as by the strict division of Roman Catholic and Protestant they could secure, they had the most absolute and entire control over every interest specifically belonging to them and subject to the action of the legislature.[47]

This being so, the true interest of Protestants was

> ...to preserve towards the religious majority a position of absolute neutrality in so far as the religious disputes of that majority are concerned....If the Roman Catholic Church is intolerant of dissent among its own membership from any of its pretensions, however extreme and to our minds presumptuous, every appeal such as that addressed by you [Galt] can but increase the influence of these pretensions and render more powerless any resistance to them. With an abstinence from interference in these disputes and continuing our alliances *on political grounds alone*, the Protestants of the Province will best maintain their own rights, and most certainly minister to the best interests of the state.[48]

Galt did not share the opinion of White, Masson, and others, that the *political* approach of the Church was a purely *theological* matter, and thus entitled to freedom, because he did not believe that the Church's intolerance could be restricted to Catholics. For Galt, the supposed toleration of the Church toward Protestants was disingenuous. There had indeed been a time when such toleration had been real, but then the Church had believed in a religiously neutral political sphere. Once it had rejected this notion, it was in effect arguing that Catholic principles ought to govern political life. This argument, Galt maintained, was a general argument, which implied general application; any claims by the Church to the contrary were purely prudential.

Galt sought to illustrate this prudence of the Church by referring to the difference between Spain and England. It was true, he argued, that in England such prelates as Newman and Manning tortured the language of the Vatican decrees to make them seem less objectionable, but in Spain they were being applied in their obvious meaning. According to Galt, the writings of Dr. Joseph Fessler, the late Secretary General to the Vatican Council, explained the differences of approach manifested by the Church in the two countries. Fessler's work "teaches, first, that the Roman Church has never absolutely withdrawn from any of her alleged franchises. And secondly that in the present age, she will not insist upon them when vigorously resisted."[49] Thus, "wherever it reigns supreme and controls the Civil Government [as in Spain, the hierarchy] is exclusive, despotic and grasping;

but when, as in England, and until lately in Canada, it is unconnected with the state, it confines itself to its proper functions of teaching piety and morality...."[50] This argument was further corroborated for Galt by the difference between the hierarchy in Quebec, where because of the Catholic majority it could entertain visions of a Spain-like dominance, and in Ontario and the Maritime provinces, where its minority status led such prelates as Archbishop Lynch to take a stand similar to that of Newman and Manning.[51]

Galt might have added that the issue was not which of the two interpretations of the documents was the correct one, but which in fact was being applied in any given case. Even if Newman and Manning were correct, Bishops Bourget and Laflèche thought differently, and it was the latter who wielded ecclesiastical power in Quebec.

In any case, the arguments of Masson and White, that the rights of Protestants were not then being assailed, were, to Galt, quite beside the point. Indeed, he openly conceded that these rights were not then being attacked, claiming that "we are confronted with a near and ominous future",[52] not that this future had already arrived, and that once the Church had brought all Catholics under control, "our turn will come," not that it had come already.[53] Unlike Masson and White, Galt seemed to be concerned not so much with actual public manifestations of intolerance, as with the character of public opinion, for he believed that it is ultimately opinion that determines action. His primary objective was to combat a certain opinion that, although it had not yet led to attacks on the rights of Protestants, would have done so once it had become the dominant opinion. And inasmuch as this opinion had implications for the civil rights of Protestants, it ceased to be a purely religious opinion.

> It is not consistent with the good government, the peace, and the prosperity of the country, that any portion of our population should be held in such bondage, and though, as a Protestant it does not reach me, still as a citizen my rights are impugned, and my civil liberty impaired.[54]

Masson and White had themselves admitted that anything touching civil rights ceased to be purely religious; they had simply not gone far enough, according to Galt, in tracing the connections between opinion and action.

The problem with the "new attitude" of the Church, as Galt understood it, was that it sought to make the politician represent primarily a religious opinion, as the attempt to create a Catholic party revealed. This, according to Galt, was the classic recipe for religious strife, for a Catholic party would inevitably call forth a Protestant reaction. The politics of the country would then become a religious politics, and parties would become religious parties. Unless there was a sphere that was religiously neutral, and in which men could exercise free thought, the majority-minority breakdown would always be on religious lines, undoubtedly a dangerous situation. Indeed, Galt saw the creation of a "Protestant Defence Association" in Quebec as a sign of things to come.[55] Elicited by the ultramontane pretensions, this association—because it was itself based on a religious principle—would have contributed to the solidification of the Catholic party, which would have further strengthened the Protestant party, and so on, with obvious results.

To put it another way, representative government, which in practice means government by majority, can only exist if the minority trusts the majority. But if majority and minority divide on religious lines this is impossible. Only if majority and minority can divide on lower level issues, which cut across religious lines, can the system work; but this depends on the various religions admitting that such a lower and religiously neutral level exists—an admission the ultramontanes were not willing to make.

If one grants the validity of Galt's analysis of the "new attitude", his conclusion seems to follow inescapably: parties based on purely religious lines would eventually form, and civil war would become an ever greater likelihood. Therefore the ultramontane doctrine that implied the formation of a Catholic party had to be vigorously opposed.

Yet if Galt was right, so was White (even granting Galt's interpretation of the "new attitude"). The political realignment that Galt was proposing would have been based on a division that transcended ordinary party politics as much as the religious division of Protestant and Catholic, and, in principle at least, would have had a similar tendency to lead to civil war.

Galt did not believe he was advocating a religious division, as is clear from his opposition to the recently formed Protestant Defence Association.

> ...considering, that it is the *civil* rights of free speech, a free press, and free political action, and not in any way religion itself which are endangered, I would suggest that a more general name might be adopted, and a much wider scope given to its action, so as to include within its sphere all those who desire the action of the State to be untrammelled by ecclesiastical influence and interference.[56]

Nevertheless, we must admit the difficulties of this opinion, difficulties that White's analysis brings to the fore. White claimed that it was not the Church that was trespassing on the secular realm, but Galt who was invading the religious sphere, and this claim has force to the extent that the liberal principle of religious freedom means that each religion must be free to define its own theology. It was to this principle, not merely to his own electoral interest, that White appealed in his defence of the ultramontanes.

The problem, as White recognized, was that the ultramontanes considered their doctrine of the subordination of state to church to be a theological doctrine. Thus, a necessary corollary of Galt's claim that in opposing this doctrine he was opposing only political, not religious opinion, is that ultramontane theology was false theology. But is not the question of what is true and false theology, a theological question, and was not Galt, therefore, trespassing on the religious realm?

From the time of Papineau and the Rebellion of 1837, this had been the standard ultramontane response to the liberal charge that the Church was illegitimately trespassing on the secular realm. A typical statement of this view is Bishop Laflèche's comment on the legal decisions, coming soon after the Galt-White debate, that a priest committed the offence of "undue influence" when, from the pulpit, he instructed his parishioners that they would be committing a sin if they voted Liberal.[57]

> ...it is evidently not the civil judge who pronounces thus on the morality of the vote, and on its conformity with, or opposition to, the law of God; for the civil law does not speak of sin....It must, therefore, be the theologian who declares that a vote cannot constitute a grave sin! Moreover, it is the *canonist* who sets the limits which the priest, in his pulpit, may not overstep when he preaches morality to his parishioners, and when he forewarns them against that which may place their souls in danger. It makes no difference that his conscience tells him that it is his rigorous duty to so warn them, and to turn them from the gravity of the sin they will commit by violating the law of God; he is nevertheless guilty of undue spiritual influence because he has passed the limits fixed by the *canonical* and *theological* judge, although the civil law speaks neither of spiritual influence, nor of sin, both of which absolutely escape its sphere of jurisdiction.[58]

Galt was well aware of this rebuttal, and in the introductory remarks to his second pamphlet he explicitly undertook to defend himself against the charge that he was trespassing on the religious sphere. In particular, he invoked the authority of Gladstone, who, in a similar debate with Cardinals Newman and Manning, had penned the following disclaimer.

> I desire to eschew not only religious bigotry; but likewise theological controversy. Indeed with theology, except in its civil bearing,—with theology as such—I have nothing whatsoever to do. But it is the peculiarity of Roman theology, that by thrusting itself into the temporal domain, it naturally, and even necessarily comes to be a frequent theme of political discussion.[59]

This quotation does not solve the problem, however, for Gladstone is saying two contradictory things. On the one hand, he tells us that he is not concerned with "theology as such"; on the other hand, he is forced to admit that he is concerned, of necessity, with "Roman theology" because it insists on "thrusting itself into the temporal domain", which *is* his concern. Gladstone is implying that "Roman theology", to the extent that it injects itself into the temporal sphere, is not "theology as such"—i.e., it is not true theology because true theology does not thrust itself into the temporal domain. But, again, the question of true and false theology is surely a theological question. Galt could not escape the ultramontane charge with his use of this quotation.

Having invoked the support of Gladstone, Galt proceeded to make a distinction between the "Roman Catholic Church" considered as its government or polity, and considered as a system of faith, claiming that it was only the former that he was criticizing.[60] This distinction was also made to exempt himself from the charge of entering the religious sphere, and thereby limiting its freedom, but it too runs into difficulties to the extent that the Catholic "system of religious faith" included a teaching about the "government and polity" of that Church. To separate them, as Galt did, implies that that aspect of Catholic theology that extends to the government and polity of the Church is not proper theology, a proposition that is open to the same problems raised by the Gladstone quotation.

Finally, Galt made the following statement near the end of his pamphlet:

> It is certainly not a religious question, but a political or civil one,...whether we shall surrender our civil rights into the hands of the Priesthood or not—whether we shall permit them to use at our elections undue influence infinitely more powerful and more dangerous than that of gold or intemperance—whether they shall dictate to us what we shall say, or read, or think, and thus gradually shackle all the energy and intelligence of our young Dominion.[61]

Galt was certainly correct in maintaining that this was a political question; but why was it not also a religious question? If salvation depends, as ultramontane doctrine taught, upon submitting certain political decisions to the Church, then surely a question of religion was involved as well. Again, to argue that it was not was to argue that the bishops were wrong about the requirements of salvation, which was plainly to enter the realm of theology.

For the ultramontanes, then, and not without reason, the liberals were very far from heeding their own doctrine of separate and equal spheres. "Without knowing it," said Bishop Laflèche, "they...jumped with both feet into the religious domain, and there they...made of themselves theologians and canonists."[62] By taking it upon themselves to define the boundary between the religious and secular realms, and hence the relationship between them, the liberals were entering upon a fundamentally theological question. To impose this definition upon the Church, moreover, as the courts were beginning to do, implied not equal and separate spheres, but the subordination of church to state. Indeed, the ultramontanes considered the liberal doctrine of equal and separate spheres to be a logical absurdity in any case. They conceded the existence of two *different* spheres, each with its own proper functions, but they refused to admit that these spheres could be entirely separate, or of equal weight. In the absence of a neutral third party, they maintained, the representatives of one of the realms had to be the final arbiter of disputes concerning the boundary between them, and this role could only fall to the superior authority. The ultramontanes were unabashed in claiming that the purposes of the secular realm were subordinate to those of the religious sphere, and that the state, though free in its proper domain, was therefore ultimately subordinate to the Church. For them, rejection of this view necessarily entailed the opposite doctrine of state supremacy; no middle ground was possible.[63]

V

It is indeed difficult to dispute the ultramontane claim that their theocratic teaching was a theological teaching, and the consistent liberal denial of this indicates that the liberal principle of religious freedom is a conditional one. For liberalism, religion is separated from the state in order to banish Great Parties and make possible the peaceful partisanship with which we are familiar. This strategy depends upon the relegation of religion to the private sphere; it cannot work unless all politically powerful parts of the community agree to leave their religious opinions at home when they enter the public sphere. As Locke knew, a tolerant regime cannot tolerate the intolerant.[64] This means that religion can be free to define itself only to the extent that its definition is congruent with the separation of church and state, or that only those theologies compatible with the liberal principle of separation can be counted as legitimate theologies. It means, further, that religion must be subordinated to the secular purposes of the state, or that the two realms, while separate, are not equal. As Walter Berns reminds us, "the term *liberalism* in its modern sense, was coined to denote the liberation from the power of church and churchmen,"[65] and the liberal "solution of the religious problem consists in the subordination of religion".[66] No one understood this more clearly than the theocrats against whom liberalism contended, including Quebec's ultramontanes. From this theocratic perspective, the subordination of religion inherent in liberalism was the worst form of theological heresy. To the ultramontanes, for example, Galt's proposed anti-theocratic party would have been indistinguishable from the Protestant Defence Association, which Galt eschewed. To the bishops, Galt's new party would not have been a secular party, but a party just as thoroughly committed to the establishment of religion as their own. It would have differed only in attempting to establish another, and in their eyes heretical religion. This is why, as White sensed, the struggle between liberalism and theocracy as such has the same warlike character as the struggle between two contending theocracies. To put it differently, the struggle against the premise of Great Party politics, in the name of peaceful party government, is itself a struggle of Great Party proportions.[67]

NOTES

[1] Harvey C. Mansfield Jr., "Party Government and the Settlement of 1688," *American Political Science Review*, LV111 (1964), passim.

[2] Alexis De Tocqueville, *Democracy in America*, George Lawrence (trans.), J.P. Mayer (ed.), (Garden City, N.Y., Anchor Books, 1969). pp. 174-5.

[3] See John Locke, *A Letter Concerning Toleration*, Patrick Romanell (ed.), 2nd ed., (Indianapolis, Bobbs-Merrill, 1955), passim, esp. pp. 17, 27.

[4] Fernand Ouellet, "Nationalisme canadien-française et laïcisme au XIXe siècle," in Jean-Paul Bernard (ed.), *Les idéologies Québécoises au 19e siècle*, (Montreal, Boreal Express, 1973), pp. 41, 42.

[5] Michel Burnet, "L'Église catholique du Bas-Canada et le partage du pouvoir a l'heure d'une nouvelle donné (1837-1854)," in ibid., p. 83; Guy Bourgeault, "Le nationalism Québécois et l'Église," *Canadian Review of Studies in Nationalism*, V (1978), p. 192.

[6] Brunet, "L'Église catholique," p. 83; Bourgeault, "Le nationalism Québécois," p. 193.

[7] Ouellet, "Nationalisme canadien-française," p. 49.

[8] Ibid., p. 42.

[9] Ibid., p. 43.

[10] Ibid., p. 44.

[11] Fernand Ouellet, "Le mandement de Mgr. Lartigue de 1837 et la réaction libérale," in Ramsay Cook (ed.), *Constitutionalism and Nationalism in Lower Canada* (Toronto, University of Toronto Press, 1979), passim; Bourgeault, "Le nationalisme Québécois," p. 193.

[12] O.D. Skelton, *Life and Times of Sir Alexander Tilloch Galt* (Toronto, McClelland and Stewart, 1969), Ch. 6.

[13] Ibid., pp. 72-4.

[14] Ouellet, "Le mandement," pp. 71-2.

[15] Philippe Sylvain, "Libéralisme et ultramontanisme au Canada française: affrontement idéologique et doctrinal (1840-1865)," in W.L. Morton (ed.), *The Shield of Achilles* (Toronto, McClelland and Stewart, 1968), p.121; Marcel Dandurand, "Les premiers dificultés entre Mgr. Bourget et l'Institut canadien de Montréal (1844-1865)," *Revue de l'Université d'Ottawa*, XXV (1955), p. 153; O.D. Skelton, *Life and Letters of Sir Wilfrid Laurier* (Toronto, McClelland and Stewart, 1965), I, pp. 17-8.

[16] Sylvain, "Libéralisme et ultramontanisme," p. 120; Nadia F. Eid, *Le clergé et le pouvoir politique au Quebéc: une analyse de l'idéologie ultramontane au milieu du XIX siècle* (Montreal, Hurtibise, 1978), p. 9.

[17] Eid, *Le clergé et le pouvoir politique*, passim and esp. pp. 80-9.

[18] Jean-Paul Bernard, *Les rouges: libéralisme, nationalisme et anticléricalisme au milieu du XIX siècle* (Montréal, Les Presses de L'Université du Québec, 1971), pp. 143, 151-2, 185-6, 222-30, 234-5.

[19] The analogy of "Catholic liberalism", and by implication political liberalism manifested by Catholics (since the two were identified by the ultramontanes), was made in the famous September 22 Pastoral, a joint pastoral letter issued by the Bishops of Quebec, at the instigation of Bishop Bourget, on September 22, 1875. See *Mandements, Lettres Pastorals, Circulaires et Autres Documents Publiés dans le Diocèse de Montréal depuis son Erection* (Montréal, J.A. Plinguet, 1887), VII, p. 206, hereafter cited as the *September 22 Pastoral.*

[20] See, e.g., *Le Nouveau Monde* (April 27, 1871), hereafter cited as "Programme."

[21] Ibid. My translation.

[22] Ibid. My translation.

[23] Ibid. The translation is taken from Mason Wade, *The French Canadians*, revised ed., (Toronto, Macmillan, 1968) pp. 353-4.

[24] Skelton, *Galt*, p. 189.

[25] Ibid., p. 242.

[26] Loc. cit., p. 189.

[27] Ibid., p. 238.

[28]Alexander Galt, *Civil Liberty in Lower Canada* (Montreal, 1876). Galt's second, and much longer pamphlet, written partly in response to Thomas White's criticisms, was *Church and State* (Montreal, 1876).

[29]Thomas White, *The Protestant Minority in Quebec in its Political Relations with the Roman Catholic Majority* (Montreal, 1876), pp. 1-2.

[30]See, e.g., the speech by Bowell in *House of Commons Debates* (February 11, 1876), p. 44, hereafter cited as *Debates*.

[31]Galt, *Civil Liberty*, p. 5.

[32]Galt, *Church and State*, pp. 15-16.

[33]Ibid., p. 28.

[34]Galt, *Civil Liberty*, p. 5.

[35]Ibid., p. 6.

[36]Loc. cit.

[37]White, *The Protestant Minority*, p. 2.

[38]Ibid., p. 3.

[39]Ibid., p. 15.

[40]Ibid., p. 11.

[41]Ibid., pp. 11-12.

[42]Ibid., p. 17.

[43]*Debates*, p. 22.

[44]Ibid., p. 25.

[45]White, *The Protestant Minority*, p. 9.

[46]*Debates*, pp. 22-3.

[47]White, *The Protestant Minority*, p. 17.

[48]Ibid., p. 19. Emphasis added.

[49]Galt, *Church and State*, p. 9.

[50]Ibid., pp. 7-8.

[51]Ibid., p. 18.

[52]Ibid., p. 28.

[53]Galt, *Civil Liberty*, p. 6.

[54]Ibid., p. 15.

[55]Galt, *Civil Liberty*, p. 16; *Church and State*, p. 40.

[56]Galt, *Civil Liberty*, p. 16. Emphasis added.

[57]Laflèche was referring to the famous undue influence cases, *Hamilton* v. *Beauchesne* (1877), 3, Q.L.R., p. 75, and *Brassard* v. *Lanuevin* (1878), 1, S.C.R., p. 145.

[58]Mgr Lois-François Laflèche, *L'influence spirituelle indue devant la liberté religieuse et civile* (Trois-Rivières, 1881), pp. 28-9. My translation.

[59]Galt, *Church and State*, p. 2.

[60]Ibid., p. 3.

[61]Ibid., p. 38.

[62]Laflèche, *L'influence spirituelle indue*, p. 29.

[63]See the *September 22 Pastoral*.

[64]Locke, *A Letter Concerning Toleration*, pp. 50-1.

[65]Walter Berns, *The First Amendment and the Future of American Democracy* (New York, Basic Books, 1976), p. 1.

[66]Ibid., p. 26. See Locke, *A Letter Concerning Toleration*, pp. 39-40, 48.

[67]For further analysis of the character of this struggle see Rainer Knopff, ''Quebec's 'Holy War' as 'Regime' Politics: Reflections on the Guibord Case,'' *Canadian Journal of Political Science*, XII (1979).

Beginnings of A Canadian Catholic Social Theory

GREGORY BAUM

Under the pressure of the Latin American Church a shift to the left has taken place in the Catholic Church's official social teaching. This shift has produced a critical social theory in the Canadian Catholic Church that deserves attention. When in January 1983 the Canadian bishops published their "Ethical Reflections on the Economic Crisis", the majority of Canadians were greatly surprised, the defenders of the existing order as well as its left-wing critics. Only a minority of Christians had followed the evolution taking place in the Catholic Church.

In the past, political scientists paid little attention to Catholic social theory. The reason for this was its abstract, *a priori* character, largely unrelated to existing social conflicts, which placed it outside the public debate going on in society. By Catholic social theory was usually meant the synthesis of social ideas produced by Pope Leo XIII in the encyclical *Rerum novarum* (1891), which drew upon reform principles developed by nineteenth-century Catholic critics of modern society.[1] This synthesis of ideas underwent a certain development by subsequent popes and Catholic social thinkers. Until the Vatican Council (1962-5), Catholic social teaching evolved only very slightly. Catholic social theory was a kind of "red Toryism". Modern, industrial society was criticized in the light of an idealized picture of the old order. What was called for was the return to virtue. Catholic social teaching repudiated political and economic liberalism; it rejected a society where decisions were made in accordance with the interests of the industrial and commercial elites; it envisaged a government made up of high-minded men, above the conflict of the classes, which would promote the common good of society and protect the poor and the weak from exploitation by the rich and powerful. Catholic social teaching defended the right of private property and the right of workers to organize labour unions. The popes saw their social teaching as a third way between liberalism and socialism, but the abstract, idealistic nature of their theory, worked out without reference to people's actual aspirations and struggles, did not generate a social movement nor produce concrete policies. There were some interesting exceptions to the rule.

On the whole, Catholics tended to read papal social teaching in the light of their own political interests. The owning classes made much of the papal defence of private property, the condemnation of socialism, the repudiation of the class struggle, and the summons to greater personal morality, while the workers and critics of society lauded in papal teaching the unmasking of economic liberalism, the defence of labour unions and labour struggles, the emphasis on the government's duty to promote the common good of society, including an economy oriented toward justice, and the call for labour codes to protect workers from exploitation. Thus Catholics in the United States made use of papal teaching to defend Roosevelt's New Deal while the bishops of Quebec used the same teaching to condemn the newly formed CCF.[2] In Quebec the Catholic clergy attached itself to the corporatist principles contained in papal teaching.[3] Corporatism presents the ideal of a cooperative, non-competitive, but hierarchical society, where social and economic policies are made by representatives of "the corporations", i.e. the bodies constituted by the workers, managers and owners of the various branches of industry. Corporatism, it was argued, promises to overcome class conflict by class cooperation. It would allow representation of people apart from parliamentary democracy. However, the promotion of corporatist theory in Quebec remained abstract. No concrete policies and no political movement proceeded from it.[4] Political scientists have tended to associate corporatism with European fascism which tried to adopt certain of its features. This was an additional reason for not paying much attention to Catholic social theory.

The Church's Shift to the Left

To understand the emergence of a new Canadian Catholic social theory it is necessary to take a brief look at the shift to the left that has taken place in the official teaching of the Catholic Church coming from the centre, from Rome. The significant turning point here is the year 1971. A Synod of Bishops held in Rome in that year produced a document, *Justitia in mundo*, that dissolved once and for all the corporatist heritage and adopted the liberationist perspective recommended by the 1978 Medellin Conference of the Latin American bishops.[5] *Justitia in mundo* (n. 1-6) offered a re-interpretation of the central Christian categories, in keeping with the biblical prophetic tradition and with modern sociological insights. We are told that sin includes "social sin", that is to say the social structures that oppress people, that conversion includes the raising of consciousness in regard to these structures of oppression (the term used is "conscientization"), and that the salvation which Christ has brought includes "the liberation of people from the conditions of oppression". The Christian message has an emancipatory thrust. Christian truth transforms. *Justitia in mundo* demands that the Church's preaching of the gospel include witness to social justice and human rights, and that the response to this gospel in faith include social action to transform society. Following the Latin American perspective, the Synodal document recognizes that the present world economic system threatens to push ever larger sectors of humanity into dependency, poverty and starvation. It is an expression of "social sin". The Synod expresses its solidarity with the peoples who under these conditions struggle for their emancipation.

The Canadian bishops made a significant contribution to the 1971 Synod of Bishops. They had already been in dialogue with Latin American liberation theology and the liberationist approach recommended by the Medellin Conference. The speech Cardinal George Flahiff, Archbishop of Winnipeg, made at the Synod contained a principle that has remained operative in the evolution of Canadian Catholic social theory ever since. Why is it, Cardinal Flahiff asked, that Catholic social teaching has had so little impact? One of the reasons for this, he believed, was its abstract and academic character.

> I suggest that, henceforth, our basic principle must be: only knowledge gained through participation is valid in the area of justice. True knowledge can only be gained through concern and solidarity....Unless we are in solidarity with the people who are poor, marginal, or isolated we cannot even speak effectively about their problems. Theoretical knowledge is indispensable, but it is partial and limited. When it abstracts from lived, concrete experience, it merely projects the present into the future.[6]

This distinction between abstract and concrete thought is of capital importance. It is much more than a critique of the inherited Catholic social teaching. It raises questions in regard to all idealistic theories, including a good deal of social science and political theory produced at universities. Abstract thought, usually associated with elitist institutions, is built on unexamined presuppositions derived from mainstream culture, and hence simply extends the present into the future. Concrete thought is generated through identification with people's emancipatory struggles and takes place at a certain distance from traditional institutions and established wisdom. How had this critical epistemology reached the Canadian bishops in the early seventies? The bishops were in touch with Christian grassroots communities in Canada (Native Peoples, welfare groups, rural poor, labour organizations, immigrants, etc.) engaged in concrete social justice struggles. Some of these groups as well as the bishops themselves were familiar with Paolo Freire's *The Pedagogy of the Oppressed* and other radical adult education projects sponsored by churches in the Third World.

In the same year as the 1971 Synod, Pope Paul VI published a letter, entitled *Octogesima adveniens*, addressed to the Cardinal Maurice Roy, President of the Justice and Peace Commission and Archbishop of Quebec City, in which he removed the taboo the Church had long attached to socialism (n. 31). Catholics have become socialists. Catholics may become socialists. The same letter also introduced a more nuanced critique of Marxism (n. 32-4). It distinguished between Marxism as total philosophy, Marxism as a style of political organization, and Marxism as a form of social analysis. While Paul VI repudiated Marxist ideology and Marxist political organizations, he appreciated Marxist sociology of oppression, if it was able to resist the temptation of reductionism built into it. This qualified recommendation of "Marxist social analysis" was confirmed by several national episcopates, including the Canadian bishops.

Octogesima adveniens also praised the new emergence of utopias (n. 37). Paul VI here followed the revisionist Marxist Ernst Bloch's understanding of utopia, not as the empty dream of a never-never land ("abstract utopia," in Bloch's terms), but as the image of an alternative society, in discontinuity with the present order, yet close enough to the as yet unrealized possibilities of the present to generate practical strategies and strengthen the motivation for political action, ("concrete utopia" in Bloch's terms). This praise of utopia implies a radical break with the corporatist imagination that had haunted Catholic social teaching for so long. The old Catholic social theory criticized the present order in the light of an idealized image of the feudal past, while the new Catholic social theory criticizes present society in the light of utopia, an imaginative society of the future, utopia being understood in the creative and yet sober sense in which it was used by Ernst Bloch. This shift of perspective profoundly influenced Canadian Catholics.

Since the early seventies, then, there emerged in Canada a new Catholic social theory. This process is part of a history that has not yet been written. In the early seventies the Catholic Church joined the other Canadian Churches in a common commitment to social justice and the search for joint social policies. The churches encouraged and eventually supported several inter-Church committees, whose task it was (and still is) to examine from a Christian perspective, various social and economic issues that profoundly mark Canadian society and its relation to the

Third World. The inter-Church committee "GATT-fly" studies issues related to trade, aid and development; "Project North" deals with rights of the Native Peoples; there are the inter-Church committees "On Human Rights in Latin America" and "A Task Force on the Churches and Corporate Responsibility". "Ten Days for Development" is an adult education project with an outreach to all the Churches. This is not a complete list. On the basis of the reports written by these committees, and in dialogue with a growing critical Christian literature on social justice in Third World and developed nations, the Churches began to formulate their own social policies. In ecumenical cooperation the Churches produced critical reports on justice in Canada which they submitted, at regular intervals, to the prime minister and members of the federal cabinet. What took place in the Protestant Churches, especially among small action groups and on the highest level of Church leadership, was the return of the old Social Gospel in a contemporary form. This evolution in the Churches, Catholic and Protestant, was grounded in a network of small groups and communities,[7] Catholic, Protestant or simply ecumenical, struggling for justice around concrete issues. Some groups mobilized Native peoples, some immigrants, some the urban poor and the rural poor, others were identified with labour struggles, others took on Quebec's right to self-determination. Cardinal Flahiff's principle that "unless we are in solidarity with the people who are poor, marginal or isolated we cannot even speak effectively of their problems", was honoured by the Canadian Churches in the development of their social position.

Equally important for this evolution in the Churches has been their association with universal Church bodies and with Third World Church groups in particular. For the Catholic Church, as we saw earlier, the radicalization of the Latin American Church and the more recent teaching coming from Rome had great importance. Again, this ecumenical history has not yet been written.

What I wish to do in this essay is quite modest, I wish to describe and analyze the emerging social theory, produced by the Canadian bishops in dialogue with many Church groups and contained in pastoral documents published by them over the years. We shall examine principally six documents, "Sharing Daily Bread," 1974, (D1), "Northern Development: At What Cost," 1975, (D2), "From Words to Action," 1976, (D3), "A Society to be Transformed," 1976, (D4), "Unemployment: The Human Cost," 1980, (D5), and "Ethical Reflections on the Economic Crisis," 1983, (D6). In this essay we shall refer to these simply as the Documents.[8] In addition to them we shall look at the handbook, *Witness to Justice*, prepared by the Social Affairs Committee of the Canadian Catholic Conference of Bishops as a teaching instrument for parishes and schools. This Canadian Catholic development has moved in a direction that has recently been confirmed by the pivotal papal encyclical, Pope John Paul II's *Laborem exercens* (1981). I have analyzed the social theory of this encyclical elsewhere.[9] Here I shall refer to it only occasionally as clarification and confirmation.

Solidarity with Society's Victims

In the Documents to be examined in this essay Canadian society appears fraught with conflicts and contradictions. "Many people agree that there is something wrong with the present social and economic order" (D3, n.3). "The maximization of consumption, profit and power has become the operative principle of this society" (D2, n.21). When looking at Canadian society the bishops focus their attention on the victims. In the corporatist imagination of past Catholic teaching, society appeared as an organic reality, the reform of which demanded the enhancement of this organicity through extended cooperation, the return to virtue and the recognition of the necessary hierarchies. In contrast with this, the newer Catholic teaching, influenced by the Latin American experience, has produced a conflictual imagination which makes people see in society first of all the victims, the structures of victimization, and the corresponding distortion of the totality.

To understand society we must stand in solidarity with its victims. The Documents deal with world hunger (D1), with Native

Peoples (D2), with the unemployed (D5), and with the other victims of Canadian society. We are told that one of the first steps in the direction of social justice is "to listen to the victims of society" (D3, n.9). If we only talk to our friends, members of our own class, if we only follow the mass media, if we only read the articles by scholars who identify with their class, we cannot come to a valid collective self-understanding. It is the victims who reveal to us aspects of our own society that are hidden by mainstream culture.

This principle is given special attention in the bishops' statement on the economic crisis. Here we look at society from the viewpoint of the unemployed, the marginal, the powerless, the workers whose jobs have become insecure and whose wages decline in effective value. The statement uses a technical term derived from Latin American Church documents. It speaks of "the option for the poor" (D6, s.1).[10] What is this option for the poor? It can be said that the Christian Church has always preached an option for the poor by calling upon people to be compassionate and assist those who have fallen into hunger and misery. The option for the poor has also had an ascetical meaning in the Catholic tradition. Many Christians, especially in religious orders, believed that by living in simplicity or even voluntary poverty, they became more open to the divine Spirit and experienced a deeper bond of brotherhood or sisterhood with humanity. In the Latin American Church, especially in the documents of the Puebla Bishops Conference (1979), the "preferential option for the poor" has acquired a clearly defined socio-political meaning.[11] The option for the poor means solidarity with the oppressed and the willingness to look at the whole of society from their point of view. The preferential option includes action and entry into a new consciousness. In the language of contemporary Catholic theology, the option is "a praxis": it begins with commitment, which in turn affects how reality is perceived, which in turn leads to further action, and so forth, the entire interaction aiming at the liberation of people from oppression.

This principle was confirmed in Pope John Paul II's encyclical *Laborem exercens* in a language chosen by himself. He wrote that the Church must call for "the solidarity *of* workers and *with* workers'', and in a later sentence for ''the solidarity *of* the poor and *with* the poor'' (s.8). The Pope argues that ''the dynamic element'' of modern society is the solidary struggle for social justice on the part of workers and the underpriviledged, joined by all who love justice, which includes, or at least should include, the entire Christian Church.

In their statement to the economic crisis, the Canadian bishops call ''the option for the poor'' the first principle of their critical reflections. They look upon Canada through the eyes of the people at the base and in the margin, i.e., through the eyes of all those who suffer injustice. The bishops reject the economic policies that define Canadian society at this time because they place the burden of the present decline on the shoulders of the workers and unemployed, the low-income people, the powerless in society. The principle of solidarity which the bishops invoke demands preferential loyalty to the underpriviledged and exploited, with a view to creating a society in which solidarity achieves truly universal dimensions.

> This option [the bishops write] calls for economic policies which realize that the needs of the poor have priority over the wants of the rich; that the rights of the workers are more important than the maximization of profit; that the participation of the marginalized groups has precedence over the preservation of a system which excludes them (D6, s.1).

This sentence reveals very clearly the shift from a corporatist to a conflictual social imagination.

Who are the victims in Canadian society? In my own terminology they are the people at the base and in the margin. They are the workers, employed and unemployed; they are people on welfare, Native Peoples, immigrant groups, refugees, the handicapped, the neglected old, and so forth. We note that because among all these categories the percentage of women is very high the greater burden is often placed on women. Among these classes, groups and peoples solidarity is not spontaneous. It is a peculiar note of Catholic social teaching that solidarity has to be created, and that this is largely a moral task. Solidarity is here motivated by a joining of collective self-interest and a commitment to social justice. We shall return to this point shortly.

Why do workers belong to the victims of society, even if they are organized in unions, enjoy relative security and are paid reasonably well? To explain this we must turn to the second principle mentioned in the bishops' statement on the economic crisis, namely "the value and dignity of labour" (D6, s.1). This is an ancient biblical principle, in the name of which the Christian Church has always honoured peasants, craftsmen, labourers, and later industrial workers, even when they were despised by the powerful in society. In recent years, however, "the value and dignity of labour" has acquired a technical meaning. The principle means that workers, because of the value and dignity of their labour, have the right to share in the decisions affecting the work process and the use of the product of their work. In previous Catholic social teaching this was sometimes referred to as "the workers' right to co-determination".[12] More recently, especially in John Paul II's *Laborem exercens*, it has been called "the priority of labour over capital". This means that workers, because of the value and dignity of labour, are co-responsible for the management of the industries and for the use to which capital and surplus value are put. Ultimately workers are meant to be co-owners of the industries. Only as workers assume such responsibility will capital and profit be made "to serve labour", i.e., serve the labourers in the industry, the technical development of the industry, and eventually the labouring society as a whole.[13]

The Canadian bishops invoke this principle several times in their statement on the economic crisis. Here we are interested in it simply as an explanation why in the emerging Catholic social theory, workers are regarded as unjustly treated even when they are organized, reasonably secure and quite well paid. In capitalist (and communist) societies workers are excluded from co-determination. The anti-democratic nature of the capitalist (and communist) organization of production violates the value and dignity of labour. Workers are prevented from being co-responsible for production and the use of capital.

Since some Canadian critics, including several Liberal MPs, have accused the bishops' statement of being "Marxist", it is perhaps important to distinguish the Catholic position from that of classical Marxism (without examining the question whether there are not revisionist Marxist theories that resemble the newer Catholic social teaching). For Marx, the origin of exploitation resided in private ownership: the owner of the industry was able to appropriate the products produced by the workers. For Marx this was theft. According to the Catholic theory, it is not the ownership question that is central. Ownership may be private (even the newer Catholic social theory defends the right to private property) or it may be, in various ways, social and public. What really counts in all these cases is the *use* of capital. How is profit employed? State ownership offers no guarantee that capital will be used to serve labour. Catholic social theory fears powerful state ownership as much as powerful private ownership. What counts is the co-responsibility of the workers and the community in determining the use of capital and profits. In the long run, according to John Paul II, the only guarantee society has that capital will be used in the service of labour is the eventual transition of private and state ownership into ownership by the workers.

Of primary importance, according to the emerging Catholic social theory, is the creation of solidarity *among* and *with* the various classes and groups at the base and in the margin of society. This solidarity is not generated by some inner necessity: it is not produced by the unfolding of dialectic intrinsic to human history. Solidarity, we noted above, is always a moral creation. One dimension of this solidarity is the collective self-interest of the victimized classes and groups; at the same time the required solidarity also transcends their respective collective self-interests. Each group must make room for the aspirations of the others, even if the struggle of these others demands some sacrifices. For instance, in terms of collective self-interest, at least on a material basis, workers derive very little benefit from the justice struggle of the Native peoples. Their struggle may even become a burden to workers. The solidarity *of* and *with* victims, advocated in Catholic social theory, demands that collective self-interest be accompanied by a commitment to social justice. Middle-class people who join in solidarity with the groups at the base and in the margin are motivated by a similar combination of collective self-interest and moral commitment to justice. Since in the long run society will be destabilized and distorted if it represses the demands for justice on the part of the exploited, the collective self-interest of middle-class Canadians, even when they are in privileged positions, calls for solidarity with the groups at the base and in the margin. This commitment is aided and strengthened by moral conviction.

Before we continue to examine the moral dimension of solidarity, we note that according to the Documents the workers, and in fact labour unions, retain the place at the centre of the justice struggle in society. We recall that Catholic social teaching has defended the workers' right to organize for almost a hundred years, beginning with Leo XIII's *Rerum novarum* (1891). The statement on the economic crisis has this to say about unions.

> Labour unions should be asked to play a more decisive and responsible role in developing strategies for economic recovery and employment. This requires the restoration of collective bargaining rights where they have been suspended, collaboration between unions and the unemployed and unorganized workers, and assurances that labour unions will have an effective role in developing economic policies (D6, s.1).

At the same time the bishops "are also aware of the limited perspectives and excessive demands of some labour unions". Labour unions are in a position of power because the workers thus organized are the producers of wealth. The bishops ask labour unions to recognize more clearly their role in the transformation of society, to reach out to the unemployed and unorganized, possibly helping them to organize, and to manifest their solidarity with the powerless and marginal groups in Canada and in the Third World. The bishops appeal here to the great moral tradition of the labour movement. If the sole purpose of unions is to enhance the terms of their own contracts, they deviate from the historical role of the labour movement as an agent for the transformation of society and solidarity with all the victims of the capitalist order.

Since the moral or spiritual dimension of solidarity is so important in the emerging Catholic social theory, we shall have to examine it more carefully. We note that this moral element may be supplied in a variety of ways. Religious people, be they Christian, Jewish, or members of other world faiths, will seek in their own traditions those elements that call for justice and solidarity. Many secular people derive this moral sense from a humanist or socialist tradition which they honour and with which they identify themselves. For others the moral dimension is drawn from the requirement of practical reason, that is, from the acknowledgement of reason as the faculty of humanity's self-liberation. Others leave their moral commitment almost totally inarticulate. Marxists in particular assume that socialist society is morally superior to capitalism and often allow this moral judgement to find expression in the indignation of their prose, but they rarely formalize the ethics implicit in their judgement and even more rarely use ethical reflection in their own reasoning. Marxists have paid a high price for their lack of ethical self-clarification.

We have noted above that the principle "the option for the poor" or "solidarity *of* and *with* the workers" has epistemological implications. Society can be correctly understood only if we study it from the perspective of its victims. To understand society in terms derived from the dominant culture entangles us hopelessly in ideology. More than that, social science itself is a reliable instrument of knowledge only if it is guided by a commitment to emancipation. In the light of this "option for the poor", the positivistic understanding of social and economic science, whether on the right or on the left, is mistaken. Positivism is in fact an ideological distortion of the quest for scientific knowledge. While this point is not explicitly treated in the Documents, it is implicit in many of their judgements and applications.

In particular, there is the insistence that ethical reflection of economic theories and policies is indispensable. Many Canadians, including some economists, criticized the bishops' statement on the economic crisis (D6) because the bishops were not economists themselves. However, according to the bishops' statement, economic science always operates out of a set of values, and for this reason ethical reflection on economic policies is imperative. The dominant economics, the theories out of which the government tailors its economic policies, has implicit in it a concept of human nature, in fact a truncated concept of human nature, one which leads to policies that damage people on all levels of society. What is required, the statement insists, is an economic science and economic policies that operate out of a more appropriate concept of human nature. The commitment to emancipation, then, is not only a principle of action, it is also a principle of social and economic science.

This emphasis on the moral or spiritual dimension (in the emancipatory sense described above), implicit in the building of society and in its own scientific self-understanding, is characteristic of the emerging Catholic social theory. In this it differs strikingly from all that is summed up under the word "necessity" in Marxism. The solidarity of the people at the base and in the margin, grounded in people's respective collective self-interests, is at the same time a moral or spiritual achievement. We have here a stress on voluntarism that brings Catholic social theory, at this point, closer to Weber than to Marx. For Christians, I am prepared to argue, human history remains open: despite the strong trends built into economic systems and political institutions, society remains open to the new, the unexpected—for good and for evil. Thus society remains open to the influence of gifted persons who create solidarity among the people and initiate qualitative social transformation—and it remains open to wicked people capable of persuading others to engage in projects of domination. Christians believe, if I may use theological language, that history remains forever open to God's grace and human sin.

Since we have moved into the field of theology, it is perhaps worth saying that in the Catholic tradition, in contrast to certain classical Protestant emphases, the love of others or *agape* has not been understood as contradicting the love of self or rational self-interest. Only exaggerated self-love has been reproved as sin. The love of others was seen as sparked by grace but grounded in a strong sense of self-possession and oriented toward new and unexpected self-fulfilment. *Agape* was not at odds with self-love. Even the love of God was understood in terms of personal self-completion. "Our hearts are restless until they rest in Thee," wrote St. Augustine in his *Confessions*. In contrast to this, and sometimes even in protest against it, some Protestant traditions defined *agape* as antithetical to self-love. Christian love and self-affirmation did not go hand in hand. While Catholics preached self-denial as the overcoming of exaggerated *and* distorted self-love, some Protestants defined self-denial as the rejection of all self-love and self-interest. In this perspective, ethics is conceived in largely sacrificial terms. It is my impression that many secular persons in Canada who come from a Protestant background continue to understand "ethics" and "morality" as a call to utter selflessness and the overcoming of self-interest. Such persons will be greatly troubled by economic theories and political policies proposed on ethical grounds, especially on Christian grounds, because they believe them to be inspired by some sort of collective self-sacrifice. It is therefore useful to recall that in the Catholic tradition (and in liberal Protestantism) ethical life, whether of persons or of societies, is not at odds with appropriate self-interest. The option for the poor, or solidarity of workers and with workers, is at one and the same time an expression of material self-interest and a commitment to emancipatory values.

Again it is Max Weber rather than Karl Marx who sheds more light on the motivation out of which people, workers in particular, struggle for social transformation. Weber suggests that a movement for social change is more effective if it is nourished by a motivation that embraces several dimensions: *zweckrational* or pragmatic self-interest, *wertrational* or commitment to value, and some form of emotion, including religious sentiment. The call to solidarity made by Catholic social teaching is, therefore, not an idealistic strategy, idealistic here being used in the Marxist sense; it is on the contrary a political policy based on people's collective self-interest to better the conditions of their lives, joined to, and often carried by, a deeper passion, the commitment to emancipatory values—which for Christians are summed up in the crucified and risen Jesus.

Lest the above remarks be misunderstood it is important to add immediately that the Documents which emphasize the moral dimension of solidarity, also communicate a good deal of suspicion in regard to traditional morality, including Christian values. The "option for the poor" calls for a conversion, a raising of consciousness, a de-coding of the values belonging to mainstream culture and middle-class Christianity. In one pastoral letter, the Canadian bishops ask Catholics to re-read the Scriptures to hear in them God's call to justice (D3, n.9). The traditional reading of biblical texts and classical Christian literature only too often tamed the critical message. The Bible was usually read with the focus on personal salvation or personal holiness on the one hand, and on the other as a set of ideals legitimating the existing order and its authorities. Christian virtues were presented as upholding society and protecting it against its enemies, whether they be critics within or aggressors without. Dissent, disrespect, deviance, and disobedience were presented as sins. In their document on the Canadian North (D2, n.25), the bishops clearly recognized that in the past the Churches were identified with the world of empire and domination, and that despite the generosity and the good will of the missionaries, Christian preaching enhanced the authorities of the rulers and increased the sense of dependency among the Native Peoples. What Church documents demand at this time, first in the Third World, and then also in Canada, is the raising of consciousness, an ideology critique of traditional Christian teaching, and a new, more authentic formulation of the gospel as God's message for human deliverance, including deliverance from oppression.

While the Documents do not explicitly promote an ideology critique of Canadian culture, they do so implicitly. They foster the suspicion that the cultural symbols and mainstream wisdom that have put their stamp on Canadian society disguise society's victims and make the present condition appear normal, appropriate, respectable, and if not perfect, at least thoroughly decent. In their statement on the economic crisis in particular, the bishops insist that there is nothing "normal" or "natural" in the present state of unemployment (D.6, s.5), that it is in fact a situation that must be called "sinful", a "moral disorder". The reason why so many Canadians do not realize the seriousness of the social and economic crisis is that they live in a culture of injustice.

It is for this reason that the bishops introduce the vision of an alternative society. They recommend alternative models of economic development (D6, s.5,6). They make use here of what Pope Paul VI called the power of utopia. Because the inherited culture imprisons us in the here-and-now and simply makes us prolong this unjust present into the future, it is important to find an imaginative, moral and scientific discourse, in a certain discontinuity with the present, that projects an alternative vision of society, one close enough to the as yet unrealized and unexplored possibilities of the present to generate political action.

From what we have seen so far, it is possible to conclude, I think, that the emerging Canadian Catholic social theory is not a theory in the classical sense at all: it is rather a critical theory, a method for engaging struggling workers and struggling groups of people in reflection and analysis so that they may define the strategy for a joint movement of emancipation and social reconstruction. With this emphasis on the lived experience of ordinary people, especially the marginal, the social theory might be understood by some as a form of populism. This would be a mistake. Popular experience is of worth only if it has been mediated by the concept of justice. Experience and analysis are inseparable. The Documents presuppose throughout that human experience is never naked or immediate: it is always mediated through forms of the imagination and paradigms derived from theory. It is the yearning for justice, even if vaguely defined, with its thrust toward universality, that provides the medium for the experience of oppression and marginalization. The populist element in the Canadian bishops' social theory—we have seen the principle enunciated by Cardinal Flahiff—is the emphasis that ordinary people, initiated into concepts of justice, are able to come to a critical understanding of their own situation, move toward an analysis of the forces that make them suffer, and make a significant contribution to the movement that seeks to liberate them.

Crisis of Capitalism

Experience calls for analysis. The Documents insist that Christians must examine the structures of injustice and search for their historical causes (D3, n.9, D5, n.7). Only if we know these causes will we be able to engage ourselves in overcoming them. The Documents suggest, moreover, that in making this analysis people begin with the injustices they experience locally, in their own community (D5, n.15, D6, s.6). What are the structures of inferiorization at the place where we live? The analysis of these ills will inevitably lead to the identification of oppressive forces operative throughout the province, the nation, throughout the world. But only if we begin this analysis locally will we get a sense that the major forces of oppression, existing in stark and terrible visibility in some parts, also affect us where we live.

How can ordinary people engage in social analysis? Since they may not have the training to do this, the Documents provide Catholics with the essential elements for such an analysis. There is in fact a growing literature in all the Churches that offer people tools of analysis and initiate them into critical thinking. The contribution of the United Church of Canada is here outstanding.[14] No political scientist has as yet studied this remarkable literature. In addition to the Documents examined in this essay, the Social Affairs Commission of the Canadian Catholic Conference of Bishops has provided guidance for Catholics in a handbook, entitled *Witness to Justice*, which provides critical introductions to various aspects of Canadian society and an appropriate bibliography.

What is characteristic of the analysis of human suffering today, found in the Documents and in the Church literature mentioned above, is that it focuses on exploitation in the economic order. Other forms of oppression become more powerful as they are related to the master/servant relationship implicit in the economic system. There are also other styles of analysis used in contemporary Christian theological literature. Contemporary neoconservative authors like to turn to Max Weber and his less brilliant followers who attribute modern alienation simply to the impact of advancing technology and bureaucracy. Technocracy dehumanizes and depersonalizes all of us, workers as well as the middle class, the poor as well as the rich. The Christian Churches as a whole, however, have opted for different tools of analysis: they have focused on economic oppression as the motor force multiplying injustices and distortions in society. Critics of the Churches have claimed that this is due to Marxist influence. I think they are correct. A passage in which the Canadian bishops repudiate Marxism as a system of thought and a philosophy of history, concludes thus: "Nevertheless, some Christians engaged in struggles for justice use what is commonly called 'Marxist analysis'. This approach can help to identify certain injustices and structures of exploitation" (D4, n.16). The Canadian bishops follow here the position of Pope Paul VI. With him they also warn of the reductionist use of Marxist analysis.

The Documents adopt the position that the social ills in Canadian society have to do with the changes going on in international capitalism.

> The present recession appears to be symptomatic of a much larger structural crisis in the international system of capitalism. Observers point out that profound changes are taking place in the structure of both capital and technology which are bound to have serious social impact on labour (D6, s.2).

Some of the pastoral documents describe this crisis in greater detail. In the statements on unemployment and on the economic crisis (D5, D6), the bishops look for the causes of unemployment in Canada. They argue that it is important that we identify these causes, for otherwise we are tempted to blame innocent people for present unemployment, for instance immigrants, women, or the workers themselves (D5, n.8). Unemployment is very largely due to the changing structure of capital in Canada (D5, n.9, D6, s.2,3). And how is capital being transformed? The two documents reply to this by listing a series of factors.

First there is the concentration of capital in ever larger corporations which allows the decisions regarding production and resources to slip into the hands of an ever-shrinking elite. Then there is the centralization of capital in the metropolitan area of

Canada, which produces regional disparity and areas of unemployment. We have Third World pockets right in Canada. Then there is the internationalization of capital. This refers to the growing ability of the large corporations to shift capital, machinery and units of production to other parts of the globe where labour is cheap, workers are unorganized and where, in many instances, military governments prevent these workers from organizing. This new trend has led to the phenomenon of de-industrialization in Canada and the United States. The documents then mention the high degree of foreign ownership of Canadian industries. The decisions regarding production are in these instances made by boards outside the country, by people who have no reason to be concerned about Canadian workers. Another cause of unemployment mentioned in the documents is one that has characterized the Canadian economy from the beginning, its almost exclusive reliance on export of natural resources rather than the manufacturing of finished products. This trend, well documented in Canadian history, has received new strength through the various mega-projects supported by the government, aimed at the export of raw materials, which provide few jobs for Canadians and leave the country in a more dependent and less developed state. Finally there is the important factor of the new technology. Under its impact the industries and their offices, including banks, are becoming increasingly capital-intensive, with devastating influence on unemployment.

Many of these factors are operative on the world scale. The Documents (D5, D6) argue that international capitalism is undergoing a qualitative change. The decisions affecting resources and production are increasingly made to protect and promote capital, even when this trend damages the well-being of the great majority. While in the New Deal capitalism since the Second World War capitalists were willing to cooperate with government to foster the welfare state, at least to a certain degree, the new phase of capitalism introduces a new brutality. Governments become obliged to follow the lead of international capital and abandon the effort to protect their people. The consequences of this change, the bishops argue, "are likely to be permanent or structural unemployment and increasing marginalization for a large segment of the population in Canada and other countries'' (D6, s.2). The bishops maintain

> that through these structural changes, ''capital'' is re-asserted as the dominant organizing principle of economic life. This orientation directly contradicts the ethical principle that labour, not capital, must be given priority in the development of an economy based on justice (D6, s.2).

The new phase of capitalism ushers in a moral crisis of major proportions. ''As long as technology and capital are not harnassed by society to serve basic human needs, they are likely to become the enemy rather than an ally in the development of peoples'' (D6, s.3).

A similar analysis of the coming phase of capitalism is found in Pope John Paul II's *Laborem exercens*. The encyclical thinks of capitalism in three phases.[15] The first one, the entrepreneurial phase, based on privately owned companies and guided by a free enterprise ideology, created modern, industrial society. Here capital had been largely organized against labour. It was a period of great suffering for working people and the poor. The second phase of capitalism was based on corporate ownership and the cooperation of society (with its schools, its systems of transport and communication), guided by a New Deal ideology. Thanks to the pressure of the workers' movement and legislation by progressive governments, capitalism in this phase reconciled itself with the welfare state. The encyclical calls this ''neo-liberalism''. Here capital was made to serve labour to a considerable degree, even though the workers themselves had as yet no direct responsibility for the industries in which they worked. The third phase of capitalism, which began with the expansion of the transnational corporations, threatens to dismantle the restraints which the previous phase had put on the rule of capital.

Beginning with Paul VI's *Populorum progressio* (1968), papal social teaching has focused on the danger of the new international, economic imperialism.[16] John Paul II underlined this line of thought. The transnationals have become so powerful that small nation-states can no longer defend the interests of their peoples; their power is such that they can even force the powerful nation-state, out of which they operate, to use political pressure and military threats to make the world safe for their business. *Laborem exercens* (n.8) foresees that the suffering, the burden of injustice, produced in this third phase will be more extensive than that caused by nineteenth-century capitalism. Yet as nineteenth-century economic oppression produced "a burst of solidarity" (n.8) that resulted in the labour movement, so, Pope John Paul II thinks, the new, more extensive form of economic oppression, will in turn produce "a burst of solidarity" and create a new movement to remake the world order.

This change in the nature of contemporary capitalism, already starkly visible in Third World countries, is, in my opinion, the infrastructural development that accounts for the shift to the left in the Church's official teaching. There is no room here to develop this theme at length. Still, it is important to search for a sociological explanation of how it is possible that the Catholic Church, an organization that in many parts of the world, especially in the so-called Catholic countries, was identified with the reactionary sector of society, has become the promoter of a prophetic, critical social theory.

The Canadian Paradox

The economic crisis in Canada is linked to the new trend of world capitalism. At the same time, the Documents also speak of the specifically Canadian elements of the economic decline. The handbook *Witness to Justice* refers to "the double paradox" of Canadian society.[17] The first paradox is that Canada is an industrial society with technological development and standard of living comparable to the great industrial nations, while it is at the same time a country that contains extended regions of underdevelopment reflecting Third World conditions. The second Canadian paradox is that while Canadians like to think of themselves as junior partners in the economic empire (in fact, Canadian-based corporations operate in Third World countries, and the Canadian national psychology tends to identify with

American interests), the Canadian economy itself has many features of Third World dependency.

The Documents repeatedly mention the high degree of foreign ownership and hence the dependent character of Canadian industrial development. More often the Documents apply the theory of dependency to analyze the structures of injustice in this country. Capitalism is seen as an economic system that creates metropolitan centres and corresponding hinterlands, where the centres enrich themselves at the expense of the outlying regions. According to the Documents, the economic conditions that produce underdevelopment in Third World countries are also at work in the creation of underdevelopment in Canada. This is clearly stated in the pastoral, "On Northern Development" (D2, n.12). In a pastoral statement of the Catholic bishops in the Atlantic Provinces, entitled "To Establish a Kingdom of Justice" (June 6, 1979), the same theory of dependency is applied to explain the poverty of the Maritime provinces a well as certain cultural and psychological trends that have gained power over people's lives. Dependency has political consequences since it places great power in the hands of a small elite that mediates the connection to the metropolitan centre; and it has a great influence on people's collective consciousness since it destroys their sense of self-reliance and the trust in their own creativity. The "double paradox" is really a double pattern of dependency, a massive, many-levelled phenomenon that is largely disguised by mainstream culture. Commitment to social justice calls for a raising of consciousness in this regard.

Christopher Lind has shown that Latin American and Canadian bishops have been greatly impressed by the dependency theory worked out by Gunder Frank and the subsequent scientific debate surrounding it.[18] What appeals to them in particular in Frank's theory, an aspect that the subsequent scientific controversy does not invalidate, is an understanding of development that is not purely economic or quantitative. According to Frank, underdevelopment is a relational reality, it is the underside of centralizing capitalist development, and as relational phenomenon it significantly damages people's lives on many levels of their existence. Moreover, the development that is sought is not defined in purely economic terms. According to Paul IV's *Populorum progressio*, the struggle for global social justice aims at "the development of peoples, not economies". Frank's theory contains, however implicitly, an ethical dimension.

In addition to being influenced by dependency theory, the Documents reflect a dialogue of their authors with Canadian social scientists, particularly those identified with what the bishops call "the New Political Economy", who combine in a creative way a neo-Marxist theoretical approach with the non-Marxist, nationalist scholarship of Harold Innis.[19] The work of Mel Watkins has here been particularly appreciated. Because Canada's prolonged colonial status, its dependence on the export of staple goods and the exploitative relations between metropolitan centres and the hinterland affect the condition of labour in Canada as well as the cultural and human aspects of Canadian society, the New Political Economy has an ethical dimension that deserves to be explored and expanded. We noted earlier that while neo-Marxist scholars believe in the moral superiority of socialism over capitalism, they are usually unwilling to reflect on this moral dimension. It is here, in ethical reflection, that the emerging Catholic social theory sees its own proper task. In their statement on the economic crisis (D6) the bishops appear to offer a set of ethical arguments for a shift of the Canadian economy in a direction similar to that recommended by the New Political Economy.

In their statement on the economic crisis, the bishops draw a picture of the present economy, which in their judgement leads to moral disaster. The present policy, they say, puts emphasis on mega-projects aimed at exporting raw materials, even though this increases the national debt and creates only few jobs. The present trend is toward unrestricted conversion to high technology and hence toward ever more capital-intensive industries. The present policy favours foreign investment. Governments offer favourable conditions to new investors and existing industries to enhance their profit in the hope that the private sector will become the engine for Canada's economic recovery. The bishops think that this hope is illusory. "Even if companies recover and increase their profit margins, the additional revenues are likely to be reinvested in labour-saving technology, exported to other countries, or spent on market speculation or luxury goods'' (D6, s.4).

According to the bishops' statement, the present economic policy leads to growing permanent unemployment: it threatens an increasing segment of the population with the loss of human dignity. What is needed, therefore, is an alternative approach. The statement uses the word ''alternative'' repeatedly. This alternative flows from a new perspective that has not only a scientific but also a moral dimension. ''An alternative approach calls for a new ordering of values and priorities in our economic life'' (D6, s.5). Or again, to find alternative ways of looking at our industrial future and organizing our economy, we need ''a fundamental re-ordering of the basic values and priorities of economic development'' (D6, s.6). The alternative is formulated primarily in an ethical discourse, although it is not idealistic. The Documents do not advocate an ethical or utopian socialism that was mocked by Marx and Engels.[20] The bishops' call is not an ethical appeal to the nation, to rich and poor alike, to be converted to the principles of justice. It is, on the contrary, a moral discourse derived from the commitment to emancipation, and it is addressed to the sector of the population constituted by the solidarity of workers and with workers. The ethical reflections are intended to help generate a social movement that could become the agent of social reconstruction.

What is the alternative direction recommended by the bishops? Instead of mega-projects and increasing reliance on staple exports, the manufacturing sector of the economy should be developed, producing goods for use by Canadians. Instead of increasing foreign ownership, self-reliant industrial development should be promoted. To overcome the concentration and centralization of capital, community ownership and/or community control of the industries should be encouraged as well as new forms of workers' management and ownership of the industries. What is advocated here is not so much increased nationalization, but the decentralization of capital. We shall return to this point further on. The bishops recommend that Canada's labour-intensive industries be saved. While it makes no sense to resist the trend toward computer technology, it is dangerous to convert industry to the new technology without plans for the workers who will lose their jobs. The bishops recommend the creation of an appropriate industrial technology, one that takes into account technological progress and the requirements of full employment. The statement also suggests that greater efforts be made to develop renewable energy sources for Canadian industries. These proposals are not intended as a definitive outline for an alternative model of economic development, which the bishops are ready to defend; they are rather proposals to foster a public debate on alternative economic models. According to the Canadian bishops, this is not the time to rely on the recognized experts in economics, for on the whole their imagination is caught within the limits of the present system. What counts at this time is to explode this confined imagination, to imagine alternatives, and to test how feasible these radical proposals are.

The Documents do not confine themselves to an analysis of economic oppression, even though they make this their focal point. They also recognize other forms of victimization in Canada, the subjugation of the Native Peoples, the marginalization of non-white minorities, the neglect of the handicapped, the aged, prisoners, and other groups in the margin. In many instances, these forms of injustice are linked to economic exploitation. Because in our society human beings are honoured in accordance with their economic productivity, people without jobs are regarded as persons below the norm and hence little attention is paid to them. But the solidarity *of* and *with* the workers includes these people. The Documents are perhaps not sufficiently sensitive to the woman's movement.

The Canadian Catholic bishops have repeatedly recognized the peoplehood of French Canadians.[21] The bishops of Quebec have written an important pastoral letter in which they defend Quebec's right to self-determination.[22] But neither they nor the Canadian bishops as a whole have tried to influence the Quebec people how to respond to the project of sovereignty-association. In their pastoral letter, the Quebec bishops insisted that the future of Quebec must be decided by Quebec people themselves, and this included the French majority as well as the Native Peoples, the English who have long been established there, and the more recent immigrants. Movements of national self-determination are acceptable from a Catholic point of view, the bishops write, only if they are not accompanied by a political ideology of national superiority and if they are effectively restrained by a commitment to respect the civil rights of the minorities.

Critical Social Theory

The emerging Catholic social theory adopts a conflict approach to the understanding of Canadian society. It regards as the dynamic element of society the movement of solidarity created by the workers and with them by all groups suffering injustice, joined by all citizens who love justice, a movement aimed at creating a society free of domination. The theory appeals to the experience of the various peoples, classes and groups that suffer under dominating structures, it proposes paradigms for interpreting these experiences, and it initiates the new members of the movement into a set of analytical tools that will allow them to link their local experience of injustice to the economic forces that define Canadian society and its relation to Third World countries. The theory is carried by an alternative vision of Canadian society, a utopia in the sense of Ernst Bloch and Paul VI, which stands in judgement over the present order, reveals the ideological distortions of mainstream culture, and strengthens people's commitment to the movement of solidarity.

At the same time, the social theory remains incomplete. While it identifies the historical agent of social change, it does not indicate the manner in which this movement might transform the existing order. One reason for this, I think, is that this Catholic social theory, while reflecting the experience of grassroots organizations, has been formulated by bishops, by men whose high office in the Church prevents them from entering more directly into Canadian politics. The Documents are written in such a way that they allow several readings, in particular a reformist and a more radical one (cf. D4, n.18). Some Catholics committed to social justice think they follow the new Catholic teaching when they become engaged in the more or less established ways of political and social reform, while other Catholics, following a more radical reading, become more restless, more troubled, and more demanding. They involve themselves in struggles around particular issues, they join one or several action groups, they work in a political party if they detect in it radical possibilities, but their deeper political intention is the creation of a movement of solidarity, possibly through and around a political party, that aims at the transcendence of capitalism.

It can be argued, I think, that the emerging Catholic social theory, is incomplete also for more profound reasons. By identifying the movement of solidarity as the agent of social change, the Documents leave to this movement the decisions regarding the way and the manner social change is to be brought about. I refer here to the Flahiff principle mentioned above: "Theoretical knowledge is indispensable, but it is partial and limited; when it abstracts from lived concrete experience, it merely projects the present into the future." Because this principle has been observed, it is possible to speak of a Canadian Catholic social theory, different in emphasis and tone from Catholic social theories worked out elsewhere. At the same time, because of this principle, the Documents offer a social theory that is incomplete precisely because it is a critical theory (rather than a theory in the classical sense),[23] one that is guided by a concrete utopia, that initiates people into the critique of the existing order, that encourages solidarity among workers and other groups struggling for justice, and fosters solidarity with workers by all who share an emancipatory ethics, a theory, in other words, that defines an approach, a style or reflection, a method. The theory offers theoretical grounds for a movement of solidarity, but then remains open to the political ideas that such a movement will generate. Catholic social theory will then apply the same critical method to test the new ideas, retaining its focus on the ethical, spiritual, emancipatory dimension of the social struggle.

Since certain critics of the bishops' statement on the economic crisis have accused it of being socialist, we must ask whether this is true. What a question of this kind means today is not very clear. Who knows what socialism is! Some people on the left think that socialism is a useful word because it symbolizes a rupture with the existing capitalist society; others on the left, with the same social and economic views, believe that the word has become politically useless because the totalitarian societies of Eastern Europe call themselves socialist. I do not wish to resolve this question. It is, however, possible to show that the Canadian Catholic social theory has a certain affinity to the social philosophy of the CCF, worked out in the thirties.

A number of Canadian economists, for instance Abraham Rotstein and Anthony Waterman, have made public pronouncements in support of the bishops' statement, in which they interpreted the bishops' social message simply as a condemnation of the government's monetary policies and a strong support for a return, possibly an enhanced return, to Keynesian economics. They think, therefore, that the critics have been needlessly hard on the bishops: their statement had nothing to do with socialism. This interpretation is not totally convincing. It is true, a certain intended ambiguity allows the statement to be read in a reformist and a more radical way; but if all it recommends is the return to Keynsian economics, one does not see the need for the emphasis on "the option for the poor" and the creation of a workers' movement of solidarity as agent of social change. The thrust of the statement points to a more drastic transformation of the Canadian economy. How else can one interpret the call for workers' management and ownership of Canadian industries?

While industrial strategy recommended in the statement calls for intelligent economic planning, we noticed that no mention was made of the nationalization of the industries. Since Pius XI's *Quadragesimo anno* (1931), Catholic social teaching has acknowledged the need for nationalization. According to this encyclical (n. 114), nationalization is necessary whenever private ownership puts so much power into the hands of an elite that governments can no longer protect and foster the common good. Yet the call for extended state ownership is not without its dangers. First, nationalization offers no guarantee that the industries will be used in the service of the labouring people. This point is made very forcefully in Pope John's II's *Laborem exercens* (n.14). Extended state ownership, moreover, puts excessive power in the hands of the government. Pluralism and freedom thrive in society only if they are inscribed in the economic infrastructure. Without a certain economic pluralism, the praise of freedom and democracy is purely idealistic. Ideas are powerful only if they are carried by infrastructural requirements. For this reason, Catholic social theory calls for the de-centralization of capital. According to the Documents, the necessary centralizing trend, the growing need for responsible and democratically controlled economic planning, must be counter-balanced by a de-centralizing trend, the cutting down to size of the giant transnational corporations. In this context the Documents recommend various forms of community ownership and workers' ownership of the industries (D5, n.14, D6, s.6). The tension between centralizing planning and de-centralizing social ownership promotes creativity and political freedom.

It is of interest to recall that the social philosophy of the original CCF movement differed from many other forms of social democracy in as much as it embraced, from the very beginning, the cooperative movement and cooperative principles.[24] In the Regina Manifesto the CCF committed itself to the promotion of cooperative ownership. The fear of a powerful centralized state bureaucracy made the early CCF advocate various forms of social ownership, some federal, some provincial, some regional or local, and some cooperative. The CCF also wished to balance the centralizing trend of economic planning with a de-centralizing trend derived from the pluralism of social ownership.

In this context it is of interest to recall that socialism advocated by the CCF retained a particular ethical tone.[25] It clearly distinguished itself from the so-called "scientific socialism" with its positivistic presuppositions. The CCF had been created by the union of several radical movements in Canada, including a strong influence of the Social Gospel, especially in the Prairie provinces. Emancipatory ethics remained an abiding principle in the CCF, which its leaders were not ashamed to invoke in their speeches. From this view, there is a good deal of similarity between the emerging Catholic social theory and the old CCF socialism.

At the end I wish to cite a concluding sentence from the speech Cardinal Flahiff made at the 1971 Synod of Bishops in Rome.

"The Church cannot be content to think of the world theoretically: it must transform it."

NOTES

[1] Cf. G. Baum, *Catholics and Canadian Socialism* (Toronto, Lorimer, 1980), pp. 71-81.

[2] N. Betten, *Catholic Activism and the Industrial Worker* (Gainsville, University Presses of Florida, 1976), pp. 46-7.

[3] G. Baum, op. cit., p. 124.

[4] Ibid., pp. 179-80. Cf. A.-J. Belanger, *L'apoliticisme des idéologies québécoises, 1934-36*. (Québec: Presses de l'Université Laval, 1974), pp. 307-27.

[5] G. Baum, "Recent Catholic Social Teaching: A Shift to the Left," in the forthcoming volume, Irving Hexham (ed.), *Religion and Economics* (Vancouver, Fraser Institute).

[6] Cardinal Flahiff's address is published in the booklet "Witness to Justice, Some Statements by Canadian Catholic Bishops" (Canadian Catholic Organization for Development and Peace, no date), pp. 1-3.

[7] Cf. Tony Clarke, "Communities for Justice," *The Ecumenist*, 19 (1981), pp. 17-25.

[8] The five documents, D2 to D6, are reprinted in G. Baum, *Ethics and Economics, Canada's Bishops on the Economic Crisis* (Toronto, Lorimer, 1984).

[9] G. Baum, *The Priority of Labour* (New York, Paulist Press, 1982).

[10] Since D6 is not divided into numbered paragraphs, I shall number the subtitles, s1 to s6, and use them in my references.

[11] A clear definition of the option for the poor is contained in the Final Document, nn. 1134-40, of the Puebla Conference. See J. Eagelson and P. Scharper (ed.), *Puebla and Beyond* (Maryknoll, N.Y., Orbis Books, 1979), p. 264.

[12] Cf. *Quadragesimo anno*, n. 65, *Mater et magistra*, nn. 91-103. Recent papal documents are available in collections such as J. Gremillion (ed.), *The Gospel of Peace and Justice* (Maryknoll, N.Y., Orbis Books, 1975).

[13] *Laborem exercens*, n. 12. The encyclical is reprinted in G. Baum, *The Priority of Labour* (New York, Paulist Press, 1982).

[14] A regular newsprint publication, called *Issue*, presenting critical assessment of social concerns, is brought out by the Division of Mission in Canada of the United Church of Canada. See also the resolutions and task force reports presented to the United Church's General Council.

[15] *Laborem exercens*, nn. 1 and 11.

[16] For an analysis, see J. Gremillion's volume referred to in Note 12, pp. 23-7.

[17] *Witness to Justice*, pp. 19-20.

[18] Christopher Lind, "Ethics, Economics, and Canada's Catholic Bishops," *Canadian Journal of Political and Social Theory*, 7, No. 3, pp. 150-66.

[19] Christopher Lind, "An Invitation to Canadian Theology," in the forthcoming *Toronto Journal of Theology*, 1. No. 1.

[20] See C. Wright Mills, *The Marxists* (New York, Dell Publishing Company, 1962), pp. 72-80.

[21] Cf. "A Letter on the 100th Anniversary of Confederation," 1967.

[22] "The People of Quebec and its Political Future," April 15, 1979.

[23]Cf. Max Horkheimer, *Critical Theory* (New York), Herder & Herder, 1972), pp. 188-243.

[24]G. Baum, *Catholics and Canadian Socialism*, pp. 19-20.

[25]Ibid., pp. 67-70.

Democratic Values

*Towards the Regime of Tolerance**

THE HONOURABLE
THOMAS R. BERGER

*This chapter represents a revised version of an address delivered at a conference on the current state of liberal philosophy, held at the University of Guelph in June of 1983.

Northrop Frye has said that "Man must seek his ideals through his social institutions". What do our Canadian institutions reveal about our ideals? This is what the constitutional debate of recent years has been about. Despite its flaws, our new Canadian Constitution and Charter of Rights, adopted on April 17, 1982, is a valuable and uniquely Canadian undertaking and represents our own attempt to articulate the philosophical ideas undergirding the Canadian polity. It is Canada's contribution to evolving notions of liberal democracy and political pluralism.

Why do we believe in Canada? What things are most important in our shared history? Here we are, twenty-four million souls scattered among the snow and scenery. Canada has persisted. Why? And why should it matter?

Some believe that the Canadian achievement lies in the utilization of our natural resources—the establishment of the fishery, the gathering of fur, the development of the grain trade, the building of an empire in timber, and now the exploitation of oil and gas and minerals on our frontiers and beyond. Here lies the Canadian achievement, in the conquest of our cold and distant landscapes and seascapes. These common tasks, it is said, are what unite us all.

I think there is more to Canada than that. I believe there is a distinctive Canadian intellectual contribution to the legal and political order, a way of enabling human rights and fundamental freedoms to prevail in a world where minority rights are constantly in danger of being extinguished and diversity is constantly under attack.

Let me offer you one man's idea of what Canada may have to contribute to the furtherance of human rights and fundamental freedoms in such a world. I speak as a resident of Vancouver where, for a majority of children in elementary grades on the east side, English is a second language, and as a resident of British Columbia with more than 200 000 citizens of Asian descent and the highest concentration of Native Peoples in any province of Canada.

We in Canada do not share the American goal, often reiterated (for example, by Michael T. Kaufman in the *New York Times Magazine*, May 15, 1983), of integration and assimilation. We believe that diversity is not inconsistent with a common citizenship. Furthermore, diversity is the condition of the world. In fact, it may be that our own experience, our own constitutional arrangements, our own mix of population, make us a more likely prototype than the United States for the world of the future.

We often compare ourselves to the United States. Because we share the same language, the same continent, and the same traditions of democracy and due process, such comparisons come easily. When we compare our record in defence of human rights and fundamental freedoms, we sometimes shrink from the result. Take for example, the expulsion of Japanese Canadians from the Pacific coast in 1942. We not only interned our citizens of Japanese descent; our Government tried, in 1945 and 1946, after the Second World War had ended, to banish them to Japan. They were not allowed to return to the Pacific coast until 1949. The United States, though it expelled the Japanese Americans from the Pacific coast, did not try to banish them to Japan, and allowed them to return to the coast even before the war had ended.

In recent years, however, it may be that we look rather better when such comparisons are drawn. In the 1950s, when McCarthyism disfigured the political landscape in the United States, and washed over into Canada, the Supreme Court of Canada stood firm in defence of the rights of political dissenters.

In the 1960s, when thousands of young Americans left their country rather than fight in a war that they considered to be unjust, they fled to Canada. Here they were given asylum, and here thousands have remained.

In the 1970s, when Vietnamese of Chinese descent were expelled from Southeast Asia, drifting over the water in search of refuge, the world took them in. The largest number, quite naturally, were received by China. A very large number were received by the United States. But it was Canada which took in 50 000, a larger number, on a per capita basis, than either China or the United States. Indeed, Canada now has the world's highest ratio of refugees to total population—one in every 324 Canadians is a refugee.

So we can see a distinctive Canadian tradition emerging. How do we square this tradition with the adoption of a Charter of Rights which many think of as a carbon copy of the United States Bill of Rights? Much has been said about the Americanization of the Canadian Constitution by the adoption of a Charter of Rights. Our Constitution and Charter, however, takes us beyond the American Constitution and Bill of Rights.

The American Constitution and Bill of Rights were adopted in the late eighteenth century. The Bill of Rights is a classic statement of liberal ideas of *individual* rights, of the political and legal rights that appertain to individual liberty. In Canada before 1982 these rights were safeguarded by the common law, and were by and large observed as faithfully here as in the United States. Now they have been included (though not altogether entrenched) in the Canadian Constitution and Charter. It is to a consideration of these provisions of the Charter that lawyers are usually drawn.

Even a cursory examination of our Constitution and Charter will show that it takes us much further than the American Bill of Rights. For instance, our Charter provides that "the rights and freedoms referred to [in it] are guaranteed equally to male and female persons''. It also includes provisions that reveal strands of Canadian federalism altogether distinct from the United States variety: the Charter enshrines the principle of equalization payments, that is, the redistribution of revenue among the provinces to ensure that Canadians in every province receive ''reasonably comparable levels of public services at reasonably comparable levels of taxation''.

Let me come, however, to those provisions of our Constitution and Charter that bear particularly on my theme. These are the provisions offering explicit protection for the rights of minorities, provisions that reflect twentieth-century notions of human rights and fundamental freedom. The rights of both of Canada's great linguistic communities have been recognized in the Constitution and Charter. The special place of the Native Peoples—the Indians, the Inuit and the Metis—has been acknowledged. We have also acknowledged the multicultural dimension of Canadian society, and another provision of the Charter, to come into force in 1985, will guarantee to every individual the right to equality under the law and the right to the equal protection of the law ''without discrimination based on race, national or ethnic origin, [or] colour''. Why have we gone to all this trouble?

In Canada we have two great societies, two nations, if you will, one English-speaking, one French-speaking. It would be a mistake to pretend otherwise. Yet we are mixed up together, and we have chosen to stay together. There are a million or more Native Peoples in our midst, claiming a measure of self-determination, and millions of new Canadians—immigrants of every ethnic and racial background and every political and religious persuasion. Thus diversity is the essence of the Canadian experience. The Constitution and the Charter reflect this diversity.

Does this leave us with a constitutional hodge-podge: protection for languages here, over there guarantees for aboriginal peoples, and, as well, an affirmation of multi-culturalism? No, these measures are the logical outcome of our history. If Quebec were to achieve independence, she would at once be faced with the very questions that confront Canada today: the rights of a great linguistic minority, the claims of the aboriginal peoples, and the place of numerous ethnic and racial groups in the life of the country.

The questions that minorities raise are not always easy to answer, and they are not always the same. Some minorities wish to integrate, some even to assimilate, and they fear that cultural distinctions will be used to exclude them from equal opportunities in political, social and economic life. Others seek to defend and protect such distinctions, fearing that their erasure will lead to assimilation and the surrender of their identity.

Our concepts of self-government acquired their present form in the nation-states of Great Britain and France, states that have traditionally been ethnically defined; we have not therefore fully realized institutional guarantees for racial, cultural, religious and linguistic minorities. In the *BNA Act*, our original Constitution, enacted in 1867, we made a beginning: in the 1982 Constitution and Charter we have made a most significant advance.

Our ideas of human rights have only recently expanded to include the rights of minorities. Governments are usually opposed to the devolution of power, to the entrenchment of diversity, to what they see as the weakening of the nation-state. This is especially so when a single, dominant people regards the state as its own political instrument. The government of such a state may regard minority languages and cultures as anomalous or transitional. In Canada, however, we have found that such diversity is the essence of the Canadian experience.

It is our good fortune that we are not all of us of common descent, that we do not speak one language only. Our idea of who we are was not fixed in a single stirring encounter. We are not cursed with a triumphant ideology; our patriotism is of the quiet sort. We have had a national flag only since the 1960s. We cannot agree on the words of our national anthem. We have no national waxworks. To some this is regrettable, but on the whole I think it is a good thing. There are, after all, 150 countries fully accoutred with flags, anthems, and all the rest, and millions ready to march in support of this or that spurious cause. Do we need any more? Perhaps we in Canada can develop a new nationalism where individuals do not need to rejoice vicariously in a sense of national power and prestige in order to authenticate their own lives.

For these reasons Canada is a difficult country to govern. There is no easy consensus. It would be simpler if we all spoke the same language, if all our children went to the same schools, if we all held the same religious beliefs, if we were all of us white. But we are not. Such diversity should not terrify us, or provoke an epidemic of xenophobia. It is our strength, not our weakness.

The struggles of Canada's minorities do not represent the whole of the Canadian experience by any means.[1] But they throw into relief the true extent of our capacity for tolerance, our belief in diversity. They sharpen our perception of ourselves—and though these struggles began, many of them, long ago, they still continue—and they may have a contemporary denouement.

Along every seam in the Canadian mosaic unravelled by conflict, a thread of tolerance can be seen. I speak of tolerance as a positive quality—not as mere indifference—of tolerance as the expression of a profound conviction about the virtues of diversity.

The crises of times past have thrown up men and women who have articulated an idea of Canada that illuminates the Canadian journey. I want to cite the words of three of these figures: Wilfrid Laurier, Angus MacInnis, and Justice Emmett Hall.

Wilfrid Laurier's career spanned the three school crises of the French-Canadian minorities in Canada. He was a backbencher in the House of Commons in the 1870s when the Acadians lost their claim to constitutional guarantees for their denominational schools. As Prime Minister he negotiated the Laurier-Greenway agreement in 1896, which gave to French-Canadians in Manitoba the right to conduct religious teaching in the public schools after hours. He was a member of the opposition again when the Ontario Government sought to limit the use of French in the separate schools of Ontario in 1912.

The disputes about separate schools in New Brunswick in the 1870s, in Manitoba in the 1890s and in Ontario in the early years of our own century were not simply disputes about religion, schools, curriculum and language. They were disputes about the place of the French-Canadians in the English-speaking provinces. In New Brunswick and in Manitoba the dispute was ostensibly over religion, in Ontario over language—two different carriers of culture. But in each case the underlying issue was the same: were the French-Canadians to have a distinct and inviolate place in the life of the English-speaking provinces, free to practise their religion and speak their language, not as a private matter, but as a matter of constitutional right, and with the same entitlement to public funds for their denominational schools as the provinces provided to the English-language public schools?

Laurier was Leader of the Opposition when Ontario sought to limit the use of French in the bilingual schools of that province. On May 9, 1916, the Liberal MP Ernest Lapointe moved a resolution in the House of Commons urging the Legislative Assembly of Ontario not to interfere with the children of French-speaking parents being taught in their mother tongue. Laurier spoke in support of that resolution. He expressed his belief that every child in Ontario ought to be able to speak English. But he pleaded for the right of the children of French parentage to a second education in a second language. The following passage appeared in his speech, delivered in English, a speech that ought to be studied in our schools today. Here is Laurier, in his seventies, still able to summon eloquence and passion:

> ...Now I come to the point where I want to speak to my fellow-countrymen in the province of Ontario. When I ask that every child of my own race should receive an English education, will you refuse us the privilege of an education also in the language of our mothers and our fathers? That is all that I ask today; I ask nothing more than that. I simply ask you, my fellow-countrymen, British subjects like myself, if, when we say that we must have an English education, you will say: "You shall have an English education and nothing else". There are men who say that in the schools of Ontario and Manitoba there should be no other language than the English language. But, sir, when I ask that we should have also the benefit of a French education, will you refuse that benefit? Is that an unnatural demand? Is that an obnoxious demand? Will the concession of it do harm to anybody? And will it be said that in the great province of Ontario there is a disposition to put a bar on knowledge and to stretch every child

> in the schools of Ontario upon a Procrustean bed and say that they shall all be measured alike, that no one shall have the privilege of a second education in a [second] language?...

Laurier was pleading for what he called "the regime of tolerance". There were no guarantees for the use of French in the schools in those days. In the new Charter of Rights, however, there is a constitutional guarantee for minority language education rights. This provision can be the means by which the French language is maintained in the English-speaking provinces. (This is important not only to French Canadians. The preservation of French-language rights in the English-speaking provinces is in the long run likely to help preserve the language rights of more than one million English-speaking Quebecers).

I have referred to the expulsion of Canadians of Japanese descent from the Pacific coast in 1942. This was not the result of a sudden manifestation of anti-Japanese feeling in British Columbia. The province had a long history of animosity toward Orientals, and a long history of discriminatory legislation. Racism had been entrenched in our political culture and was enshrined in federal and provincial statutes. Waves of anti-Oriental feeling had many times lapped at the homes of Japanese Canadians. Pearl Harbor generated a wave of anti-Japanese hysteria which was to sweep the Japanese Canadians away, to disperse them and to destroy their communities.

Throughout 1941, as war with Japan drew closer, Members of Parliament from British Columbia urged the federal government to take drastic measures against Canadians of Japanese ancestry. Only one MP from the province, Angus MacInnis of the CCF, defended the Japanese Canadians. Here is MacInnis speaking in the House of Commons on February 25, 1941:

> If we are to have harmonious and friendly relations between the oriental population and the rest of our British Columbia citizens, we must stop discriminating against and abusing the orientals. We must find some common ground on which we can work, and I think it can be found. Is there any reason, if we should get into difficulties with Japan on the Pacific coast, why the Japanese in British Columbia should be interested in helping Canada, after

> the way in which we are treating them? I am satisfied that if we treat the Japanese and our other oriental citizens aright, we shall get their loyalty, because they are no longer orientals in the accepted sense of that term. They would feel as much out of place in Japan as we would. I know them, speak to them; I visit them and have them in my home, and I have not the slightest doubt that what I say is correct. If we are to avoid the troubles that other countries have had with racial minorities, then we must take a realistic view of the situation in British Columbia and attempt to make these people feel at home among us. We will secure their loyalty by fairness and kindness and by the practice of those other attributes which we exercise in our relations with other people.

But when the war came, the clamour against the Japanese Canadians prevailed over the few voices that appealed to reason; all together, 21 000 people, three-quarters of them born in Canada, were evacuated from the west coast and interned. After the war, in 1945 and 1946, the Government of Canada sought to revoke the citizenship of Canadians of Japanese origin and to deport them and their families to Japan.

These measures were racist. That is a word perhaps too often used nowadays. But we can understand its true meaning, and the danger it represents, by reference to the case of the Japanese Canadians. A group were singled out, solely on the ground that they were of a different race than the majority, and subjected to cruel and degrading laws—even to the extent of denying them their citizenship. Prime Minister Mackenzie King wrote in his diary, after Hiroshima, that it was "fortunate that the use of the [atomic] bomb should have been upon the Japanese rather than upon the white races of Europe".

But there were, at last, protests against the government's policy, and these soon spread throughout the country. On January 24, 1947, Prime Minister King gave in. He announced that the government would not carry out its deportation program. But by this time almost 4000 evacuees, half of them born in Canada, had sailed for Japan.

It was not until 1949, four years after the war had ended, that the network of discriminatory legislation erected over the years by the federal and provincial governments was dismantled. Japanese Canadians were free at last to take their rightful place in Canadian life.

Looking back, it is easy to condemn those who called for evacuation, internment, and deportation of the Japanese Canadians. But what would we do today if some other minority were the object of racial hatred? It is not enough to say that it won't happen again. In a crowded world, Canada will continue to be a land to which peoples from all over the world, of every race, wish to come. And they are coming, from every continent.

The racial virus has so far been kept in check. There has been no attempt in any province to erect a network of discriminatory laws and regulations. There are human rights commissions at the federal level and in every province. And there are the provisions of the Charter of Rights. These give minorities the confidence to speak out, to protest the violation of their freedom, and to assert their claim to rights we have all been taught they should enjoy.

The Constitution, the Charter, and the law do not, however, provide complete protection for racial minorities. It would be difficult to draft a statute that did. Equality for racial minorities depends, in the end, on the attitudes of the citizenry.

Let me now turn to an issue which has in recent years deeply engaged Canadians. I refer to the question of Native rights. This takes us back to the beginning of Canada's history, to the occupation of a continent already inhabited by another race, with their own culture, their own languages, their own religion, their own way of life. The issue of Native rights is the oldest question of human rights in Canada and, at the same time, it is the most recent—for it is only in the last decade that it has entered our consciousness and our political bloodstream. In that decade, however, Canadian federalism has found it possible to embrace an expanding concept of Native rights.

It was not always so. The struggle of American blacks, though a mighty event in the history of the United States, is in its own way almost unique in this hemisphere. It was—and is—a struggle for equality through integration. On the other hand, the 500 year long struggle of the Native Peoples of North and South America presents a quite different and in some ways more difficult issue: how to provide the means for aboriginal peoples who wish, as a collectivity, to remain distinct and yet contemporary peoples in the midst of dominant societies founded on European ideas of liberal democracy. Canada now acknowledges its obligations to address this issue.

This has happened because the belief of the Native Peoples that their future lay in the assertion of their own common identity and the defence of their own common interests proved stronger than any had realized. When the suit brought by the Nishga Tribal Council of British Columbia to establish their aboriginal title reached the Supreme Court of Canada in 1973, all six judges who addressed the question supported the view that the Nishga's title had been recognized by English law in force in British Columbia at the time of the coming of the white man. In the judgement of Mr. Justice Emmett Hall in the *Nishga* case you will find that sense of humanity—that stretch of the mind and heart—which enabled the Court to look at the idea of Native claims and to see it as the Native Peoples see it. This, of course, required some idea of the place of Native history in our own history. It had been urged that the Nishgas were at the time of contact, a primitive people "with few of the institutions of civilized society, and none at all of our notions of private property".

Mr. Justice Hall rejected this approach. He said:

> The assessment and interpretation of the historical documents and enactments tendered in evidence must be approached in the light of present-day research and knowledge disregarding ancient concepts formulated when understanding of the customs and culture of our original people was rudimentary and incomplete and when they were thought to be wholly without cohesion, laws or culture, in effect a subhuman species. This concept of the original inhabitants of America led Chief Justice Marshall in his otherwise enlightened judgement in *Johnson v. McIntosh*, (1823) 8 Wheaton 543, which is the outstanding judicial pronouncement on the subject of Indian rights, to say: "But the tribes of Indians inhabiting this country were fierce savages whose occupation was war...". We now know that that assessment was ill-founded. The Indians did in fact at times engage in some tribal wars but war was not their vocation and it can be said that their

> preoccupation with war pales into insignificance when compared to the religious and dynastic wars of "civilized" Europe of the 16th and 17th centuries.

Mr. Justice Hall concluded that the Nishgas had their own concept of aboriginal title before the coming of the Europeans and were still entitled to assert it today. He said:

> What emerges from the...evidence is that the Nishgas in fact are and were from time immemorial a distinctive cultural entity with concepts of ownership indigenous to their culture and capable of articulation under the common law having "developed their cultures to higher peaks in many respects than in any other part of the continent north of Mexico".

The American media penetrates Canadian life so completely, we have a tendency sometimes to think that our own issues of race relations must be defined in the same way as they are in the United States. Thus many of our legal scholars and political scientists think only in terms of replicating American experience. In 1969, the Government of Canada adopted a policy of integration and assimilation for Canada's Native population that was based on American policy, developed in the 1960s, towards blacks. In 1973 the Government of Canada acknowledged that a quite different policy was called for.

In January 1981, all parties in the House of Commons agreed that the aboriginal rights of the Native Peoples should, together with their treaty rights, be entrenched in the Constitution. This provision is now a part of the new Constitution, albeit with the qualification that recognition is limited to "existing" rights.

The entrenchment of the rights of the Native Peoples is thought by some to be anomalous. Why should they have any rights not enjoyed by other Canadians? To provide a formal place within the Constitution for aboriginal peoples is said to be an affront to the conventions of liberal democracy. Yet we have taken an irrevocable step here too, acknowledging at last what the Native Peoples have said all along, that they have the right to a distinct and contemporary place in Canadian life. Indeed, in March of 1983 a constitutional conference was held in Ottawa between the Prime Minister and the Premiers of the provinces and the leaders of Canada's Indian, Inuit and Metis peoples.

What could be more relevant to the contemporary world? In every country in North and South America there are aboriginal peoples who will not be assimilated, and whose fierce wish to retain their common identity is intensifying as industry, technology and communications forge a larger and larger mass culture, extruding diversity.

Our determination to preserve our two linguistic communities, our recognition of the distinct position of the Native Peoples, our policy of ethnic multiculturalism—all these may be regarded, by some, as anomalies. But the recognition of such "anomalies" may in time constitute Canada's principal contribution to the legal and political order. J.E. Chamberlin, author of *Harrowing of Eden*,[2] has said that "Canada is Canada not only because of its unique commitment to French and English cultures, but because of its unique commitment to native nations". Constitutional protection of French and English makes the way easier for other languages, because it negates the idea of a monolithic culture. In the same way, the guarantees to the Indians, the Inuit and the Metis exemplify the Canadian belief in diversity. In this way the interests of the two linguistic communities, and of the aboriginal peoples, merge with the idea of multiculturalism.

I have been discussing minority rights, but the question is not limited to this. There is also the question of the health of the body politic. For minorities make a *positive contribution*, indeed an *indispensable* contribution, to the life of the nation. Dr. Ralf Dahrendorf, Director of the London School of Economics, speaking at Atkinson College, York University, on September 29, 1979, said:

> What is surprising is that modern societies with their opportunities of affluence, their experience of terror, their values of citizenship rights and the rule of law still seek that homogeneity which breeds boredom and kills creativity. What is behind this desire today? Why is it that people seem to find it difficult, at the

> end of the 20th century, to live with others who differ from them in language, culture, religion, colour?

Questions of human rights in Canada are linked to questions of human rights around the world. Our own successes and failures, our own attempts to accommodate minorities, are important not only to ourselves. If people of differing languages, races, cultures, and religions can live together harmoniously within a federal state embracing half a continent, perhaps they may learn to live together harmoniously in the wider world.

The new Constitution and Charter, though they seek to come to grips with these questions, do so only imperfectly. No constitution or charter can resolve these great questions of human rights and fundamental freedoms. In a sense they are never resolved. But the Charter will offer minorities a place to stand, ground to defend, and the means for others to come to their aid. The Charter is, to adopt a phrase of Professor W.R. Lederman's, "a...landmark on a continuing journey, but it is in itself neither a beginning nor an end". I believe that journey is a journey towards the regime of tolerance that Wilfrid Laurier dreamed of, towards a nation—and a world—where diversity is regarded not with suspicion, but as a cause for celebration.

As F.R. Scott, a Canadian who is at once one of our finest constitutional lawyers and one of our finest poets, has said:

> If human rights and harmonious relations between cultures are forms of the beautiful, then the state is a work of art that is never finished.

NOTES

[1] I have discussed minority rights and dissent in Canada in my book, *Fragile Freedoms: Human Rights and Dissent in Canada*, published by Clarke Irwin in hardcover (1981) and revised in softcover in 1982. It is coming out in Quebec in French in 1984.

[2] J.E. Chamberlin, *Harrowing of Eden: White Attitudes Toward Native Americans* (New York, Seabury Press, 1975).

The Development of Social Democracy in Canada

NORMAN PENNER

Social democracy as an ideology and a movement developed in most capitalist countries in the nineteenth century as part of the growing class consciousness of the proletariat, then experiencing the worst features of the industrial revolution. It developed almost simultaneously with the first attempts of factory workers to form unions, and expressed the recognition by the most advanced among them that unions were not enough, but had to be accompanied by the workers taking an independent part in political battles in order ultimately to capture political power.

By the end of the nineteenth century the most powerful social-democratic parties in Europe adopted Marxism as their ideological and theoretical foundation and elaborated their long-term programs with Marx's teachings as basic. Fundamentally such parties believed in the revolutionary overthrow of the capitalist states and the re-making of all aspects of industrial society in the socialist image and in the working-class interest. Most of these socialist parties formed a loose international federation which has become known as the Second International. They attracted to their ranks some of the most brilliant intellectuals in Europe and America and many of them became the leading representatives and spokespersons of these parties.

But not all socialist-minded workers or radical intellectuals accepted the Marxist idea, nor even agreed that the aim of social-democratic parties should be socialism. This certainly was the case in Britain where the Labour Party was officially formed in 1906 as a federation, which while it admitted some Marxist groups as affiliates, did not endorse socialism nor did it recognize the class struggle as the motor of social change. There were many diverse currents within the Labour party then, including Marxism, Fabianism, labourism, Christian socialism, among the most conspicuous, but the party's program was more liberal and reformist than anything else.

It was not until 1917, after the Russian Revolution, that a split took place in the world socialist movements, as a result of which social democracy became regarded as the non-Marxist or even anti-Marxist segment, while the extreme revolutionary wing under Lenin's leadership called itself Communist. From the First Congress of the Communist International in 1919, social democracy became an epithet by which Leninists derided their protagonists, and social democracy became the definition of socialists who believed "in evolution rather than revolution" and who adhered to the parliamentary rather than the revolutionary path, by which to attain the goal of socialism.

Social-democratic ideas were brought into Canada mainly by immigrant workers from Britian, the United States, and Central and Eastern Europe. As a result there appeared in the last part of the nineteenth and first part of the twentieth centuries Marxist parties,[1] Independent Labour parties, and parties based on Henry George's idea of a single tax, and the beginnings in 1917 of a national Canadian Labour Party sponsored by the Trades and Labour Congress of Canada. But the advent of the Russian Revolution brought about the formation of a Communist Party in Canada in 1921, and it was not until 1933 that a national party based on the later definitions of social democracy was formed under the name of the Co-operative Commonwealth Federation (CCF).

The CCF took a different path than most social-democratic parties, certainly different from the British Labour Party which was solidly based on trade union support, and was almost from the outset the political expression of the working class or at least a larger part of it. The CCF had rejected the idea of a labour party, as proposed by the Trades and Labour Congress (TLC), because it would have cut itself off from the radical farmers, especially in the West, where agrarian revolt had taken place immediately after the First World War, and where there was every potential for another revolt as a result of the severe impact the Great Depression was having on these same farmers in the thirties. The CCF started as a loose federation of labour political groups, farmers associations, co-operatives, a few trade unions, and some important academics. They were able in spite of sharp differences to agree on a program, and finally to establish a national party, which had been in the works at least thirty-five years. The fact that it has become the third party in Canadian politics shows that its existence responds to real needs which are felt and expressed by a section of the Canadian people.

The contradiction between labour and capital in the early twentieth century, one of several sources of acute conflict in the developing Canadian society, often resulting in the use of the Army against the workers,[2] produced various responses in the political arena. One response already noted was the growth of socialist parties based on Marxism. Another was the development of independent labour parties which exerted pressure on the organized labour movement to try to form a national labour party. There was also the emergence of the social gospel movement in which several prominent Protestant ministers, mostly in Winnipeg and influenced by Salem Bland, principal of Wesley College (Winnipeg), associated themselves very closely with the labour movement and influenced labour to enter more vigorously the field of political action. All of these ramifications ultimately helped produce the CCF. But simultaneously with these developments a shift was beginning inside the major capitalist parties away from nineteenth-century Toryism to a form of liberal reformism. It was this shift that proved to be decisive in slowing down and reducing the effectiveness of the movement towards a national social-democratic party.

The two main architects of liberal reformism in Canada were Mackenzie King and O.D. Skelton, both Ph.D. graduates of Harvard. King was the labour expert of the Liberal Party from 1900 on, and Skelton was Professor of Political Science at Queen's University in Kingston. They joined forces after 1921 with King as Prime Minister and Skelton as his senior civil servant to reshape the Liberal Party of Canada. Among other things that each had done in preparation for this role were Skelton's important work *Socialism—A Critical Analysis* published in 1911 and characterized by Lenin as the most objective treatment of socialism by "a bourgeois professor" and King's *Industry and Humanity* in 1918, a plea for conciliation rather than confrontation between labour and capital, a work that has been described as "the first and only book on politics of a classical character produced by a Canadian".[3]

In 1913, Skelton had issued a warning to Canadian capitalists in an article in one of the leading financial journals in Canada, entitled "Are We Drifting Into Socialism?". The main argument in this article was that the capitalists should urge the adoption by governments of reform measures to head off the more extreme demands being made by the working class and its organizations:

> Not only are these policies not necessarily socialistic; they are the best bulwarks against socialism. They are homeopathic cures, vaccinations against its growth. For private property today is on the defensive. It has no heaven-born sanction. It will endure only so long as it proves socially beneficial. The hour of social as well as political democracy has come. The ideal which will prevail, the ideal shared by socialists and individual reformers alike, is the organization of industry in the interests of the masses of the people. Our existing order will endure if it can be made and can be shown to be true, that private property is a better means of attaining this end than collectivist property. It must be shown that within the existing framework of society we can combine private initiative and private energy with social control and social justice. Every tax-dodging millionaire, every city slum, every instance of shady high finance or of overworked and underpaid employees is a potent argument for socialism. Remove the grievances—and they are many, even though exaggerated out of all perspective by the socialist—and the socialist has lost his best ammunition.[4]

Later that year Gustavus Myers, an American Marxist, already at work on his epic *History of Canadian Wealth*, commented on

Skelton's article in the *International Socialist Review*. He called Skelton one of the "super-agents of Capitalism who, foreseeing the coming of Socialism, are scientifically instructing their capitalist class how to take measures to ward off the genuine Socialist movement." Myers warned the socialists not to fall into the trap of fighting for immediate reforms, because that just "makes Capitalism more palatable to those whom it exploits and to give it an attractive appearance of respectability....Professor Skelton solemnly advises capitalists to turn themselves into a reform party and outdo all other reformers. This can be easily done, for whereas other reformers can merely agitate from the outside, the capitalist class has the power to enact whatever reforms suit its purposes."[5]

Mackenzie King published *Industry and Humanity* in December 1918, completing it after the Russian Revolution, in a period of great unrest throughout the world, including Canada, as a result of the war. The theme of the book according to Fern and Ostry is summed up in the following passage from it:

> It is not alone a new dawn Labour and Capital may summon forth; they can create a wholly new civilization. Let Labour and Capital unite under the inspiration of a common ideal and human society itself will become transformed. Such is the method of creative evolution....Let Labour and Capital unite under the ideal of social service: the work of continued production will go on; not only will it vastly increase, but the whole complexion of Industry will become transformed. No longer will Industry be the battleground of rival and contending factions; it will become the foundation of a new civilization in which life and happiness abound.[6]

In April 1919 Professor R.W. MacIver of the University of Toronto published *Labour in the Changing World*[7] in which he addressed himself to the same problem but with a different approach.

> ...today labour feels a new consciousness of power. It has widened its claims, its horizon is no longer limited to a living wage.

> It demands a share in prosperity and a voice in the control of industry.[8]

In another passage MacIver might have been addressing himself to Mackenzie King when he declared that:

> anyone who today speaks of the essential identity between capital and labour, is convicted thereby of either simplicity or hypocrisy. For how can there be identity of interest between two parties one of which seeks to diminish what the other seeks to augment, to one of which accrues all of the joint product that it can withold from the other?[9]

Between the statements of King and those of MacIver lies one of the principal differences between liberal democracy and social democracy. Yet as it turned out both statements were correct in their historical setting. As Gustavus Myers pointed out the capitalist class is capable of making many concessions to the working class, and so long as it can make such concessions there can be a reconciliation of sorts between labour and capital. At any rate this is the idea that King was trying to sell to the Canadian bourgeoisie.

Because of the major theme of his book, Mackenzie King felt that the Winnipeg General Strike, which took place from May 15 to June 26, 1919, would be seen by many as a confirmation of his warnings about the need for conciliation, and that this in turn would help King win support for the leadership of the Liberal Party which was to be decided at the Convention scheduled for August 1919. There is little doubt that this factor did influence delegates to vote for King and, but for that, he might have been deprived of the 43 votes which was his final margin of victory. In his celebrated essay, "Conservatism, Liberalism, Socialism in Canada: An Interpretation," Gad Horowitz asserts that "King's *Industry and Humanity* and the Liberal platform of 1919 mark the transition of English Canadian Liberalism from the old individualism to the new Liberal Reform."[10]

The unrest and discontent that had emerged toward the end of the First World War involved the labour movement, the farmers, and the French Canadians. Authoritarian Toryism, at that time the dominant ideology of the ruling elites, had undermined the ideological basis of social order and opened the floodgates to a rapid rise of radicalism. Labour unrest produced a strong demand for a political party expressing the working-class interest. But while labour was debating its political position, the farmers revolted and produced provincial farmers' parties which by 1921 had become the governments in Ontario and Alberta, and a national farmers' party called the Progressive Party which emerged from the general election of 1921 as the second largest party in the House of Commons.

The debate within the labour and socialist movement on the nature and shape of a working-class party ran into obstacles which proved insurmountable at the time. In September 1917 the Trades and Labor Congress under socialist leadership had voted to establish a Canadian Labour Party, but in 1918 with a new pro-Liberal leadership the TLC began to drag its feet on implementing the resolution of 1917. After the Bolshevik victory of November 1917, the majority of members of the Marxist groups favoured a party on the Russian model rather than on the British. A significant group headed by J.S. Woodsworth opposed both models and began to agitate for what he called "the Canadian way".

Under the heading "Organizing Democracy in Canada" Woodsworth, in a number of articles in the *Western Labour News* starting in the issue of August 23, 1918, laid out the basis and program for "a genuine people's party in which farmers, industrial workers, returned soldiers and progressives could all find a place". Canada, he said, unlike Britain was not "predominantly industrial" and consequently "a labour party could not, unaided, hope to obtain power". To found a purely labour party, without the farmers, would be premature and doom the new party to isolation from the start. Yet it was perfectly clear to Woodsworth in outlining a proposed program for a people's party, that it would be clearly a social-democratic party emphasizing socialization of the railways, of the mines and other natural resources, of the banks and insurance companies, and the "progressive" socialization of manufacturing establishments.[11] Such a party, he wrote, would have as,

> our ultimate object...a complete turnover in the present economic and social system. In this we recognize our solidarity with the workers the world over....This is frankly "revolutionary" but does not look at all in the direction of a violent bloody revolution....Such a change we hope will be accomplished in this country by means of education, organization, and the securing by the workers of the machinery of government.[12]

Woodsworth was very precise and all embracing in his outline of the main demands which such a party would inscribe in its platform. These were:

> 1. Socialization of railways, telegrams, express companies, elevators, docks, stockyards, cold storage plants, and other public services of transportation and communication;
> 2. Socialization of mines, timber limits, fisheries, water-powers, electric, and other natural resources socially operated;
> 3. Socialization of banks and insurance companies;
> 4. The organization of the distribution of food products and raw materials;
> 5. Taking over of existing munition works and the utilization of these for producing supplies for public works;
> 6. The progressive socialization, that is, the bringing under national, provincial, or co-operative ownership and control of manufacturing establishments and commercial institutions;
> 7. The expropriation of unused lands;
> 8. In case of socialization or expropriation suitable provision to be made for the present owners;
> 9. During the transition period between private ownership and public ownership, public revenue to be derived from the following sources: a) Rent of privately used land or other resources not socially operated, b) A steeply graduated income tax, c) Large private estates at the death of the present owners to revert to the state; and
> 10. Management of industries to be under the joint control of committees representing the administrative body and those engaged in the industry.[13]

But after laying out in these articles the need for a people's party rather than a strictly labour party, it was clear that Woodsworth visualized such a third party to be a socialist party with a program much more socialistic than the British Labour Party and certainly drawing a sharp distinction between his program and that outlined by Mackenzie King in his 1918 book, *Industry and Humanity*.

But King's advocacy of liberal reformism was to prove decisive in winning back to the Liberal fold a large section of the farmers' movement. More than that, the leadership of the TLC and substantial sections of the American Federation of Labor in Canada became supporters of King politically and were able to prevent the affiliation of their unions to any form of social-democratic party. During the years from 1921 until his defeat in 1930, King devoted a lot of attention to Woodsworth and his small labour group and succeeded in convincing people who might otherwise have supported Woodsworth that there was not that much difference in their social programs. In the crucial vote of June 1926 when Woodsworth traded his support to King in exchange for old-age pension legislation, his action according to a biography of King,

> aligned the Left in Canada with the Liberal Party as a lesser evil than the Conservative. King's earlier radicalism, generally forgotten, had built a tacit alliance which might save him now, would certainly profit his party in due season....The Liberal Party was moving leftward. It would move much farther than Woodsworth dared to hope.[14]

The parliamentary struggles which were fought out in the House of Commons during the decade 1921-30 set the stage for the eventual formation of a social-democratic party. Woodsworth battled with King for the support of the farmers' groups and ended up winning 11 out of the original 65. He developed a social-democratic position on major Canadian themes. He championed the cause of labour. His many speeches on the status of Canada and its economy constituted a major contribution to a social-democratic political economy of Canada. Two major weaknesses in his position however were a complete failure to understand Quebec and the national question and, associated with this error, his continued insistence on strong powers for the central government even though that was strongly opposed by Quebec. These positions were later adopted by the CCF and carried forward by the NDP.

Woodsworth also had differences with the Independent Labour Party (ILP) which he represented in the House of Commons from 1921 until it became part of the Co-operative Commonwealth Federation at its foundation in 1933. Some of these differences surfaced when Woodsworth applied to join the Winnipeg Centre branch of the ILP in 1921, after a long absence from Winnipeg interrupted only by his return to help in the Winnipeg General Strike. The immediate difference arose out of a seemingly technical point, when his application was held up until his membership in the Federated Labour Party (FLP) in British Columbia (which he helped to found) could be classified. Even though there was no national party, several ILP members felt that since J.S. Woodsworth had not resigned from the FLP, he should not be allowed to join the Manitoba ILP![15] This was finally settled and the way opened for Woodsworth to become a candidate of the Manitoba ILP in the Winnipeg Centre riding. He was denounced by the Trades and Labour Council of Winnipeg which objected to Woodsworth's support for, or at least his failure to fight, the One Big Union which had retained some strength in Winnipeg. Moreover, the TLC considered that by running under the ILP banner Woodsworth had badly undermined the Canadian Labour Party, which the Labour Council supported.

There were other differences, and these were reflected in part in the Manifesto of the Manitoba ILP. This manifesto was much more moderate than the articles Woodsworth wrote in the *Western Labour News*, referred to above. The Manitoba manifesto was labourist rather than socialist, and while there was nothing in it that Woodsworth could disagree with, he wanted it to go further. This was seen in an article he wrote for the *Canadian Forum* in 1925, as part of a series which that magazine was publishing about the possibilities of a new party. Woodsworth cited the program of the Manitoba ILP as a model, but whereas that program had fourteen points, he added an extra point which he was later compelled to give up, "Opposition to all encroachments of Capitalist Imperialism".[17]

The differences Woodsworth had with the ILP were expressed in his arguments with A.A. Heaps who was elected to the House of Commons in 1925 as the ILP candidate for Winnipeg North, and who held that seat until 1940. The biography of A.A. Heaps, written by his son Leo, explains the differences between Woodsworth and Heaps in these terms:

> The major political difference between the two was that for Woodsworth every capitalist was suspect as a wicked exploiter of labour. He seemed unaware that men could come from a background of wealth and still possess a sensitivity and a troubled conscience towards the ills of mankind. Heaps could genuinely befriend and respect Bennett, while Woodsworth was intellectually unable to do so.[18]

Another difference according to Heaps' biography was Heaps insistence that the new party that Woodsworth was working towards should be a labour party based on the British model.

> Heaps advocated a Canadian Labour Party that would represent the legitimate aspirations of labour. But the CCF did not listen to Heaps. Instead it took a wrong turn in the thirties.[19]

When the CCF was finally formed in 1933, it adopted the *Regina Manifesto* as its program. This was very similar to the original program which Woodsworth had listed in his series of articles in the *Western Labour News* in 1919, referred to above. There were included however some additional points which Woodsworth had not inserted but with which he was in full agreement. One was "security of tenure for the farmer upon his farm on conditions to be laid down by individual provinces....". Another was section 12 entitled Freedom:

> Freedom of speech and assembly for all; repeal of Section 98 of the Criminal Code; Amendment of the Immigration Act to pre-

> vent the present inhuman policy of deportation; equal treatment before the law of all residents of Canada irrespective of race, nationality or religious or political beliefs.

The entire manifesto, especially the last paragraph, was a resounding victory for Woodsworth:

> No CCF Government will rest content until it has eradicated capitalism and put into operation the full programme of socialized planning which will lead to the establishment in Canada of the Co-operative Commonwealth.

There is no doubt that the unity which finally emerged to form the CCF, with its clearly socialist program, was made possible by the onset of the Great Depression, and the consequent increased militancy of a section of labour, radical intellectuals, and farmers who were particularly hit by poverty, evictions and foreclosures.

But while this radical program was accepted after much debate at the founding Convention in 1933 it was not the Marxist-oriented delegates and their criticism of the program that ultimately triumphed. Rather it was a powerful group of intellectuals who began shortly after the death of Woodsworth to propogate the need for a more moderate statement of the CCF aims and means. They were headed by David Lewis, M.J. Coldwell, and Frank R. Scott, who argued that the *Regina Manifesto* was a product of the worst years of the Depression and ought to be changed to bring it up to date. At the 1944 Convention, the first big change in the CCF program took place with the adoption of a draft which contained some important new formulations. These limited socialization to "key industries which are monopolistic in operation." "For the first time," according to Lewis, "the CCF officially recognized the idea of a mixed economy."[20]

After this victory, this group pressed for further changes in the *Regina Manifesto* and by 1956 had succeeded in replacing the *Regina Manifesto* with an entirely new one known as the *Winnipeg Declaration*. The *Regina Manifesto* had stated clearly the aim of the CCF to be the "eradication of capitalism", and committed itself to the means by which this would be done, namely by the socialization of the Canadian economy through the Parliament of Canada when the socialists had won a majority. The *Winnipeg Declaration*, however, eliminated these explicit statements in favour of a more general declaration of its commitment to humanitarian goals, without being committed to any particular means by which these goals would be realized.

The difference between the two manifestos is seen particularly in the last paragraphs, which indicate the different emphases that permeate both documents. *The Regina Manifesto* ended with this ringing call:

> No CCF Government will rest content until it has eradicated capitalism and put into operation the full programme of socialized planning which will lead to the establishment in Canada of the Co-operative Commonwealth.

The Winnipeg Declaration ends with a motherhood statement that any party in a democratic society could endorse:

> The CCF will not rest content until every person in this land and in other lands is able to enjoy equality and freedom, a sense of human dignity, and an opportunity to live a rich and meaningful life as a citizen of a free and peaceful world. This is the Co-operative Commonwealth which the CCF invites the people of Canada to join with imagination and pride.

David Lewis vigorously maintained that the new statement of principles was no new departure in content but merely in the wording. Nevertheless even the less sophisticated reader would see that the framers of the Declaration felt it necessary and desirable to water down the socialist content of the original manifesto. In arguing on behalf of the *Winnipeg Declaration*, Lewis quotes approvingly the speech which R.H.S. Crossman made at the Convention, on behalf of the British Labour Party:

> Ironically enough, it is the socialists and the trade unions of the world who have saved capitalism from its inevitable collapse by

> raising the standard of living of the masses, which was required to create a new form of capitalism such as we see it today.[21]

Thus stated, one can draw the conclusion that instead of "eradicating capitalism" which was the main aim of the *Regina Manifesto*, the CCF leaders in 1956 felt that their purpose was the reform of capitalism, for the well-being of the people, and even in the interests of the capitalists themselves.

The CCF and its successor the NDP, like all social-democratic parties, reflects various ideological currents within its ranks. As a result there is a constant battle going on within the party, sometimes bitter, other times milder, but never muted. The most important schism in recent years took place between 1969 and 1972 with the emergence in the NDP of a fast-growing faction popularly called the Waffle. It wanted to make the NDP more socialist and more nationalist. It tied the question of socialism to the growing domination of Canada by United States capital.[22] But while it finally disintegrated as an organized movement, it left behind it an active left group in the NDP as seen in the Convention of July 1983, which was held symbolically in Regina, exactly 50 years after the formation of the CCF.

David Lewis in his memoirs attributes the problem of the CCF and NDP to three factors: the reformism of Mackenzie King, the constant attacks on the party by the Canadian Communists, and the failure of the CCF or NDP to win any serious support in Quebec. Lewis felt that the politicians of the two major parties, and particularly Mackenzie King, borrowed the ideas put forward by the CCF, and made them Liberal planks.[23] That is not however a completely accurate assessment. The fact is that Mackenzie King in his *Industry and Humanity* of 1918 put forward many proposals which the CCF later adopted, but within a social-democratic framework.

There is no doubt that Mackenzie King's liberal reformism paid off in delaying the advent of a social-democratic party and, after its formation, in limiting its size and effectiveness as a parliamentary force. He was not as successful as Roosevelt, whose bold policies in the New Deal destroyed the Socialist Party and the populist parties in the United States, and won the adherence to the Democratic Party of most of the trade union leaders including those who had been members of the Socialist Party. King proceeded in what looked like the same direction, but without the speed and decisiveness of Roosevelt. His policy of conciliation made him appear as a moderate, leaning slightly to the left. The Communist Party believed in King's reforms and stated that King "had supported progressive policies...and was susceptible to mass pressure...", and therefore should be supported.[24]

But it must be noted here that another factor in making King appear almost radical was the reactionary nature of the Tory leaders he confronted: Meighen, Bennett, Manion, and Drew. The hatred Bennett engendered during his five years in office, for example, caused many voters who might otherwise have voted for the CCF, to cast their ballots in the 1935 election for King as the lesser evil.

The conflict between the Communist Party of Canada and the CCF, as David Lewis states in his autobiography,[25] took a lot of time and much effort on the part of the CCF and especially from David Lewis who made the fight against Communism one of his main themes. But the fight actually began before the formation of the CCF, when in 1921 the Communist Party of Canada was formed as a unit of Lenin's new Communist International, and adopted the Conditions of Affiliation to the CI, one of which was that all Communist parties "must recognize the necessity of a complete and absolute rupture with reformism and the policy of the 'Centre'; and that they must carry on propaganda in favour of this rupture among the broadest circles of party members."[26] From 1921 until 1933, there was no national social-democratic party in Canada, and the Communist Party of Canada (CPC) had a clear field to win the support of class conscious workers. It carried on a relentless struggle against social democracy and social democrats, accentuated in 1928 by the Sixth Congress of the Communist International when Stalin coined the epithet "social-fascist" to characterize social democracy throughout the world, and elevated the fight against social democracy to be the *main* task of all Communist parties.[27] While this slogan was abandoned in 1935, in favour of the tactic of the "united front", Canadian Communists never officially condemned the slogan, even after the Communist Party of the Soviet Union, under Khruschev, said in the book *Fundamentals of Marxism-Leninism* (1963):

> In 1928 Stalin went so far as to declare the Left Social Democrats "the most dangerous carriers of bourgeois policy in the working class" and he introduced additions in this sense into the theses of the Sixth Congress and the Tenth Plenary Session of the Executive Committee of the Communist International, thereby forcing the Communist Parties of the capitalist countries onto a path of sterile sectarianism.[28]

The Communist Party of Canada officially adopted Stalin's characterization at its own Convention in 1929. In fact when describing Woodsworth, Jack MacDonald, then General Secretary of the CPC, in his report to that Convention, used almost the same words that Stalin had used in describing social democracy the world over:

> Woodsworth is one of the most dangerous elements in the working class. The fact is that he is the main representative of the bourgeoisie in the ranks of the working class, yet a large number of workers look upon him as a real champion of the workers.[29]

The Communist Party has never recognized that it made any errors in its characterization of the CCF, and though it changed its tactics many times with regard to the CCF, in its latest account of its history published in 1980 it still places all of the blame on the leadership of the CCF for the poor relationship which existed between the two parties.[30]

The appeal of the CPC for a united front with the CCF in the thirties won some support within the CCF including some fairly prominent leaders of the CCF, but was rejected for a number of reasons. One of the most important reasons why the CCF rejected these appeals vehemently was their fear that a united front would be looked upon as identifying the CCF with the Communists, thereby blurring the distinction which men like Woodsworth, Lewis, Scott and others felt was essential to maintain.

In that respect, they were probably correct. The kind of socialism that was already becoming evident in the USSR, including executions, assassinations, and fake trials, increased the difference between democratic socialism and communism, and it was felt that these differences would tend to be obliterated in the minds of most Canadians if the CCF had entered into joint activities with the Communists. Nevertheless, in elected bodies and in other forms the CCF and the Communist Party did fight for similar measures such as unemployment insurance, repeal of Section 98 of the Criminal Code, aid to republican Spain, support for Canadians who went to fight for Spain, support for the single unemployed and their epic "On-to-Ottawa" trek, and so on. This was a period of *de facto* united front activity, while at the same time each party felt it necessary to denounce the other, publicly.

But the main factor which made it impossible to envisage any kind of organic unity, even on the most fragmentary basis, was the fight between the CCF and the CPC for political support from the newly organized industrial unions. The Communists had succeeded in organizing the first CIO unions in Canada starting in 1935, and when the CCF began to take these unions seriously and sent in organizers as the CPC had done, a fierce struggle got underway which lasted for almost 20 years, with the CCF ultimately victorious. As a result most of the Communist-led unions were expelled from the central labour federations, or were captured outright by the CCF with the support of the international officers of these unions.[31] There is no doubt that the CCF benefitted in this struggle by its support for the "cold war", although this is not to suggest that its support for the cold war was motivated by the desire to get closer to the main leaders of the international unions. But it helped.

Many members of the CCF rejected in part or in whole the propaganda that posited the Soviet Union as the only threat to world peace and overlooked the aggressive imperialism of the United States which was deploying its armed forces throughout the world. But the main leaders of the CCF supported wholeheartedly the foreign policies of the Canadian and American governments, particularly NATO, the war in Korea, and the rearmament of West Germany.[32] At the same time the cold war propaganda rebounded somewhat against the CCF as seen in its drop in popular support. The fierce anti-communism of the period had a spill-over effect by which many people reacted against all forms of socialism. (See Table showing percentage of popular vote obtained by the CCF-NDP for the years 1949, 1953, 1957 and 1958, at the end of this essay.)

With the impending merger of the Trades and Labour Congress of Canada and the Canadian Congress of Labour in 1956, the CCF entered into negotiations to have the new Canadian Labour Congress adopt the CCF as its political arm. This was one of the compelling reasons for the *Winnipeg Declaration*. To succeed in achieving this alliance, it was necessary to satisfy the more conservative representatives of the American Federation of Labour (there was no problem with the Congress of Industrial Organizations, affiliated with the CLC) by a program that was much less socialistic than that of the CCF hitherto. Out of these negotiations the New Democratic Party emerged as a reconstructed CCF, with a structure that would enable trade unions to affiliate *en bloc*, and with a watered down program to match. But this change has not brought about the desired result of winning the working-class voters away from the Liberal Party.

In the twenty years of its existence, the NDP has continued to confront the problem of the differences between social democracy and liberalism. It could not relate to Quebec nationalism, and found itself irrelevant in the sweeping changes of the Quiet Revolution even though these changes were of a radical and social-democratic character.

Nowhere is the NDP's dilemma more conspicuous than in its support for Trudeau's constitutional package. This support made the party, once again, unable to relate to Quebec. In fact it strongly opposed Quebec on the issue. It also placed the federal party in a position hostile to the provinces where it had enjoyed wide support in four of the provincial legislatures. The national party's support of the constitutional package resulted in a major split at two recent conventions, July 1981 and July 1983. The split was not the usual left-right split. The opposition also consisted of people like former Premier Alan Blakeney of Saskatchewan, the party organizations in Alberta and Quebec, and approximately fifty per cent of the Ontario delegates.

The NDP finds itself in a trap of its own making. Oddly enough it was warned about such a trap in 1960 by Pierre Trudeau who was then not in the Liberal Party, but close to the CCF. In an article written for a CCF publication, Pierre Trudeau warned it not to be associated at all times with support for a strong central government, at the expense of the provinces.[33] His main theme was that the CCF, which is strong in certain provinces, should be flexible enough to advocate provincial rights. "Left-wing thinkers have too often assumed that fundamental reform is impossible without a vast increase, in law or fact, of the national government's area of jurisdiction".[34] But this view, Trudeau held, has "considerably harmed the cause of reform". It has harmed the CCF in its relation to Quebec because it wrongfully limits the Quebec case to one of protecting cultural and language rights which it then says are quite capable of being defended in Ottawa rather than Quebec. But Trudeau pointed out in 1961 that Quebec's rights include the right to self-government, not just cultural rights, and the former must be defended as well as the latter.[35]

Yet the support of the CCF for a strengthened central government in the thirties had much more validity for a social-democratic party than it has now. It was fighting then to have the central government assume powers necessary to alleviate the effects of the Great Depression. It had even more validity in the early fifties when the party was advocating a full welfare state, which the federal government was in a better position to implement. But no such issue is involved in the present debate. In fact, the federal government is reducing its contribution to the federal-provincial program of joint expenditures for social legislation adopted during the fifties, and is using its strong fiscal powers to aid the big business sector of the economy.

The changes which have taken place throughout the world in the past two decades have presented challenges to the social-democratic parties in advanced capitalist countries which have been met in vastly different ways. On the one hand there has been an upsurge in the strength and power of some parties, as in

France, Greece, and Spain. But at the same time there has occurred a serious split in the British Labour Party, where much of the right wing which had dominated the party for most of its history has left to form a new party which it calls the British Social-Democratic Party.

In Canada during this period, the New Democratic Party has been fluctuating in its popular vote and number of elected members (see Table at end of essay). It has been the government at various times in three of the four Western provinces, and in one period from 1972 to 1975 it held these provincial governments at the same time. There is no doubt that the position the NDP federal caucus took to support Trudeau's constitutional package caused a serious schism within the party, particularly between those who place their emphasis on provincialism and those who still regard a strong central government as almost a religion. There are those who demand a total recasting of the party into a radical, clearly socialist, and militant one recognizing and advocating self-determination for Quebec, and breaking with NATO.[36]

All of these currents surfaced strongly at the Fiftieth Anniversary Convention of the NDP held in Regina in July 1983. What came out of this Convention, however, was the same as what went in. The differences are still there. They were not resolved, and will undoubtedly become accentuated as the political and economic crisis which has gripped Canada continues to deteriorate, and the onslaught against the welfare state and against the trade-union movement sharpens.

There are differences within the NDP over its economic policies, social legislation, and even about the role of the trade unions in the party. But there are other issues which have also surfaced, and which have created sharp differences within the party and among people who normally vote NDP. Some of the more recent examples are the NDP stand on constitutional reform, its attitude toward self-determination for Quebec, its stand on abortion and free choice, and its attempt to restore French rights in Manitoba.

These divisions present a real dilemma for the NDP. True to its character as a social-democratic party, it takes in people who can unite around much of the NDP program, but who come in with somewhat different perceptions of what the NDP's role ought to be. In the West, where the Liberals are practically extinct both provincially and federally, the NDP has been able to win some Liberal votes and even to recruit Liberals into the party. But this has created or accentuated those differences which are much more difficult to resolve.

Another dilemma which has been referred to earlier, is the absence of any real influence of the NDP in Quebec. With or without this influence, the NDP cannot continue to be an English-only movement or party. It must either incorporate into its program self-determination for Quebec or, what would be the same thing, maintain fraternal relations with a party of Quebec social democrats, on the only basis which would be meaningful, namely the NDP recognizing the fact that Quebec is not just a province but is also a nation.

The NDP has changed its attitude to foreign policy from the cold war stance in the forties and fifties, to become the only party in the House of Commons to adopt positions against United States involvement in Central America and Chile and against the testing of the Cruise Missiles on Canadian soil. In general it supports the peace movement and the movement's opposition to nuclear weapons. But in spite of great pressure from within the NDP and from the peace movement, it still supports Canada's membership in NATO which in fact ties Canada and the others to follow the dangerous road along which the United States, as the real leader of NATO, is taking its so-called "partners".

There is no doubt that to be effective in this period the NDP will have to become more militant than before, and to operate on a scale wider than orthodox parliamentarianism allows. It must include in its program the new issues of the past two decades—women's rights, feminism, Native rights—and fight for them whether in power or not.

It can and probably will accept much of that challenge, particularly if pressure from the trade-union movement, women's groups, and other non-parliamentary bodies increases. In those conditions, the NDP and whatever social-democratic party emerges in Quebec, by working together with these non-parliamentary bodies could fulfill, in part at any rate, the expectations many people have had about the role of social democracy in Canada, but which have been only partially fulfilled.

Percentage of the popular vote obtained by the CCF-NDP on the federal level and in its four best provinces in provincial elections

G denotes that the CCF/NDP formed the government.

FEDERAL VOTES

1935	9%
1940	8%
1945	16%
1949	13%
1953	11%
1957	11%
1958	9%
1962	14%
1963	13%
1965	18%
1968	17%
1972	18%
1974	15%
1979	18%
1980	20%

PROVINCIAL VOTES

British Columbia

1933	31%	1960	34%
1937	30%	1963	29%
1941	35%	1966	35%
1945	40%	1969	35%
1949	37%	1972	40% **G**
1952	32%	1975	39%
1953	32%	1979	46%
1956	30%	1983	49%

Manitoba

1936	12%	1962	15%
1941	17%	1966	23%
1945	35%	1969	38% **G**
1949	25%	1973	42% **G**
1953	17%	1977	39%
1958	20%	1981	48% **G**

Ontario

1934	7%	1959	17%
1937	6%	1963	16%
1943	32%	1967	26%
1945	22%	1971	27%
1948	27%	1975	29%
1951	19%	1977	28%
1955	17%	1981	21%

Saskatchewan

1934	25%	1960	40% **G**
1938	22%	1964	40%
1944	55% **G**	1967	44%
1948	46% **G**	1971	55% **G**
1952	55% **G**	1975	40% **G**
1956	44% **G**	1978	48% **G**
		1982	38%

NOTES

[1] Norman Penner, *The Canadian Left* (Toronto, Prentice Hall, 1977), pp. 40-76.

[2] See S.M. Jamieson, *Times of Trouble: Labor Unrest and Industrial Conflict in Canada 1900-66* (1971), p. 9; Desmond Morton, "Aid to the Civil Power; The Canadian Militia in Support of Social Order" in *Canadian Historical Review*, 50 (1970), p. 407; Norman Penner (ed.), *Winnipeg 1919: The Strikers Own History of the Winnipeg General Strike* (Toronto, Lorimer, 1975).

[3] Henry Fern and Bernard Ostry, *The Age of Mackenzie King* (London, Heinemann, 1955), p. 246.

[4] Professor O.D. Skelton, "Are We Drifting into Socialism?" in *The Monetary Times* (January 1913).

[5] Gustavus Myers, "Only One Goal" in *International Socialist Review*, 14 (October 1913), pp. 214-15.

[6] Passage from Mackenzie King, *Industry and Humanity*, cited in Fern and Ostry, op. cit., p. 274.

[7] R.W. MacIver, *Labour in the Changing World* (New York, Dutton, 1919).

[8] Ibid., p. 33.

[9] Ibid., p. 28.

[10] Gad Horowitz, *Canadian Labour in Politics* (Toronto, University of Toronto Press, 1968), pp. 3-57.

[11] J.S. Woodsworth, "Organizing Democracy in Canada" in *Western Labour News* (August 23, 1918).

[12] J.S. Woodsworth "What Next?" in *Western Labour News* (July 25, 1919).

[13] J.S. Woodsworth "What Next?" in *Western Labour News* (August 8, 1919).

[14] Bruce Hutchison, *The Incredible Canadian* (Toronto, Longmans, 1952), p. 113.

[15] Minutes of Independent Labour Party of Manitoba, 1920-23, in Public Archives, Ottawa: Aug. 4, 1921, Aug. 11, 1921, Sept. 1, 1921.

[16] *Western Labour News*, editorial, "A Dangerous Alternative" (October 14, 1921).

[17] J.S. Woodsworth, M.P., "Grandsons of Confederation" in *The Canadian Forum* (April 1926), pp. 205-7.

[18] Leo Heaps, *The Rebel in the House* (London, Niccolo, 1970), p. 118.

[19] Ibid., p. 117.

[20] David Lewis, *The Good Fight* (Toronto, Macmillan, 1981), p. 250.

[21] Quote from R.H.S. Crossman in Lewis, *The Good Fight*, p. 448.

[22] Robert Hacketts, "A History of the Ontario Waffle" in *Canadian Dimension*, 15 (October-November 1980) and John Bullen, "The Ontario Waffle and the Struggle for an Independent Socialist Canada: Conflict in Canada" in *The Canadian Historical Review*, LXIV, No. 2 (June 1983).

[23] David Lewis, op. cit., p. 293.

[24] British United Press dispatch, March 1, 1938, quoting Norman Freed, member of the Dominion Executive, Communist Party of Canada. Also see Penner, *The Canadian Left*, pp. 165-6.

[25] David Lewis, op. cit., p. 107.

[26] Lenin, *Selected Works*, X (New York, International Publishers, 1943), pp. 200-6, 207-13.

[27] See Jane Degras (ed.), *The Communist International Documents*, II, Report of the Sixth Congress, Communist International.

[28]*Fundamentals of Marxism-Leninism*, 2nd edition, (Moscow, Communist Party of the Soviet Union, 1963), p. 347.

[29]Quoted in N. Penner, *The Canadian Left*, p. 148.

[30]*Canada's Party of Socialism*, written by a Committee of leading members of the Communist Party of Canada (Toronto, Progress Books, 1980).

[31]I.M. Abella, *Nationalism, Communism, and Canadian Labour* (Toronto, University of Toronto Press, 1973).

[32]David Lewis, op. cit., pp. 347-9.

[33]Pierre Elliott Trudeau, "Practice and Theory of Federalism" in Michael Oliver (ed.), *Social Purpose for Canada* (Toronto, University of Toronto Press, 1961), pp. 371-93.

[34]Ibid., p. 372.

[35]Ibid., p. 375.

[36]See Documents of 12th Federal NDP Convention, June 30-July 3, 1983, Regina, Saskatchewan. Also see *The Commonwealth*, Saskatchewan NDP Journal, issue of July 13, 1983.

DEPARTMENT OF POLITICAL STUDIES

TO: All Members of Regular Faculty

FROM: C. Pentland, Political Studies

DATE: 24 November 1989

RE: <u>Tenure Recommendations</u>

The deadline for recommendations in respect to tenure is imminent. Therefore it is imperative that colleagues who propose to comment get their letters to Shirley Fraser immediately.

C. Pentland

/bm

Variations on the Democratic Theme

RALPH NELSON

If, in the interwar period, the practices of democratic states had lent some credence to the propriety of considering them decadent, the end of the Second War brought to a close the epidemic of dictatorships which assailed Europe and saw the image of democracy refurbished. And, in fact, we find a proliferation of democracies, the most remarkable feature of which was the contrast between liberal democracy and the new species, people's democracy. If the survival and existence of democracy no longer seemed in doubt, its essence, however, became problematic.

In Canada where the political system was as likely to be described as responsible government as it was political democracy, the new prestige of the word democracy is reflected particularly in the focus adopted in Comparative Politics. (The most famous introduction to the study of Canadian Government and Politics, R.M. Dawson's *The Government of Canada*, managed to dispense with the term democracy altogether.)[1] An examination of the development of democractic thought from the end of the Second World War to the present reveals the interplay of many influences, both native and external. On the one hand, we may speak of the development of Canadian political thought along the lines of the British tradition, or growing out of the Innis school. On the other hand, external influences, such as that of American political sociology, were felt.[2] Given the fact that the American political science community is so large, plus the fact that the expansion of Canadian universities led to the recruitment of social scientists from across the border, it is hardly surprising that there has been such a penetration. It is no secret that these influences have often been viewed negatively.[3] But, in addition, there has also been a notable influence of some European models in the effort at a self-understanding of Canadian democracy.

Our task is to examine the development of democratic thought in Canada during this period, paying particular attention to both its evolutionary aspects—let us say development along a certain line, by expansion or modification, so to speak—and dialectical aspects, reactions in most instances to predominant patterns. After an attempt to discern these vectors, a tentative evaluation will be offered. Perhaps it would be better to call it a stocktaking of where we stand in regard to the meaning of democracy in the last quarter of the turbulent twentieth century.

A reasonable point of departure would be a review of two important works in Comparative Politics produced by experienced teachers of political science after considerable reflection. We refer to J. A. Corry, *Democratic Government and Politics* (1946),[4] and Alexander Brady, *Democracy in the Dominions* (1947).[5] Dealing with institutional aspects of the political system, these studies are notable for their emphasis on the interest group phenomenon in politics. Nor was such a concern eccentric at that time.[6] Neither of these writers was inhibited by the neat positivist compartmentalization of description and evaluation. Indeed, they both sought to understand what was going on in various democratic systems, but they also wanted to weigh and to judge, to point out that certain tendencies might be unsatisfactory and others salutary. If this struck some as old-fashioned, it was because Corry and Brady studied politics with a practical orientation.

Based on twenty-five years of inquiry, Corry sets out to examine "regimes of freedom",[7] political democracy. He passes in review such notions as the enlargement of individual freedom, popular control over the government, government as servant rather than master, the rule of law and the will of the people. However, his focus appears to be on the contrast, if not the conflict, between the common interest, on one hand, and individual and group interests, on the other. It is significant that Corry utilizes phrases like "the common interest", "the national interest", "the common good" and "the public good" at a time when such concepts were being rejected by pluralists as vague or simply devoid of meaning.[8] In this critical perspective, while it was acceptable to speak of group interests, and of individual interests, of course, the trend was to reject the notion of some supervening public interest. At the other extreme was Rousseau's concept of democracy which denied the political legitimacy, though not the political existence, of "particular wills". Corry's approach is singular in trying to grasp both sides of the antinomy: to reconcile "the common interest and particular conflicting interests."[9]

The problem, then, is that society is characterized by the collision of group interests and yet the political task is one of integration. The two party system becomes in this situation "an agglomeration of interest groups".[10] Interest groups seek representation either through a functional type of representation or through influence and pressure. We have the clear impression that the public good consists precisely of "a delicate equilibrium of interests"[11] or, as Corry writes, "democratic government has always been involved in maintaining an equilibrium between groups".[12] Given the group perspective, political analysis may examine the role of the party system or that of the government itself. If it is the case that parties have become little more than combinations of interest groups, Corry feared that "the party system on which democracy must rely to direct the government and to ensure that it obeys the will of the people shows signs of disintegrating in the face of diverse demands of pressure groups of various kinds".[13] Thus, its integrative function is threatened.

On the other hand, the government, the executive, acts as a mediator in this system. Different pressure groups have varying access to the administration, the extent obviously a topic for empirical investigation. In the pluralist state, as we know it, such groups act to control the custodians so that regulators become, in effect, partisans. Though the executive must take into account the views of organized pressure groups, the clear inference is that it should resist being colonized and controlled by powerful interests.

If group life is at the centre of Corry's analysis of Canadian democracy, it is also the factor he uses to describe the threat posed by totalitarian regimes to liberal democracy, for such regimes "cannot tolerate independent group life".[14] Under such regimes, the pressure group is eliminated. If totalitarian intolerance threatens liberal values like freedom of association, the pathology of liberal democracy consists of the abuse of this freedom, particularly through lobbying. Lobbying is not just described in Corry's work; it is evaluated and, on the whole, is viewed negatively. While empiricists have come to accept lobbying as a fact of life, Corry may be critical because he detests the tactics used by lobbyists, because lobbyists attempt to dominate the state and are thus inimical to the establishment of a balance. In short, he attacks the choice of means, the lack of moderation, the threat to the public interest implicit in the lobbying process. In order to deal adequately with this issue, we should require a deontology to distinguish between proper pressure tactics and improper ones. As it is, we are left with a rather vague attack on the lobbyists as an unsavoury political influence. Corry's view of lobbies is perhaps the best instance of that combination of description and evaluation which marked a generation's approach to the study of democracy. It is an attitude shared by Alexander Brady.

Brady has more to say about democratic ideology than Corry does, even though he notes how that ideology tends to be muted in Canada.[15] He views political problems in terms similar to those of Corry, but is perhaps more sociological in articulating his views on pluralism. It is significant that Brady mentions two facets of pluralism, or what has been called its ambiguity. English political pluralism tended to stress the autonomy of the group as "the principal bulwark against state absolutism".[16] Brady discusses briefly the opposition between pluralism and statism which is characteristic of the English pluralist perspective with its concern for the ability of voluntary or spontaneous associations "to act apart from the state",[17] rather than being controlled by it or having its margin of activity severely reduced. However, having noted that aspect of pluralism, Brady is mainly concerned with pluralism in the North American sense with its focus on the group as capable of influencing government policy in order to benefit its members. In the pluralist perspective, then, there is a competitive situation between individual and group opinions and interests, where parties function as "composite groups"[18] to draw together various interests, not only to gain electoral victories, but also to further the task of achieving national unity through government. Brady seems optimistic about the integrative process, "the reconciliation of contending interests",[19] despite the dispersive force of self-regarding groups. There is an explicit normative theory here which defends the idea of the public interest, castigates the methods employed by lobbyists and indicates how Parliament may be reduced "to play the menial role of delegated broker for private interests",[20] when it should exercise an autonomous role. If there is a shortcoming in Brady's exposition, it is the lack of a developed normative theory of pluralism. Perhaps because of the extent of his comparative analysis, we find him somewhat chary in exploring the implications, both analytical and normative, of Canadian pluralism. However, both Corry and Brady have contributed to examining the pluralistic dimension of Canadian democracy, and Brady anticipates to some extent the important empirical studies of interest group activity in the sixties and seventies.

When we turn to Henry Mayo's *An Introduction to Democratic Theory* (1960),[21] there are significant differences in approach from the previous studies. First of all, Mayo's work may be called a "pure" theory of democracy, not in the sense in which pure is opposed to applied, but in the sense in which the pure is the unmixed, the unadulterated. Where Corry and Brady operate in a comparative perspective, Mayo does not, even though he does make some comparisons between political systems. Secondly, in the earlier studies there is a strong sociological cast to the pluralist analysis of democratic government, while Mayo makes reference to the current concepts of political sociology without really adopting a sociological perspective. We shall see that his approach is individualistic.

Mayo calls his study "a small effort at a comprehensive theory of democracy".[22] He distinguishes between an operational (explanatory) and a normative (justificatory) approach to democratic theory and, on balance, tries to present both sides, following David Easton's idea that "a complete political theory, then, we may say explains and justifies a political system".[23]

Mayo excludes the philosophical or "way of life" approach of a Dewey, for example, and excludes as well a discussion of democracy in legal terms, like sovereignty. As a political system, that is, as "one more answer to the question of how the political policy decisions are made and should be made",[24] democracy is specified by its method. And indeed method, according to Mayo, "becomes the chief distinguishing mark of a political system".[25] Democracy, then, its not specified by what it aims at, or should aim at, that is, by its purposes, results or consequences. Mayo seems to endorse wholeheartedly Schumpeter's famous conception of democracy as a method, as well as the notion that political theory gains from imitating economic theory, and Mayo's concept of effective choice has a Keynesian ring to it. What we must look for in modern society is not an imitation of Athenian democracy, but its appropriate counterpart. What participation was to Athenian democracy "the effectiveness of the popular control over the rulers or decision-makers" becomes in modern democracy.[26] Although Mayo does accept much of Schumpeter's theory, he apparently does not accept the latter's idea about the non-involvement of the people between elections: effectively Schumpeter tells the people to mind their business and leave the decision-makers alone. Such a theory both explains and justifies a democratic political system. Mayo avoids the question as to whether such a description of the political system justifies calling it democratic, rather than merely liberal. Nor does Mayo bring in the sociological dimension implicit in the Schumpeterian notion of democracy as elite competition, being consistently individualistic in his methodology.[27]

Negatively, the most salient feature of Mayo's theory is his contention that democratic theory can do without the concept of representation. Yet Mayo uses the term throughout his introduction and thus has not shown us what to put in its place. Furthermore, we must agree with S.J. Benn that Mayo's analysis of the notion of representation is "superficial", particularly when Hannah Pitkin's investigations are considered.[28] Leon Dion is more sympathetic with Mayo in understanding the problems associated with speaking of the elected representing the electors, but still doesn't believe that the term can be dispensed with.[29] Mayo maintains that democracy is not just the process by which certain decision-makers are chosen; it is popular control over the decision-makers. But how is that control to operate? How will the performance of decision-makers be judged and appraised? To what extent can it be said that they have received leads and instructions from the electorate? All of these questions would have to be inspected to give depth to the notion of popular control. Mayo obviously has a distaste for concepts like that of "the popular will" which Schumpeter considered a component of what he called "classical democratic theory". In fact, Mayo is generally critical of many aspects of citizenship theory and even argues that actual practice is a refutation of some of the norms of citizenship theory, for instance that citizens have a duty to vote.

Mayo's critical, if not sceptical, turn of mind is apparent when he deals with methods, values and purposes in democratic theory. As noted above, he accepts the idea that democracy is essentially a method. However, this acceptance implies a number of values such as the peaceful adjustment of differences, orderly succession of rulers, emphasis on minimizing coercion, respect for equality, diversity, freedom and equity.[30] But if democracy is value-laden, Mayo firmly rejects any assertion that there are democratic purposes, or stated differently, that there are specifically democratic goals, and he does so repeatedly. Perhaps his most succinct formulation is that "a democracy is a political system devoted to no goals as such".[31] This is another example of how democratic theory, in his eyes, resembles economic theory. They both are non-teleological. Moreover, Mayo shares the American pluralist view that statements about a public interest are partisan and inane.

Democratic theory also implies a certain conception of law and obligation. Mayo argues that the citizen's obligation to obey laws (and presumably other directives) in a democracy is not derived from the aim and content of such laws, but is based merely on their source. Thus, it is reasonable to conclude that we are obliged to obey duly constituted authorities. This seems to follow from his previous premise that democracy has no aims of its own, that it does not furnish us with any criteria by which we might be able to evaluate the content of a law. The least that can be said of such a theory of obligation is that it is terribly narrow.

While Mayo has intended to develop a general theory of democracy, rather than an American or Canadian theory of democracy, he does examine some aspects of democratic theory which are relevant to an understanding of the Canadian tradition. He observes that John Calhoun's theory of concurrent majorities, or something similar to it, has been applicable in Canada.[32] He suggests that federalism as it operates in Canada involves a modification, if not a violation of the democratic norm of majority rule, and the same of course is true in the American political constitution because of the Connecticut Compromise which established the makeup of the Senate. However, having noted the applicability of the concurrent majorities principle, Mayo does not examine the question in an historical context as the spokesmen for consociational democracy will do later.

Finally, Mayo briefly summarizes the Marxist critique of liberal democracy and its important distinction between real democracy and formal, or sham, democracy. In a companion work to the *Introduction to Democratic Theory*, *Introduction to Marxist Theory* (1960), Mayo deals at greater length with the problem in an essay entitled "Democracy and Marxism". Mayo notes that Marxists tend to distinguish between two uses of the term "democracy": the first in which democracy is seen as a "form of government or political system", that is, the term has a political reference, while there is a second sense in which the term is used, this time "with an economic and social reference".[33] Mayo is generally critical of Marxist theory, and particularly negative about its teaching on the absence of autonomy in the politics of liberal democracies, where politics is nothing but an instrument of class domination.

It is precisely the Marxist approach that has been adopted by the most celebrated political theorist of democracy in Canada, C.B. Macpherson. Macpherson first set out the main lines of what he calls the political economy approach to democracy in his study of *Democracy in Alberta* (1953). The central social phenomenon underlying Macpherson's analysis is the "opposition of class interests" in a "mature capitalist economy".[34] He assumes that only socio-economic cleavages give rise to political parties. Classes are described as "significant entities".[35] The class theory is contrasted with pluralistic theory as we find it, for instance, in the group theory analysis of Corry and Brady. Macpherson speaks of the "class problem of democracy",[36] meaning that politics in contemporary liberal democracies is not simply to be understood in a pluralistic way as adjustment, "but also (and more fundamentally) one of expressing and containing the conflict of class interests".[37]

If a class divided society seems to need a party system if democracy is to be maintained, and the clash of class conflict moderated, does the absence of class divisions then entail the disappearance of a party system? It would seem so, for in the Alberta case, the "absence of any serious opposition of class interests within the province meant that alternate parties were not needed either to express or to moderate a perennial conflict of interests".[38]

What is clear is Macpherson's analysis is that the term democracy primarily refers to "a social order in which there was no exploitation of man by man or class by class";[39] political democracy is defined in terms of the function it performs when this other concept of democracy as a social order is not present, that is, when there is persistent class conflict. In fact, we have three distinct definitions: social, moral and political.[40] As to political democracy, Macpherson does talk about several kinds which are relevant, in his opinion, to an understanding of Albertan politics. However, in *Democracy in Alberta* Macpherson does not offer us a full-scale typology or set of models of democracy, as he does in his later works.

If we accept "the concept of democracy as a means, a method or type of political organization and responsibility",[41] we can then distinguish between delegate and plebiscitarian democracy. Macpherson does not elucidate the basis of this distinction, nor does he pretend that the division is exhaustive. (We may note that in *The Real World of Democracy*, he makes conceptions explicit which were only latent in *Democracy in Alberta*.) Delegate democracy occurs "when the electorate attempts to treat the elected members of the legislature as instructed delegates".[42] Democracy, in this perspective, becomes "the control and instruction of elected representatives by the groups which nominated and elected them"[43]. Plebiscitarian or plebiscitary democracy, as defined by Macpherson, occurs when "the people give up their right of decision, criticism, and proposal, in return for the promise that everything will be done to implement the general will".[44] This is a definition of plebiscitary democracy which differs in important respects from what the term means in France.[45] We may then say that in one of these notions, representatives are really given no authority at all since they are issued instructions or orders, while, in the second case, they are fully empowered to make decisions because of their pledge to implement the general will. If the former conception hearkens back to the Lockean tradition, or that version of it which Edmund Burke criticized in a memorable letter to the Electors of Bristol, the second seems to be of Rousseauian origin, but a Rousseau reconciled to the principle of political representation.

Macpherson must address the issue whether a "single mass party" transcends the party system or is simply a hypertrophy of it. He obviously rejects "an outright totalitarian one-party rule",[46] but, leaves us in some doubt as to his definitive view about the appropriate politics of a non class-divided society. This issue, however, is central to his treatment of democracy in the Massey Lectures, *The Real World of Democracy* (1965).

Macpherson, in what is generally considered his most important work in political theory, *The Political Theory of Possessive Individualism* (1962), had already shown his interest in developing typologies, sets of categories or models, to deal with and evaluate different stages of social evolution. In *Possessive Individualism*, Macpherson distinguishes between customary or status society, simple market society and possessive market society.[47] He describes a binary concept of the moral value system, or conceptions of man, opposing possessive individualism and the developmental perspective of John Stuart Mill and T. H. Green, an opposition apparently based on the significant difference between having and being. In *The Real World of Democracy*, Macpherson approaches the question of political typologies in a systematic way.

First of all, Macpherson's distinction between a liberal conception of democracy and two non-liberal variants presents serious methodological problems. Leaving aside Maurice Cranston's quip that Macpherson had succeeded where Wilson failed by making the world safe for democracy,[48] the methodological question concerns the purpose served in political inquiry by calling three different kinds of political systems by the same name. Unless there is some residual unity, despite the striking differences, which would justify imposing a common name, Macpherson, in fact, only succeeds in showing that liberal democrats, Leninists and some followers of Rousseau use democracy in completely different senses. How are we to escape from the ambiguity of the term "democracy" as a general category in which each of these political systems would have its place? Macpherson says that they have one feature in common, "they share the same ultimate moral end",[49] that is, they all accept a self-realizations ethics, even though there are differences in "the scale of values."[50]

If we define democracy in terms of this ultimate end, we may discover that forms of government which Macpherson would not consider democratic in any way, pursue, or claim to pursue, this goal.[51] Thus Macpherson's criterion of end is too broad to specify the meaning of democracy. Moreover, if we adopt Macpherson's earlier notion of democracy "as a means, a method or type of political organization and responsibility",[52] then the differences between the three forms are more paramount than any similarity.

Pennock has noted that little by little the Third-World variant of democracy has been modified and then played down in Macpherson's later writings.[53] This variant was a more fully articulated version of plebiscitarian democracy. If at first Macpherson stressed its Rousseauist character, he later identified it as Robespierrean. Macpherson's remarks both about Third-World and Soviet systems are so general and so vague as to provide only a sketchy basis for comparisons with Western democracies.

However, the crucial distinction in *The Real World of Democracy* is between democracy as a form of government and as a kind of society. If we adopt the former as a criterion, democracy means a system of government which embodies the politics of choice within a competitive party system. Clearly, liberal democracies fit this description, while the so-called non-liberal variants do not. However, Macpherson does something rather curious in a series of lectures on the "real world" of democracy. He begins to talk about the *possible* world of political democracy when he elaborates on the conditions under which the Soviet Union could become democratic. Thus he perpetuates a practice which consists in judging liberal democracies on their performance and socialist systems on their ideals and aspirations.

If we adopt democracy as a certain kind of society as a criterion, a society consisting of a certain set of relations between individuals, the liberal democracies in Macpherson's eyes are least democratic while he seems to accept the claim that the Soviet Union embodies a classless society. Nowhere do we find a political system which can genuinely be considered democratic in both senses.[54]

In any case, "liberal democracy is the politics of choice".[55] It corresponds to societies of choice, competitive societies. If, on the one hand, we have the politics of choice without the classless society, and on the other, the classless society without the politics of choice, are we not looking for a synthesis in which the two are combined? Was this not precisely what was at stake in the Prague Spring in which the government of Czechoslovakia was seeking "socialism with a human face"? But, if this is the goal, Macpherson seems to be in a dilemma: once the competitive, class-divided, exploitative society is transformed into the co-operative commonwealth (to bring out an old war horse), do we any longer have any need of the politics of choice and, if we do, then perhaps class divisions are not the only cleavages which lead to political competition and the politics of choice. This difficulty is based on what is perceived to be the ultimately reductionist character of Macpherson's approach which conceives of the society-polity relation in terms of origin and derivation or, in Marxist terminology, infra and super structure. Perhaps what

Macpherson is getting at is that the appropriate political system for the classless society is really a form of plebiscitary democracy, for then, and only then, is a real general will possible. Thus linking up Macpherson's earlier remarks on plebiscitarian democracy and his examination of the so-called Third-World variant, the significance of the "third way" is neither historical nor empirical, but normative. It is offered as a norm for the appropriate and adequate political system of the classless society.

Democratic Theory: Essays in Retrieval (1973) indicates the extent to which the main themes of Marxist theory have been adopted by Macpherson. Here again the political economy approach is wielded with his usual adroitness. As applied to democratic theory, the approach once again involves treating the concept of democracy as referring primarily to a kind of society rather than a system of government. Macpherson shows little sympathy with either the preoccupations or the contributions of empirical political theory.

Once again, Macpherson squares off by opposing the two antithetical ethical systems, the one based on the conception of man as a "consumer of utilities"—our old friend possessive individualism—and the other, on the conception of man as "an enjoyer of his human attributes".[56] Macpherson had always shown a great deal of symphathy for J.S. Mill and T.H. Green, and in this collection, we find that Macpherson maintains that Marxian theory would be much improved were it to be combined with these two philosophers' theory of self-realization. Adapting Green's theory, leaving aside what is outworn in it, would complement that basic truth of Marx and together effect a synthesis in which socialism becomes the equal right to the means of self-development. As Parekh says, "Macpherson seems to wish to create a socialist *society* in order to realize liberal man. He himself says that his basic concern is to 'retrieve' the ethical values of liberalism, and it is largely because they cannot be realized in capitalist society that he wishes to replace it with a socialist one".[57]

It should be pointed out that the typology employed throughout *Democratic Theory* does not differ essentially from *The Real World of Democracy*. However, Macpherson now admits that the

African—Third World—form might be better described as in transition to democracy rather than as actually democratic. This variant of democracy beings to fade from sight. Yet not only does Macpherson continue to focus on democracy as a kind of society, but he alludes to political democracy as "merely a mechanism of choosing and authorizing governments"[58], a curious way of describing a political system for which men and women are willing to suffer and even die in Czechoslovakia and Poland, and the successful establishment of which in Portugal and Spain has brought those previously isolated countries into the European community. It is probably only in English-speaking countries with a long democratic tradition that democracy can be considered "merely a mechanism".

The last full-blown statement on democracy by Macpherson is to be found in *The Life and Times of Liberal Democracy* (1977). Here Macpherson leaves behind his concern with democratic theory in a global perspective, limiting himself to a study of those democratic models pertinent to a liberal society. He has now developed a series of models parallel in some ways to the models of society found in *Possessive Individualism*. In dealing with models of democracy in the liberal (democratic) context, Macpherson operates on the assumption that man is formed by the society in which he lives and the political system is fitted to that society, or, if it is not suitable to it, one must look for another which will be. The underlying assumption is that in a capitalist class-divided society, there are two contrasting models of man: man conceived as an infinite consumer and man "as a being capable of developing his powers or capacities".[59] If the former model, based on market assumptions, is to be replaced by the latter, there must be a transition to a non-capitalist society. However, Macpherson limits himself to a call for a change of consciousness when he comes to propose prescriptions for action.

Four models of democracy are proposed to us: the protective, the developmental, the equilibrium and the participatory model. The first, associated with the names of Bentham and James Mill, seemed realistic during the heyday of classical political economy since it adopted the idea of man "as he had been shaped by market society".[60] Developmental democracy, identified with J.S.

Mill's theory of democracy, and later with Lindsay, Barker and Dewey, was bound to fail because its conception of man and its ethical quest for a free and equal society aimed at self-realization was in contradiction with the harsh realities of capitalist society. In short, the ideals of developmental democracy, which Macpherson endorses, cannot be realized under capitalism. Model Two requires that a model of society be realized before it is implemented, while Model One was fitted to an existing model of society. Indeed, we shall find that Models One and Three differ from Models Two and Four because they are realistic rather than idealistic.

The Third model, equilibrium democracy, "the pluralist, elitist equilibrium model,"[61] in contrast to Mill's developmental model, is accurate and adequate, but since it minimizes participation, it is questionable to consider it democratic. In Schumpeter's formulation, it is even questionable whether it should be called a system of responsible government.[62] It is characteristic of Macpherson, by the way, to argue that the relationship between equilibrium democracy and the kind of society in which it flourishes is not a contingent, but a necessary connection, as if no other political system would do. Mature capitalist society *requires* a form of elitist democracy. There are some reasonable doubts whether such a proposition has been demonstrated in Macpherson's treatise.[63]

The fourth model is clearly envisaged by Macpherson as a consummation devoutly to be wished, but the model is presented in an inchoate form. Macpherson recognizes that it differs from the others in being less specific and, we may add, in being based on a number of suppositions and counterfactuals. In the light of Macpherson's search for the appropriate political system for a non class-divided society, the proposal for a participatory democracy marks an apparent abandonment of an earlier option, plebiscitarian democracy, and a partial integration of another option, delegate democracy.

Macpherson is aware of the danger of circularity in proposing a form of participatory democracy, since without greater participation "a more equitable and humane society" cannot be attained.[64] Yet political systems have hitherto been considered as derivations from, or reflections of, a certain kind of society. Macpherson's escape from circularity by recourse to the notion of reciprocal causality only partially overcomes the difficulty. If we must wait until considerably more social equality has been achieved, along with a transformation of consciousness which shall turn us into "exerters and enjoyers" rather than "consumers", are we not speculating about a political system only when "the life and times" of liberal democracy has ended? It does not appear that Macpherson supports a kind of participatory incrementalism which will usher in a new order, but a leap, whether brought about by a revolution or some other dramatic means. In examining the interrelations between and among political, social and cultural factors, Macpherson seems to give priority to a cultural change involving a "new awareness" of "the image of man" and when that has occurred, and only then, can social and political transformations follow.[65] The only kind of revolution Macpherson unequivocably favours in this work is cultural.

But what about the participatory models themselves? How does Macpherson deal with the notorious obstacles to the establishment of a more participatory polity? Macpherson, of course, does not confine himself to the possibilities of political participation in the narrow sense, but also briefly examines some notions of workers' control. The inquiry touches on how such a system will come about, what structure it will have, and how it will be operated. We shall only examine the structural issue here.

In the first sketch, Macpherson presents a model of "a pyramidal system with direct democracy at the base and delegate democracy at every level above that".[66] The scheme is reminiscent of G.D.H. Cole's plan for a participatory democracy. However, Macpherson discusses the political structure as if he were dealing with a classless society. There would be no political parties.

In the second sketch of a participatory democracy, Macpherson adds political parties to the pyramid, for he is now willing to entertain the possibility that "even in a non-class-divided society, there would be issues around which parties might form".[67] He refers to Czechoslovakia in 1968 as a case in point. One wonders if Macpherson himself is aware of the distance he has come from his treatment of party competition in *Democracy in Alberta*. But perhaps it was just a temporal lapse, because, in the final analysis, the second sketch is just a stage on the way to the achievement of the first. When the good society arrives, its political system will be participatory, pyramidal, with representatives who are delegates, but without political parties. Macpherson's mood is upbeat and optimistic both about cultural-social transformation and the possibilities of a modified kind of participatory democracy; it is not direct democracy in any complete sense. The reasons for his optimism, however, do not stand up under scrutiny.

Despite the fact that Macpherson continues to depreciate the political meaning of democracy—"merely a mechanism for choosing and authorizing governments or in some way getting laws and political decisions made"[68]—in order to emphasize democracy "as a kind of society",[69] the four models are indeed models of political democracy. Macpherson's combination of Marxism and liberalism has been commented on by several critics,[70] but the limitations of his approach are worth noting. Macpherson usually operates within the Anglo-Saxon philosophical and political tradition. Even his Marxism is of the rather unsophisticated variety which is widely current in English-speaking countries. His "parochialism" no doubt accounts for the absence of any reference whatsoever to Tocqueville in a book on the life and times of liberal democracy. But his theoretical perspective ignores as well a theory of democracy that many consider particularly appropriate in understanding the operation of democratic government in Canada, and that some have justified for its contribution to political stability. We refer to consociational democracy. Since this conception, like other pluralist interpretations of democracy, does not award any priority of socio-economic or class divisions over others (ethnic, cultural, religious, for instance), Macpherson would undoubtedly find it one more ideological attempt to ignore the fundamental social fact of liberal democracy. Accordingly Macpherson would see it as one more attempt to blunt social conflict and impede the movement toward the harmonious society.

Macpherson's analysis is fundamentally grounded in a sociology of classes of a Marxist kind. The background to consociational theory can be situated in a sociology of elites. Though Mayo adopted Schumpeter's definition of democracy as basically a method, he did not stress the process as elite competition. However, this is the tag which has been attached to Schumpeter's revised notion of democracy.

From pluralism, a logical though not a temporal progression, leads to the contemporary emphasis on elites. First of all, the pluralist conception of society remains somewhat vague until one specifies that the real political actor is not the group itself, but the group leader or representative. While the group leader interacts with party or other political officials, he also maintains various relationships with his followers. Contemporary elite theory, claiming to be empirical rather than normative, that is, not concerned with whether those on top should be there, but with how they behave in various contexts, originates in the attempts of Michels, Mosca and Pareto to counter the arguments of both Marxists and certain kinds of populist democrats.

Revised democratic theories, like that of Schumpeter, understand, then, the electoral process as consisting of a competition between elites in a free political system. This account of democracy, and this is largely the case with Mayo's account as well, does not concern itself with the governmental process in which elites must also cooperate. However, the two theories may be considered as complementary: elite competition at one level, elite cooperation at another.

Arend Lijphart, a Dutch political scientist educated in the United States, noted that there is another side of democratic elitism which may not be so important in the United States, but which is paramount in segmented societies like Austria, Belgium, Holland and Switzerland.[71] The theory of elite accommodation or consociational democracy is this other side. In the tradition of elite accommodation, "the political leaders engage in coalescent rather than adverserial decision-making".[72] The conditions which tend to insure political stability in the United States will not be conducive to promoting stability in segmented societies, that is, where there are hostile societal segments, as the

Flemish-Walloon division in Belgium. Or to state it slightly differently, stability there requires the choice of "segmented pluralism over American pluralism".[73]

The first systematic foray in applying the elite accommodation or consociational model to Canada was made by S.J.R. Noel in 1971,[74] followed by Robert Presthus in 1973,[75] and Kenneth McRae in 1974.[76] Noel observed that there were advantages in trying to understand Canadian politics from "a European perspective",[77] and that this perspective would offer an answer to a problem apparently insoluble in terms of ordinary North American pluralism.

> By what means, therefore, has the Canadian federal system been able to achieve the minimum level of harmony between its regional component which, despite the lack of a strong national identity, has allowed it to maintain itself and function with relative effectiveness for more than a century?[78]

This harmony has not been achieved by appeals to the masses, nor by stimulating popular participation, for these actions would only serve to exacerbate an already delicate situation. The alternative would be cooperation between and among the political leaders of the segments—ethnic or regional—in Canada in order to foster national unity, more concretely, "to maintain the national political system and make it work".[79] The focal point of this process in the Canadian political system is the federal Cabinet. According to this logic, a decline of elitism and the rise of participatory democracy could harm Canadian federalism "if it leads to a situation in which the mass of the people are unwilling to accept the inter-elite accommodations made by their political leaders".[80] Noel foresaw the danger of a situation in which a conflict between the Parti Québécois and a federal Liberal government, elected with strong Quebec support, would result in turning from elite accommodation to mass appeals. This is pretty much the scenario of the Quebec Referendum of 1980. (The prime minister, at one point, had also spoken of a referendum.) It would seem that the use of the referendum in Canada has usually been destabilizing.

Robert Presthus discusses the theory of elite accommodation in Canada in the well-travelled pluralist path which bears on relations between interest groups and governmental elites. His aim is analytical rather than normative. His thesis is to show why limiting participation may be functional as when stability is achieved through "the ability to transcend at the elite level the cleavages existing at the subcultural level".[81] While Canada, in his opinion, does meet the general requirements of consociational societies, Presthus' study seems more taken up with the vertical relation between groups, parties and government than with the horizontal relation between governing elites. Nevertheless, he reiterates Noel's contention that the federal Cabinet is at the centre of elite accommodation, particularly through the constitutive use of representational criteria, such as proportionality.

In his findings, Presthus observes that elite accommodation reinforces the status quo. On one hand, it has negative consequences for democratic participation because it discourages mass participation which might be destabilizing, and, on the other hand, it insures "a virtual monopoly of access by established groups which tend to enjoy major shares of political resources".[82] The end result is what Presthus refers to as "a quasi-participative political culture insofar as the ordinary citizen is concerned".[83]

Kenneth McRae's approach to elite accommodation in Canada is more historical showing that the patterns of segmentation in Canada have shifted from a religious to a linguistic base. The compromises embodied in the *British North America Act* have their counterparts in the area of decisions about the language of education and work in the twentieth century. McRae notes that for elite accommodation to work, it is important that political parties be not narrowly identified with any one segment. The locus of consociational politics in Canada must "normally" be sought "not in compromises *among* parliamentary parties but in accommodation *within* the party in power and in the mechanism of the federal system".[84] In this respect, Noel, Presthus and McRae are in agreement.

However, McRae notes that there are major divergencies from the consociational model in the Canadian case. To take a notable difference, while political parties in other segmented societies reflect subcultural bloc values, and are instruments of popular mobilization, this is not generally the case in Canada. Yet, McRae argues "despite these differences [between Canada and other segmented societies studied] the use of the consociational model helps to differentiate Canadian politics from its usual Anglo-American context and permits new insights at both the analytical and normative levels".[85]

A more rigorous method of testing whether or not Canada can be considered as a consociational democracy is employed by Arend Lijphart in a kind of summing up of the findings of the previous inquiries into consociationalism in Canada. No doubt elite cooperation is the hallmark of a consociational system based on segmental cleavages. But there are four characteristics of a consociational polity: government by a grand coalition, mutual veto or a "concurrent majority rule", proportionality "as the principal standard of political representation", and a high degree of segmental autonomy.[86] In the Union Government, before Confederation, or at the time of Confederation, it could be argued that all four characteristics were present, even though segmental autonomy was *de facto* rather than *de jure* or formal. Today only the last two criteria are applicable to the Canadian political system: proportionality and segmental autonomy. The inference is clear; Canada was more consociational before 1867 than it is today. Yet it might be thought paradoxical to celebrate a political system which ended in political deadlock and the search for a new political constitution. In any case, Lijphart, commenting on the work of Presthus and McRae, believes that the correct description of the Canadian political system is "semiconsociational democracy".[87]

Democratic theory, as we have seen, may progress by a process of evolution, that is through continuity and refinement, or it may advance through a dialectical process in which one theory emerges in contradiction, that is, in strict opposition, to another. In the last decade there have been both kinds of progress. The 1970s were marked by a strong reaction to the non-participatory, hence non-democratic aspects of the reigning orthodoxies: elite competition and elite accommodation. But there has been also an extension of elite analysis, usually in a critical spirit, to the study of what has been termed the "state elite" in state-centred models of democracy.[88]

It is convenient to date the reaction to democratic elitism in Canada to the reception given Carole Pateman's *Participation and Democratic Theory*.[89] It was recognized that the predominant notion of democracy was democratic elitism or the elite competition model. A consensus had developed among the exponents of this model that we should no longer be concerned about political apathy, the decline of citizenship, the domination of elites, but realize how "functional" or useful such apparent anomalies are for a stable democracy. Furthermore, arguments were marshalled by these exponents to show why a more participatory form of democracy was not feasible either. Many of the arguments have been accepted by advocates of participatory democracy and accordingly the stress has been on "a viable theory of participatory democracy"[90] with hopes being raised about the democratization of the work place, or "industrial democracy" in an older vocabulary. Several Canadian political writers contributed to the Benello-Roussopoulos collection, *The Case for Participatory Democracy* (1971).[91] The aim of the collection was to examine ways in which democratic process could be introduced into "the major organizations of society, public *and* private".[92] George Woodcock expounded on the idea of radical democracy, Christian Bay elaborated the concept of freedom first developed in *The Structure of Freedom* (1958), and Dimitrios Roussopoulos examined the urban commune.[93] H.B. Wilson, in *Democracy and the Work Place* (1974), discusses the movement towards industrial democracy, or worker self-management, a topic which was thoroughly studied throughout the decade of the seventies.[94]

For an analysis of participation from a philosophical perspective, there is a significant essay by David Braybrooke published in 1975.[95] Finally, we have seen the important theoretical contribution to the literature of participatory democracy by C. B. Macpherson at a time when the impetus toward a broad-ranging notion of participatory democracy had begun to wane. There had never been much hope for the replacement of the existing political system by the kind of pyramidal structure advocated by Macpherson. Sanguine expectations about worker self-management, inspired by Yugoslavian workers' control (see Pateman), hardly persisted into the eighties. The system of elite competition at the political level and the authoritarian nature of North American labour-management relations were more intractable to change than some had at first believed. At least holistic schemes for participatory democracy, either at the political level or in the work place, have tended to be abandoned in favour of some measure of reform of liberal democracy as we know it. The weakening of the power of the trade unions during this period has precluded any concerted efforts on their part at improving a situation in which the worker is denied any role in decision-making.

Despite the failure of many schemes for increasing political participation—conceived in a broad sense to include industry—there are some indications that the cause of participatory democracy has not been lost. The distrust of government, because of its perceived failures to manage the economy, or the environment or to provide certain basic forms of protection, have mobilized certain segments of the population. The causes these groups espouse may not be considered progressive. The fact that participation may not further one's favourite causes no doubt will lead to a loss of enthusiasm in participation by those who see participation primarily as a means to the achievement of radical goals. However, for the convinced political democrat, self-government, and hence popular participation, must be considered as an end.

An important step in fostering a more modest and realistic form of participatory democracy is taken when the conceptual muddle which allows "democratic elitism" to be considered as a genuine form of democracy is cleared up. As Hugh Thorburn pointed out, "there is nothing inherently democratic about pluralism; rather it is a liberal doctrine favouring freedom of association and the free play of interests, in which the strong dominate the weak".[96] A disjunction has occurred between the term "liberal" and the term "democracy" so that liberals fear the populace and deny any sound political judgement to the common man, and "radical" democrats criticize the basic tenets of liberalism. Several recent studies have made an important contribution to the task of demystification which democratic theory requires today.

The dialectical development in democratic thought in Canada may seem to confront us with a choice between the elite competition model, on one side, and a participatory model too closely patterned after classical instances of direct democracy, on the other, so great is the tendency to oppose one extreme to another. But there is a third way and we are indebted to William Mishler for pointing it out.[97] First of all, it is necessary to dispel certain attitudes and positions encumbering democratic thought: the strict separation of analysis and evaluation, the idea that democracy has no purposes of its own, the idea that there is one single classical theory of democracy, and that an elitist theory of democracy is the only kind we can reasonably expect to have. Mishler proposes a threefold division in which a representative model of democracy stands beside classical and elitist models. If "the role of citizen participation in the political process" is at the core of current debate over democratic theory, the representative model of democracy differs from elitist theories precisely because it offers vistas of participation denied by the latter.[98] Mishler is aware that an empirical theory is needed in order to ascertain what are the citizen's capabilities for participating as well as the opportunities available. However, the representative model of democracy is frankly normative and, in a co-authored study which appeared in 1982,[99] the Mishler theory is more clearly delineated. Democracy essentially "is a system of government by and for the people, in which political authority derives from citizen participation in governmental decisions".[100] Since it is generally agreed that the ancient mode of direct democracy is no longer applicable in the modern world, the choice is between the elitist and representative models of democracy. The former is based on a Burkean notion of representation, while the latter draws its inspiration from J.S. Mill.[101]

How do these two models agree and how do they differ? Both maintain that government will be in the hands of a minority, that those who govern "should be popularly elected and guided by a conception of the public interest".[102] The last feature, be it noted, would not be accepted by either Schumpeter or Mayo. Since the conception of the public interest varies in each case, this could be reckoned more a contrast than a similarity.[103] The salient differences bear on who should govern, how much and what kind of participation should occur, and on what relations should obtain between the representatives and those they represent. In the elitist case, the representative is fit to rule because he or she is qualified to ascertain what the public interest should be and how it is to be obtained. In the opposite case, since the public interest is defined in terms of "needs and wants", the representative receives directives from the public and presumably makes decisions about how those goals are to be achieved.[104] It is assumed that the elitist model will defend the status quo, while the representative model would be open to innovation.

In the elitist model, the representative would, one imagines, be judged on the basis of personal characteristics or success in maintaining stability, while the representative model would require that the representatives give an account of their stewardship in terms of how well popular directives had been carried out. In the final analysis, "political participation is a defining characteristic of representative democracy" (the representative model),[105] it is not of the elitist model.

Whatever shortcomings these recent studies may have from a theoretical point of view, they do raise important questions about democracy through an analysis of the theory of representation. Along with Corry, Brady and Macpherson, it is asserted that democracy does indeed have purposes of its own. It cannot be defined merely as a means, and Macpherson may simply be alerting us to the poverty of such a conception when he denigrates democracy as merely a form of government. Most of the literature on democratic theory in Canada insists on the need for a sociological dimension, that is, an analysis of social agencies beyond the actions of lone individuals. Needless to say, there is no agreement as to whether pluralism, class theory or elite theory best provides this basis. Corry and Brady used pluralism, Macpherson class theory, the consociationalists elite theory, and some combination of these theories has also been used. Although most of the writings surveyed favoured greater participation, considerable differences exist between and among these writers concerning appropriate avenues and venues.

Perhaps the fundamental issue, however, concerns the political capabilities and tendencies of ordinary people. If we share the negative view of the "masses" as prone to fall for sinister demagogic appeals, as incapable of sound political judgement and as a threat to stable government, we shall continue to be satisfied with a theory and practice that minimizes participation. But if we have a more affirmative view of the "people" as generally well-intentioned, capable of making a reasonable political choice if they possess sufficient information, and providing an impetus to needed change, we shall certainly endorse a more participatory political system. For as has been stated so well, "democratic theory always has been predicated on faith; faith in the capacity of people for self-government".[106]

NOTES

[1] The omission is interesting in view of Dawson's remark elsewhere that "the first and most important characteristic of Canadian government is that it is a democracy....Government in Canada rests on the will of the people and is—ideally at least—at all times responsive to their opinions". R.M. Dawson, *Democratic Government in Canada* (Toronto, University of Toronto Press, 1949), p. 3.

[2] Alan C. Cairns discusses these influences in "Political Science in Canada and the Americanization Issue," *Canadian Journal of Political Science*, VIII (June 1975), pp. 191-234. For a somewhat different view, see Allan Kornberg and Alan Tharp, "The American Impact on Canadian Political Science and Sociology," in Richard A. Preston (ed.), *The Influence of the United States on Canadian Development* (Durham, N.C., Duke University Press, 1972), pp. 55-98.

[3] To mention but one such objection, particularly relevant to our theme, see C.B. Macpherson, "After Strange Gods: Canadian Political Science 1973" in T.N. Guinsburg and G.L. Reuber (eds.), *Perspectives on the Social Sciences in Canada* (Toronto, University of Toronto Press, 1974), pp. 52-71.

[4] J. A. Corry, *Democratic Government and Politics* (Toronto, University of Toronto Press, 1946).

[5] Alexander Brady, *Democracy in the Dominions, A Comparative Study in Institutions* (Toronto, University of Toronto Press, 1947).

[6] R. Pendleton Herring, *The Politics of Democracy* (New York, Rinehart, 1940), was an important predecessor, but the approach gathered momentum in the 1950s with David Truman's *The Governmental Process* (New York, Alfred A. Knopf, 1951) and a number of similar studies. G. David Garson has devoted a study to the phenomenon, *Group Theories of Politics* (Beverly Hills, Sage Publications, 1978).

[7] J. A. Corry, op. cit., p. 1.

[8] See G. David Garson, op. cit., Chapter 4.

[9] J. A. Corry, op. cit., p. 197. Later, Corry reiterates his position: "The job of the democratic politician is to reconcile the conflicts [of interests and wills] by compromise in a policy that is tolerable to nearly all, even if congenial to few." *The Changing Conditions of Politics* (Toronto, University of Toronto Press, 1963), p. 55.

[10] J. A. Corry, *Democratic Government and Politics*, p. 189.

[11] Ibid., p. 208.

[12] Ibid., p. 209.

[13] Ibid., p. 432.

[14] Ibid., p. 437.

[15] Alexander Brady notes that Canadians "take the ideological basis of their democracy for granted. Their democratic ideals are commonly an unexpressed premise". Op. cit., p. 64.

[16] David Nicholls, *Three Varieties of Pluralism* (New York, St. Martin's Press, 1974), p. 2. The book is particularly valuable for the comparison of the two dominant types of pluralism. For Nicholls' study of English pluralism, see *The Pluralist State* (New York, St. Martin's Press, 1975). Chapter 8 of this work also deals with the two pluralisms.

[17] A. Brady, op. cit., p. 8.

[18] A. Brady, "Parliamentary Democracy" in A. Brady (ed.), *Canada after the War* (Toronto, Macmillan Co., 1943), p. 34.

[19] A. Brady, *Democracy in the Dominions*, p. 104.

[20] Ibid., p. 421.

[21] Henry Mayo, *An Introduction to Democratic Theory* (New York, Oxford University Press, 1960).

[22] Ibid., p. v.

[23] Ibid., p. 11.

[24] Ibid., p. 29.

[25] Ibid., p. 30.

[26] Ibid., p. 60.

[27] This is best expressed when Mayo insists that "it is individuals who vote and their votes can be courted, often over the heads of their group leaders. It is parties and legislatures, not interest groups which resolve the group conflicts". Ibid., p. 165.

[28] S.I. Benn in a review of *An Introduction to Democratic Theory* in *Political Studies*, 9 (1961), p. 208.

[29] Léon Dion, *Société et politique; la vie des groupes*, tome 1, *Fondements de la société libérale* (Québec, Les Presses de l'Université Laval, 1971), p. 310.

[30] Henry Mayo, op. cit.; pp. 218-43.

[31] Ibid., p. 249.

[32] "Doubtless Calhoun's theory of concurrent majorities, or minority veto, was an impossible one to put into *law*, but something closely resembling it is at work in the United States political system, the Canadian and perhaps other." Ibid., p. 202.

[33] Henry Mayo, "Democracy and Marxism," *Introduction to Marxist Theory* (New York, Oxford University Press, 1960), pp. 264-5.

[34] C.B. Macpherson, *Democracy in Alberta, Social Credit and the Party System* (Toronto, University of Toronto Press, 1953), p. 241.

[35] Ibid., p. 226.

[36]Ibid., p. 241.

[37]Ibid., p. 241.

[38]Ibid., p. 21.

[39]Ibid., p. 46.

[40]The moral concept of democracy as a goal is a "non-exploitative, just, co-operative and political order in which no organization would have to exercise power...". Ibid., p. 48.

[41]Ibid.

[42]Ibid.

[43]Ibid.

[44]Ibid., p. 233.

[45]Observing that a plebiscitary democracy is not just a dictatorship which doesn't bother to submit its policies to the electoral process, Georges Burdeau says that "on the contrary, it doesn't just use elections as a means by which the leader comes to power; it makes them an instrument of government. Far from being obliged to remain silent, the people are kept breathless by being constantly consulted. Only the people are not asked *what* they want, but *who* they want". *La Démocratie* (Paris, Éditions du Seuil, 1956), p. 56.

[46]C.B. Macpherson, op. cit., p. 247.

[47]C.B. Macpherson, *The Political Theory of Possessive Individualism, Hobbes to Locke* (Oxford, The Clarendon Press, 1962), pp. 49-61.

[48]Maurice Cranston, "Ethics and Politics," *Encounter* (June 1972), p. 20.

[49]C.B. Macpherson, *The Real World of Democracy* (Toronto, Canadian Broadcasting Corporation, 1965), p. 37.

[50]Ibid., p. 60.

[51]"Since every government, however autocratic, claims to pursue this ideal, it is difficult to see if there is any to which Macpherson would deny the coveted description 'democratic'." Bhikhu, Parekh, *Contemporary Political Thinkers* (Oxford, Martin Robertson, 1982), p. 66. Steven Lukes is also critical of this aspect of Macpherson's thought in his essay "The Real and Ideal Worlds of Democracy", Alkis Kontos (ed.), *Powers, Possessions and Freedom, Essays in Honour of C.B. Macpherson* (Toronto, University of Toronto Press, 1979), pp. 139-52.

[52]C.B. Macpherson, *Democracy in Alberta*, p. 48.

[53]J. Roland Pennock, *Democratic Political Theory* (Princeton, Princeton University Press, 1979), pp. 515-16, n. 12.

[54]A comparison between Macpherson's intentions and those of Maurice Duverger would be fruitful. See the latter's *Modern Democracies: Economic Power versus Political Power* (Hinsdale, Ill., The Dryden Press, 1974) and *Lettre ouverte aux socialistes* (Paris, A. Michel, 1976).

[55]C.B. Macpherson, *The Real World of Democracy*, p. 33.

[56]C.B. Macpherson, *Democratic Theory: Essays in Retrieval* (Oxford, Clarendon Press, 1973), p. 4.

[57]B. Parekh, op. cit., p. 72.

[58]C.B. Macpherson, *Democratic Theory*, p. 51.

[59]C.B. Macpherson, *The Life and Times of Liberal Democracy* (Oxford, Oxford University Press, 1977), p. 48. Pennock says that Macpherson sees the theoretical mixture of two views of the human essence "in conventional democratic theory as a weakness. An important argument of my book, on the other hand, is that the mixture is part of democracy's strength. Man's nature is to want *both* to consume *and* to create. To build

a theory on a contrary assumption would be to build upon a false foundation." J. Roland Pennock, op. cit., p. 138, n.

[60]C.B. Macpherson, *The Life and Times of Liberal Democracy*, p. 43.

[61]Ibid., p. 77.

[62]John Plamenatz, *Democracy and Illusion* (London, Longman, 1973), pp. 115-29.

[63]In a review of *The Life and Times of Liberal Democracy*, J. Roland Pennock taxes Macpherson with having failed frequently to produce evidence and support for his arguments. J. Roland Pennock, *Political Theory* (November 1978), pp. 555-8.

[64]C.B. Macpherson, *The Life and Times of Liberal Democracy*, p. 94.

[65]Ibid., pp. 101-3. He refers to "a new awareness" on p. 101 and "the image of man" on p. 103.

[66]Ibid., p. 108.

[67]Ibid., p. 112.

[68]Ibid., p. 5.

[69]Ibid., pp. 5-6.

[70]B. Parekh, op. cit., pp. 72-3 and Steven Lukes, op. cit., pp. 151-2.

[71]Arend Lijphart, "Consociational Democracy," *World Politics*, 21, No. 2 (1969), pp. 207-25.

[72]Arend Lijphart, *Democracy in Plural Societies: A Comparative Exploration* (New Haven, Yale University Press, 1977), pp. 99-100.

[73]F.C. Engelmann in a review of Kenneth McCrae (ed.), *Consociational Democracy: Political Accommodation in Segmented Societies*, in *Canadian Journal of Political Science*, VIII (June 1975), p. 335.

[74]S.J.R. Noel, "Consociational Democracy and Canadian Federalism", Kenneth McRae (ed.), *Consociational Democracy: Political Accommodation in Segmented Societies* (Toronto, McClelland and Stewart, 1974), pp. 262-8. This is a reprint of an article which appeared in the *Canadian Journal of Political Science*, IV (March 1971), pp. 15-18.

[75]Robert Presthus, *Elite Accommodation in Canadian Politics* (Toronto, Macmillan of Canada, 1973).

[76]Kenneth McRae, op. cit.

[77]S.J.R. Noel, op. cit., p. 262.

[78]Ibid., p. 263.

[79]Ibid., p. 264.

[80]Ibid., p. 267.

[81]Robert Presthus, op. cit., p. 13.

[82]Ibid., p. 352.

[83]Ibid.

[84]Kenneth McRae, op. cit., p. 250.

[85]Ibid., p. 260.

[86]Arend Lijphart, *Democracy in Plural Societies*, p. 25.

[87]Ibid., p. 119.

[88]By state-centred we refer to a growing body of literature concerning the degree to which the state may be considered autonomous or subordinate. Dennis Olsen, *The State Elite* (Toronto, McClelland and Stewart, 1980), raises questions about the state elite in Canada similar to those raised by C. Wright Mills about the state elite in the United States. Like a previous study, Leo Panitch (ed.), *The Canadian State: Political Economy and Political Power* (Toronto, University of Toronto Press, 1977), the orientation is

Marxist. Eric A. Nordlinger, *On the Autonomy of the Democratic State* (Cambridge, Harvard University Press, 1981), is critical of the Marxist approach in Chapter 8.

[89]Carole Pateman, *Participation and Democratic Theory* (Cambridge: Cambridge University Press, 1977). Typical of the reception given the study are two reviews, one by F.C. Hunnius in *Canadian Forum* (March 1971), p. 444, and another by Vaughan Lyon in *Canadian Journal of Political Science*, IV (December 1971), pp. 583-4.

[90]Vaughan Lyon, op. cit., p. 444. Michael Margolis, *Viable Democracy* (Markham, Penguin Books Canada Limited, 1979), seems rather pessimistic about the possibilities for greater participation. See remarks on pp. 185-7.

[91]C. George Benello and Dimitrios Roussopoulos (eds.), *The Case for Participatory Democracy: Some Prospects for a Radical Society* (New York, Grossman Publishers, 1971).

[92]Ibid., p. 4.

[93]George Woodcock, "Democracy, Heretical and Radical," pp. 11-25; Christian Bay, "Freedom as Tool of Oppression," pp. 250-69; and Dimitrios Roussopoulos, "The Organizational Question and the Urban Commune," pp. 317-27, Benello and Roussopoulos (eds.), op. cit.

[94]H.B. Wilson, *Democracy and the Work Place* (Montreal, Black Rose Books, 1974).

[95]David Braybrooke, "The Meaning of Participation and of Demands for It: A Preliminary Survey of the Conceptual Issues," J. Roland Pennock and John W. Chapman (eds.), Nomos XVI, *Participation in Politics* (New York, Lieber-Atherton, 1975), pp. 56-88. Braybrooke has also written an important book on values and purposes in democratic theory, *Three Tests for Democracy: Personal Rights, Human Welfare, Collective Preference* (New York, Random House, 1968).

[96]Hugh B. Thorburn, "Canadian Pluralist Democracy in Crisis," *Canadian Journal of Political Science*, XI (December 1978), p. 724.

[97]William Mishler, *Political Participation in Canada* (Toronto, Macmillan of Canada, 1979).

[98]Ibid., p. v.

[99]Allan Kornberg, William Mishler and Harold C. Clarke, *Representative Democracy in the Canadian Provinces* (Scarborough, Prentice-Hall Canada Ltd., 1982).

[100]Ibid., p. 2.

[101]Ibid., p. 3. One might argue with the statement that Burke advocated a form of elite democracy instead of just inspiring it. For a recent study of Mill's theory of democracy, see Dennis F. Thompson, *John Stuart Mill and Representative Government* (Princeton, Princeton University Press, 1976).

[102]Ibid., pp. 3-4.

[103]Kornberg, Clarke and Mishler do state that "their differing concepts of the public interest and how it is discovered should be underscored". Ibid., p. 5.

[104]Ibid., p. 5.

[105]Ibid., p. 270.

[106]Ibid., p. 282.

French Canada

*Currents of Nationalism in Quebec**

DENIS MONIÈRE

*Translated by Christine Brooks and Stephen Brooks.

An understanding of the national problem in Canada and other advanced capitalist societies is possible only when two theoretical snags are avoided. The first involves reducing nationalistic claims to the status of cultural/linguistic issues brought about by ethnic differences. This thesis is generally supported by groups which lean towards maintenance of the status quo. The other snag is that of assimilating nationalism within bourgeois ideology and capitalism, and thereby postulating that only the conflict between classes and the passage from capitalism to socialism will allow the resolution of the national question. This position is generally defended by the Marxist-Leninist left. These two conceptions miss part of the reality and, paradoxically, proceed by the same logic in their concrete application.

In our opinion, contemporary nationalist movements express a popular resistance to the development of capitalism in its monopoly phase. They represent above all an opposition to the logic of political centralism inherent in the process of capital concentration. They express also a vision of society that questions the logical consequences of world domination by commodities; in other words, general manipulation, the remoteness of decision-making centres and standardization through programmed consumption.

Nationalist ideology has certainly corresponded conjuncturally to the growth needs of the market economy, in justifying the increase in the supply of labour, abolishing the limits of the feudal world, and creating a unified market. However, nationalism in the bourgeois sense of the term includes the negation of national differences and constitutes in reality a process of national oppression. From this perspective, nationalism cannot signify the affirmation of a specific identity; an ethnic, linguistic and cultural difference based upon control over material factors. Rather, historically it has meant acculturation, regression and folklorization of ethnic, linguistic and cultural differences. Bourgeois nationalism is essentially unifying and centralizing. The practice in certain so-called socialist states is not different in this regard. We have said that nationalism is an ideology, conjuncturally bourgeois, which is to say that it is not essential to capitalism with its expansionist and generalizing tendencies. The relationship between liberal ideology and nationalism is paradoxical. Consistent with the necessities of capital reproduction and accumulation, liberalism affirms unifying categories and therefore the reduction of differences. Nature, the Universal Declaration of the Rights of Man, Progress: these categories reflect and justify the expansionist/imperialist necessities of capitalism. Hence, during the first phase of its domination the bourgeoisie rests upon the creation of a nation-state. But its capital accumulation activities tend to transcend the nation-state framework since the development of capitalism engenders monopolistic tendencies and the export of capital. Capital does not identify with the nation. It is a-national, and tends to be transnational.

In the monopoly and imperialist phase of capitalism, nationalist movements become obstacles to the realization of conditions necessary for the survival of capitalism. This implies reinforcement of the processes of standardization and the policy of centralization. Control over the power of the state thus becomes the immediate object in the class struggle. In Canada, the crisis of national unity is the manifestation of a class struggle between the Canadian bourgeoisie and the technocratic "petite bourgeoisie québécoise", with which a large part of the Quebec working class is associated.

The national problem evolves in time and space. One cannot confine it within an absolute logic or assign it a single meaning. The content of nationalist ideology will vary as a function of the characteristics of concrete situations and the social forces which they express.

Throughout the history of Quebec the content of nationalism has varied a good deal. In order to understand the reasons for these variations, as well as the nature of Quebec nationalism as it has developed since the Quiet Revolution (1960), it is crucial to trace the principal currents of this nationalism and to situate them within an economic and social context. It is therefore necessary to point out the various parameters of ideological change and to place in relief the significant turning points in our evolution as a people.

That the national question is still alive in Quebec is due to the fact that decolonization never took place. The northern territory of America was first colonized by France which progressively settled the shores of the St. Lawrence. Later, the conquest of Canada and colonization by the British checked and distorted the process of national emancipation. The French in North America, contrary to settlers in most other colonies of the Portuguese, Spanish and English, were unable to attain the political sovereignty necessary to the life of a people.

Thus, to understand the evolution of Quebecois nationalism the effects of colonialism must be understood. The process of colonization implies that a society is conquered and subjected to an external power which, by its military and technical might, imposes a social and economic order that is informed by exogenous ends. In other words, the conquered society must serve the interests and the economic development of a foreign metropolis.

This foreign control over the riches and the economic life of the colonized society is accompanied by the formation of a double social structure, with one level superimposed upon the other. Moreover, one level is superior to the other and differentiated by nationality and, in many cases, by the mode of production. This unequal relationship involves a double system of authority, institutions, norms, and behaviour: that of the dominant colonial population and that of the subordinate colonized society. In the long run, colonial domination brings about structural distortions in the colonized social system, folkorization of its culture, and important changes in the development of its ideologies. Because of the double process of colonization brought about by the Conquest and the social disturbance which resulted from it, the evolution of political and social thought in French Canada is distinguished from that of other societies.

England had not engaged in seven years of war in North America simply to replace the French flag with the British flag at the Citadel of Quebec. Military operations always have economic objectives. In this case it involved the elimination of competition from French-Canadian fur-trading merchants by capturing the immense territory of New France which spread from Quebec to Louisiana. This operation also permitted the population of the New England colonies to expand towards the West.

The change of metropolis took away from French-Canadian merchants the economic basis they had relied upon. Indeed, the society of New France was decapitated, with its most dynamic class removed. The Conquest impeded the development of a French-Canadian bourgeoisie and brought about the progressive ruination of the businessmen who remained in the conquered colony. With the change in metropolis from Paris to London these remaining merchants were cut off from sources of capital, supplies, and markets. Not having reliable associates in the new metropolis, French-Canadian merchants lost control of the fur trade. They became merely subcontractors, selling their merchandise to the English merchants of the colony. Marginalized in the commercial sphere they left the big profits to others and contented themselves with the crumbs by becoming suppliers of raw materials. They also lost, little by little, the internal trade of the colony (e.g., wine and spirits). Their stores were empty, previous orders to France not having been delivered, and for lack of credit they could not restock from the new metropolis. Thus, the English merchants became commercially dominant with French Canadians confined to the role of subcontractors even in the domestic trade.

French Canadians also lost control of the state apparatus which, through the device of military supplies, played an important role in the economic life of the colony. The Conquest therefore had the effect of transferring economic and political power to a social group outside of the class structure of the colony. A new clique was in power, that of the English merchants who were to profit from state contracts and their monopoly over trading concessions. French Canadians were forced to withdraw to the country and leave the most profitable sectors of the economy to the new masters. French-Canadian society was forced to rely upon its own strengths and to fall back on agriculture, cottage industry, and small trade in order to survive.

British political domination and the changes in external economic relations led to the formation of two superimposed social structures: a colonial social structure, the material basis of which rested upon commercial trade and control over political power, and a colonized social structure based on subsistence production.

Thus, on the social level, the Conquest had the effect of eliminating the ruling class of French-Canadian society, replacing a developing francophone bourgeoisie with an anglophone bourgeoisie, and allowing the formation of a double structure of classes differentiated by both nationality and the mode of production. The French-Canadian social structure retained indelible marks of the circumstances that resulted from the Conquest. These circumstances favoured the co-optation of a decadent social group, viz. the clerical aristocracy, characterized by a non-creative economic condition and by an ideology of collaboration and conservation. The conquerors tried to assign the guidance of French-Canadian society to this group. Until 1850 the clerical aristocracy was unable to impose its political authority on the people. It was challenged by another class, namely the professional petite bourgeoisie which opposed both the British oligarchy and its ally, the francophone clerical aristocracy. Due to colonization there occurred a distortion in the extent to which economic relationships were mediated by political relationships. This conferred considerable weight and relative autonomy to the petite bourgeoisie which, according to the circumstances, oscillated between the interests of the people and those of the bourgeoisie.

This situation had a distorting effect on both the ideology of the anglophone bourgeoisie and that of the francophone petite bourgeoisie. With the establishment of a representative assembly in 1791 this latter group used the new political institutions to defend the economic interests of French Canadians and promote its own social advancement. The political struggles which occurred in the early nineteenth century placed in opposition two conceptions of the nation and two concepts of economic development in Quebec. From this opposition was born French-Canadian nationalism.

Nationalism in the Commercial Phase of Capitalism

At the beginning of the nineteenth century there occurred market contraction and a decrease in the price of furs, such that by 1810 the lumber trade replaced that in furs. From 1815, exports of squared timber experienced a dramatic increase on account of the British protectionist policy. This policy led to a transfer of British capital to Lower Canada (Quebec), which was invested in the exploitation of forest resources. French Canadians could not profit from the development of this new economic sector because only the English merchants had access to the commercial network of the metropolis (London). Our economic role was to supply cheap labour and produce wealth for others. For their part the English businessmen attempted to use the colonial state in support of their ventures. Even at that early date, control of public resources and the use of taxes were the stakes underlying political struggles between the assembly, which represented the people, and the executive, representing the interests of the British Crown and those of the anglophone merchant bourgeoisie which controlled 90 per cent of the colony's economy.

This bourgeoisie desired to complement its economic power with control over political power. But because colonialism implies domination over a majority by a minority, the English merchant bourgeoisie was unable to support the struggles for the establishment of a democratic political system through the achievement of responsible government. Bourgeois democracy, based on the principal of representation and delegation of powers, did not function to the advantage of the English bourgeoisie since it implied that power depends upon numbers (i.e., the majoritarian principle). In a colonial situation the majority is formed by another nationality, and its interests diverge from those of the colonial bourgeoisie.

The content of the ideology of this English bourgeoisie was unlike that of the other bourgeois groups. In general a bourgeoisie is nationalist, democratic and progressive. However, in Quebec between the Conquest and the middle of the nineteenth century, the Canadian bourgeoisie was comprised of English businessmen who controlled the lumber trade, the banks and the transportation network, and who could not play this democratic and progressive role. Because of the colonial situation, involving the domination of the English minority over the French majority, the merchant bourgeoisie was unable to impose its political hegemony by relying upon popular support. Instead, it had to ally itself with the bureaucratic class and use the powers of the executive and legislative councils, neither of which was responsible to the people, to promote its class interests. Consequently, there existed a contradiction between the bourgeoisie's aspirations for control of the state through the establishment of parliamentary democracy, and the material basis of its situation, viz. colonial oppression.

The political thought of the English bourgeoisie suffered from the following dilemma. Its interests compelled this class to demand parliamentarism and the establishment of a representative assembly as existed in those colonies whence most merchants came. But how were they to justify a legislative assembly that would exclude from its ranks 99 per cent of the population? If equal rights were accorded the French, they would control the assembly. If French Canadians were excluded from representation in the assembly, there would be the risk of alienating the population.

In order to transform Canada into a colony of English inhabitants it was necessary to encourage massive English immigration. And to attract these immigrants they had to be given the same rights they enjoyed in the metropolis. The dilemma was how to give these rights to those who emigrated from the metropolis, while withholding them from the conquered population. Assimilating the French Canadians through English immigration meant giving the same rights to those in the conquered colony as in the other colonies. To concede these rights meant returning power to the French Canadians, for they were in the majority. Colonialism was opposed to democracy. As long as the French Canadians formed a majority the bourgeoisie would resist the establishment of a liberal democracy and prefer to support an aristocratic regime and an alliance with the *Château Clique*. Thus, democratic rights would not be recognized in Canada until the numerical strength of the French Canadians was diminished. With the arrival of the Loyalists in 1791, the representative assembly was established. Then in 1848, when it became clear that French Canadians would comprise a minority within the framework of the United Canadas, the principle of responsible government was put into practice.

Similarly, the Canadian bourgeoisie could not be nationalist because its prosperity always depended on external markets, British or American according to the times. Unlike most colonial bourgeoisies this class was reluctant to break the colonial tie to the metropolis. English Canadians' sense of belonging was defined much more in relation to the Empire than in relation to Canada.

The effect of ideological distortion also shaped the francophone petite bourgeoisie. First of all, it became the carrier of liberal ideology and nationalism. This class played the ideological role that is usually played by the national bourgeoisie. It demanded democratic and republican institutions, responsible government, the end of the colonial tie, and the secularization of society. Through this project of national emancipation the professional petite bourgeoisie attacked the power of the merchant bourgeoisie, the collaborating clergy, and the bureaucratic oligarchy.

The members of this new class were products of the people. These professionals were for the most part sons of farmers who had certain of their children educated in schools and colleges. Education and politics were for them the only means of social advancement, given that other sectors were closed to francophones. Consequently, they inclined towards the liberal professions, becoming lawyers, notaries, and doctors. But these educated young people, possessing great hopes, did not always find work. Their professions were overcrowded and Canadian society could not integrate them nor satisfy their aspirations since the army, the navy, private and public administration, and engineering were proscribed careers, reserved for the elite of the colonial social structure. Due to the colonial situation the distancing of the petite bourgeoisie from the peasant masses was not realized. They had to support one another in order to protect their economic positions.

Frustrated in their aspirations, economically threatened by the congested service sector and by the agricultural crisis which affected their clientele, these young professionals rapidly became conscious of their interests. They found in political action an outlet where they could exercise their talents and through which they could impose their leadership and their vision of the world which, in these circumstances, corresponded to the material interests of the *habitants*. Behind their political demands for responsible government, which meant access to public offices, and their goal of national emancipation stood a social struggle.

The ideology of the petite bourgeoisie had two main characteristics: nationalism and liberalism. This last theme had a particular connotation due to the superposition of nationalities and the specific character of the colonial social structure. The French-Canadian petite bourgeoisie made use of political instruments usually demanded by the merchant bourgeoisie, in order to keep the latter in check. It dissociated political liberalism from its economic objective, i.e., the development of commerce. Consequently, there was an incongruence between the ideological superstructure and the economic base. The professional petite bourgeoisie adopted the political ideology of the bourgeoisie but, because of the colonial situation, it was unable to ally itself with this class and accept its hegemony. The petite bourgeoisie preferred to ally itself with the people, for they provided it with an economic foundation. It was the farmer who payed for the services of notaries, lawyers, doctors and small businessmen, and therefore this professional class had a stake in defending the economic interests of the farming class. French-Canadian members of the assembly considered that political power should promote the development of agriculture, while the anglophone capitalists felt that it should serve business. During this period one witnessed therefore a class struggle which was at the same time a conflict between nations. All the parliamentary battles that followed carried the mark of this antagonism which placed two social structures in opposition to one another.

This antagonism was reflected at several levels. There was a conflict between two economic experiences, the one based upon agriculture and limited to Quebec, and the other founded on commercial capitalism within a pan-Canadian perspective. On the political level, the opposing sides used different powers to defend their respective interests. The executive and legislative councils were used by the English Canadians, and the assembly by the French Canadians. The latter were opposed to the Empire and aspired to independence, while the English Canadians relied upon the metropolis and wished to maintain the colonial connection. Finally, French Canadians opposed immigration in order to check the growth of the English population, while the English supported immigration as a source of manpower and, indirectly, as a means of swamping and assimilating the French-Canadian population. Until 1837 the legislative assembly was the usual scene for these confrontations. French-Canadian members used the legislative power to undermine the economic interests of the commercial bourgeoisie. The quarrel over financing the canalization of the St. Lawrence illustrated well the dialectic of the struggle, a struggle which was at once social and national.

The completion of the Champlain canal in 1822 and the progress of the Erie canal threatened the commercial hegemony of Montreal's English merchants with competition from American capitalists. The English-Canadian bourgeoisie considered it urgent that channels of communication with Upper Canada be opened, and a pan-Canadian commercial unity be created. These businessmen counted on using the state and public funds to realize this project. However, the French-Canadian delegation did not share this view of the appropriate orientation of economic development. It refused to finance this project from the people's money. This refusal was made even more frustrating for the commercial bourgeoisie by the fact that Upper Canada already had begun construction of its part of the canal system.

In brief, one can state that the main characteristics of the ideology of the petite bourgeoisie were political liberalism, laicism, and national emancipation. The thought of Louis Joseph Papineau is revealing of these three dimensions of the ideology of the professional petite bourgeoisie.

L. J. Papineau developed a political vision which aimed at control of the state by the petite bourgeoisie. Papineau was conscious of the incompatibility between a democracy which would serve French Canadians, and the maintenance of the colonial connection. For Papineau, parliamentary institutions and responsible government signified the possibility for French Canadians to control the political system and use it to support the development of French-Canadian society. Papineau's thinking was centered on Lower Canada. He never envisaged a Canada comprising all the English colonies. Moreover, he opposed the pan-Canadian perspective of the commercial bourgeoisie.

Papineau's nationalism included an economic dimension, for he aspired to found a French-Canadian economic order that would serve primarily the interests of Lower Canada. The *Patriotes* whom Papineau led were opposed to the domination of commercial capitalism and extroverted economic development, i.e., development determined by the foreign market of the metropolis. They attempted to establish a system of economic development centred on Lower Canada, oriented towards satisfaction of the basic needs of the population.

The Rebellion of 1837-8 was thus an attempt at democratic revolution within the framework of a colonial state. Due to the distinctive nature of the class structure, the professional petite bourgeoisie was called upon to act as the driving force of political progress, rather than the bourgeoisie as was the case in England, France and the United States.

The liberating political nationalism upheld by the *Patriotes* was crushed militarily. In terms of consequences, the failure of the Rebellion brought about a modification of the relationship between social forces in Lower Canada. First of all, it signified the victory of the commercial bourgeoisie over the professional petite bourgeoisie. Henceforth, capitalism would be able to develop without impedement and with the support of the state. The commercial bourgeoisie was then enabled to exercise its hegemony and, privileged through the new constitutional arrangements, it became a propagandist for the democratic ideal. There no longer were any obstacles to the establishment of responsible government within the framework of a United Canada. The failure of the *Patriotes* thus permitted the resolution of the contradiction between the English bourgeoisie's aspirations of liberal democracy and its position of colonial dominance.

Furthermore, following the defeat of this French-Canadian lay elite the Catholic Church assumed the leadership of French-Canadian society. The ideological and political power of the clerical elite and the petite bourgeoisie in neither case rested on control over the means of production, i.e., capital. It depended on subordination to and collaboration with another social structure wherein lay economic power. At the centre of the great Victorian compromise the Church left control of the economic sector to the commercial bourgeoisie and took upon itself social and ideological control. Political and honorific positions were left to the professional petite bourgeoisie.

With class alliances modified, the professional petite bourgeoisie, under the influence of its moderate faction, developed a new strategy. Essentially, this was centred on conservation through subordinate collaboration. Within the framework of a United Canada and responsible government, the petite bourgeoisie abandoned its alliance with the people in order to offer its services to the commercial bourgeoisie which, in exchange for this submission, allowed access to the civil service. With a new economic base, the professional petite bourgeoisie thereafter subscribed to a defensive nationalism which used blackmail arguments to obtain positions in the apparatus of the state.

The failure of the Rebellion thus led to union of the two Canadas, and accelerated the inferiorization of French-Canadian society. Dynamic and liberating resistance, based on the aspiration to build a politically independent and economically autonomous

French-Canadian society along the shores of the St. Lawrence, was succeeded by conservative and defensive resistance. The struggle for survival replaced the struggle for independence. "Sensing that they might well become a minority, the Quebecois no longer aimed towards an independent society, but towards the conservation of their culture."[1]

Nationalism and Industrialization

Between 1840 and 1867 there occurred the great ideological turning point in French-Canadian society. The main components of the ideology that would dominate Quebec for a century were developed under the pressure of economic, social and political transformations following from the defeat of 1837-8. This event reinforced all the effects of the Conquest of 1760 and ensured the economic, social and political inferiorization of French Canadians.

The second half of the nineteenth century was characterized by the structural transformation of the Canadian economy which, dependent upon external foreign influences, became oriented progressively towards industrialization. From the international perspective, this period corresponded to the second phase of capitalist expansion. This manifested itself in Canada through the massive influx of first British and later American capital which was invested in railroads.

The primacy of light industry and the dependent/extroverted character of economic development characterized this first phase of industrialization in Quebec. Entrepreneurs, markets, technology and capital came from outside Quebec and were controlled by anglophones. Small trade and agriculture, which had been at the centre of the economic life of French Canadians, allowed for neither sufficient capital accumulation nor the formation of a financial and industrial bourgeoisie capable of taking advantage of the industrialization process. Quebec was able to contribute only its natural wealth and its cheap labour force. Moreover, the constitution of the federal state ensured the industrial bourgeoisie of policies which conformed to its interests.

Canadian Confederation was, in large part, a product of capitalism which required a larger market and access to public resources in order to develop. To bring about this artificial market, enormous investments in the infrastructure were necessary, investments which were beyond the capacity of private enterprise. Therefore, the federal state was used to extort from the various provincial populations the funds necessary to put the railroad companies on their feet financially. It was mainly Ontario that benefited from the transport revolution. In 1867 Quebec had 925 kilometres of railway track compared to Ontario's 2242. Adolphe Chapleau said at the time that the province of Quebec had never been favoured like Ontario. This imbalance in treatment partly explained the backwardness in the industrial and urban development of Quebec, and may be read as an extension of the effects of the Conquest. Furthermore, the national tariff policy of 1879 increased from 17.5 to 30 per cent the entrance duty on finished and intermediary goods, the main effect of which was to stimulate industrialization in Ontario where heavy industry was developing.

Despite Quebec's backwardness, Quebecois society was becoming industrialized, demonstrated by the fact that from 1851 to 1896 production in the secondary sector grew from about $2 million to $153.5 million. But in general, the industries taking root were linked to the exploitation of natural resources or the production of necessities intended for immediate consumption (i.e., food).

Industrialization is always accompanied by urbanization. Thus, between 1901 and 1921, Quebec's urban population increased from 39.6 per cent to 56 per cent of the total population. As early as 1901 agriculture employed only 38.5 per cent of the active labour force. Movement to the cities and the establishment of a working class resulted from the need for a concentrated industrial labour force, and from the arrival of successive waves of immigrants. The proletarianization and urbanization of French Canadians was belated. Thus, they had to integrate into an urban milieu already dominated by anglophones.

While Quebec was being industrialized to the profit of English-Canadian and British capitalists, the clerical elite and the petite bourgeoisie were developing a vision of society which was diametrically opposed to the reality of the material world. In order to preserve its economic and social basis, this elite tried to convince French Canadians to remain farmers despite the poor prospect and material conditions associated with this type of activity. The elite ideology denied industrialization, urbanization, modern advances, and state intervention. Instead, it urged French Canadians to remain on the land.

This unrealistic ideology, carried by a class whose domination depended upon its subordination to and collaboration with another social structure, rationalized the chronic powerlessness of the colonized population by magnifying and idealizing the consequences of its exploitation and alienation. In other words, the effects of the colonial situation were taken as postulates in this world vision, and the whole of French-Canadian society was assigned an unrealistic destiny which had as its sole object the justification of domination by an effectively powerless class incapable of leading the way to autonomous economic development.

Thus, in the industrial phase of capitalism the dominant ideology was out of touch with the structural tendencies of the society. There was an opposition between the process of capitalist industrialization and the dominant ideology produced and propagated by the Church and its lay ideologists who adhered to a traditional model of society based on agriculture and small property holders. The dominant ideology of this period had, therefore, a behind-the-times character. It was underdeveloped in relation to structural transformations which influenced the particular development of ideologies in Quebec.

From 1850 to 1950, French Canada was dominated by an ideology of conservation and a nationalism that was essentially cultural and dedicated to the defence of religion, language and institutions. We were poor, but chosen by God for a grand spiritual and moral mission: to Christianize America and carry the torch of civilization. This is what Monseigneur Paquet declared at the beginning of the century:

> (We) are not only a civilized race, we are pioneers of a civilization; we are not only a religious people, we are messengers of the spirit of religion; we are not only dutiful sons of the Church, we

> are, or we should be, numbered among its zealots, its defenders, and its apostles. Our mission is less to handle capital than to stimulate ideas; less to light the furnaces of factories than to maintain and spread the glowing fires of religion and thought, and to help them cast their light into the distance.[2]

The unrealistic character of the dominant ideology resulted from the national and social domination exerted upon French-Canadian society by British colonization. Due to the economic and political structures imposed through colonization, the industrialization and urbanization process was carried out almost exclusively by English and American capitalists. The clerico-petit bourgeois class was not equipped to play the same role, nor to take on the management of economic development to its own profit. Threatened and panic-stricken, this class preferred to withdraw into itself, and deny modern advances which therefore escaped us as a people. It took refuge in a world of illusions and celestial hopes. As compensation for our economic inferiority a grand destiny in North America was prophesied for us. In a confused way it was felt that the business world, the factory and the city belonged to others. This was a system in which French Canadians had no place, being deprived of their own dynamic and hegemonic bourgeoisie.

Through this ideology of denial the clerico-petit bourgeois class sought to resist the social, political and ideological changes which were demanded by industrialization. Rural depopulation struck the country petite bourgeoisie, which saw its economic foundation disintegrate. Fewer farmers meant fewer business possibilities for the shopkeeper, the doctor, the lawyer and the notary. Similarly, in the city small industrial and commercial concerns were threatened by extinction because of the tendency towards the concentration of capital. Furthermore, in the city it was more difficult for this elite to maintain its ideological control and preserve its political influence since the industrial world was dominated by the English language and materialist values.

We think that the unrealistic character of this dominant ideology, as well as the monolithic quality of social and economic thought among French Canadians, can be explained by the fact that the power of the French-Canadian dominant class was not based on private ownership of the means of production, but rather on the responsibility for social control and the management of local affairs delegated to it by the Canadian financial bourgeoisie. Since the clerico-petit bourgeois class had no control over the development of economic structures, its ideology did not have as its main function the legitimization of the bourgeoisie's economic and social domination. This class did not have to define itself in terms of the development of productive forces, but rather in terms of the maintenance of its position within society's superstructure. It aimed to preserve the rural and Catholic character of Quebec because this condition gave it legitimacy in the hierarchy of authorities. The content of nationalism would likewise be defined from this perspective. Thus, the clerical elite and the petite bourgeoisie clung to a model of pre-capitalist society while the dominant economic forces, which were mostly foreign, were those of the monopoly phase of capitalism.

The dominant traits of French-Canadian nationalism since 1867 are the belief in the theory of a compact between the two nations, the denial of a link between the state and the nation, and the defence of the constitutional status quo and provincial autonomy. This constituted a set pattern of thinking which held the constitution to be sacrosanct and defended its provisions in spite of the changes and new requirements created by economic and social development. It was therefore a nationalism of survival, dedicated to the defence of the Canadian legal framework and defined in cultural terms. This nationalism shared in the ideology of conservation, conceiving of the French-Canadian population as the carrier of a culture, "a group that has an instructive history, which became a minority in the nineteenth century and that has a duty to preserve the heritage it received from its ancestors to be passed on intact to subsequent generations. Essentially, this heritage is comprised of the Catholic religion, the French language and an indeterminate number of traditions and customs. The golden age of this ideology is the past."[3] This was a mystical nationalism which appealed to the providential mission of a chosen people in legitimizing the existence of the nation.

Nationalist thought of that period was the expression of the political powerlessness which French Canadians experienced within a legal framework in which they were a minority and subject to a dynamic that they had no control over. In this context all change was perceived as a threat and automatically triggered a defensive reaction. This dialectic led to unrealistic thinking in that it compelled a collectivity to retire within itself and cling to plans or approaches that were contradicted by the facts. The nationalism of French Canadians was at once Canadian and French Canadian. It was Canadian because, unlike the anglophones, French Canadians have always been anti-colonialists and little attached to relations with the British Empire. In this connection, Henri Bourassa became a passionate defender of Canadian independence. This question was of distinctly minor importance for English Canadians, who affirmed above all their imperial solidarity and, consequently, their anti-French feelings. This difference was expressed very clearly by the newspaper *La Presse*, with reference to the Boer War: "We French Canadians belong to only one country...Canada is for us the entire world. But the English have two homelands; one here and the other overseas". Similarly, Henri Bourassa conceived of himself as a Canadian above all. He dreamt of a Canada in which the two founding nations would be in stable equilibrium. Bourassa became the advocate of a pan-Canadian nationalism based on the mutual respect of the two races. His Canadian nationalism was based upon the existence of two distinctly separate cultural nationalisms. These were to be dissociated from politics and remain free from any connection with the state. The latter was to have a neutral role, situated above the two nations and maintaining a balance between them. This was an idealistic conception of nationalism and the state since it involved a denial of politics. Indeed, this nationalism was trapped within unsolvable contradictions because it denounced pro-imperialist sentiments, social prejudices, the chauvinistic attitude of the English and their attempts at assimilation and the violation of minority rights, without recognition of the causes of these phenomena. Power relations are assigned no place in this world view. Bourassa refused to accept the logic of majoritarian democracy and, more importantly, to understand its consequences. He admitted to being disillusioned with Confederation, yet he continued to act as if it could be made to work.

Finally, Bourassa's nationalism shared in the messianic dimension of that period's thought. Bourassa believed in the civilizing and spiritual mission of French Canada in North America. He considered that this messianism could only be realized within the framework of federalism. For this reason he was opposed to independence for Quebec since, according to Bourassa, French Canada required a continent-wide dimension in order to meet its spiritual vocation. From this perspective, the role of Quebec was to come to the aid of francophone minorities in other provinces. For Bourassa, federalism was justified by messianism, and both the state and the nation were to comply with higher purposes and be placed in the service of divine Providence. In fact, the interest of the Church came before those of the nationality. It therefore comes as no surprise to learn that Bourassa's nationalism had greater rhetorical impact than practical influence, and did nothing to stem the demographic decline and the economic inferiority of French Canadians. On the contrary, it weakened them by maintaining the myth of good relations and the illusions of pan-Canadianism.

Another trend of this period was to oppose the "more Canadian" nationalism of Bourassa, with a nationalism which was more French Canadian. This latter orientation can be explained by the fact that, during the 1920s, the attention of the French-Canadian elite was diverted from the federal scene and trained upon Quebec as the effects of demographic and political inferiorization began to be felt. This reaction was brought about by a decline in the governmental influence of French Canadians under the Borden Conservatives, and by successive defeats in the struggle for the rights of French minorities outside Quebec. After conscription and the submission of French Canadians to the force of superior numbers and Ottawa's political strength during the First World War, relations between Quebec and the rest of Canada deteriorated to the point that a member of Quebec's National Assembly, J.N. Francoeur, proposed the withdrawal of Quebec from Confederation. The views of Canon Lionel Groulx embodied this collective awareness.

Groulx sought to justify the continued existence of the French-Canadian nationality, and to discover in its history the Ariadnean thread of French Canada's destiny. He desired to redress the inferior condition of his people through an interpretation of its history. Groulx considered the history of French Canada to be the guarantor of unity, cohesion and national identity.

This past, which traces its roots back to the old French regime, defines our essential being and the values that we must preserve. For Groulx, the French colonists did not constitute a people of trappers and adventurers. They were above all an agricultural people. The exemplars of this society were the settler, the evangelist and the protector (i.e., the cult of Dollard des Ormeaux). In this respect, Groulx glorified the Church's role as protector, a logic which led to a nationalism of conservation. The main foundation of this doctrine was that Catholicism must be preserved at all costs. Groulx had searched the historical record to demonstrate the beneficial role of religion and the bishops in French Canada.

On the constitutional level, and notwithstanding a temporary flirtation in the 1920s with the dream of an independent French state *(la Laurantie)*, Groulx remained faithful to the dogma of traditional nationalist thought: Quebec belonged within Canada. For Groulx Canadian Confederation was tantamount to the "resurrection of French Canada", because it restored Quebec as a political entity.

Influenced by the spirit of the times, he predicted in *Notre avenir politique* the eventual collapse of Confederation. However, Groulx did not care to push the matter. Rather, he considered that Quebec must relentlessly defend *provincial autonomy* on both the economic and political levels. Groulx attacked politicians who were more concerned with the relentless defence of the interests of their party than those of the nation. In his opinion, parties weakened the nation and were divisive factors. Only the Church could bring about unity in the nation.

As with Bourassa, messianism constituted an essential part of Groulx's nationalism. The providential mission of French Canadians consisted in the development of agriculture, representing spiritual values in America, and propagating the Catholic faith. This chosen people was to become the missionary of Christ. Messianism seems to be the refuge of threatened cultures and embodies in illusion their hope for liberation. Despite its many setbacks, French Canada must never despair, for God is its protector and saviour.

The main leitmotifs of this ideology were: Heaven is the essential thing; we are poor; we are Catholic and French; the English exercise a crushing economic power over us and are responsible for our subordination and our decline as a nation. But this French-Canadian nationalism was unarmed and sterile due to its refusal to resort to politics in order to transform aspiration into reality. It was subordinate to religious ends. Indeed, in this ideology even economic activity was directed by spiritual values and must serve the moral order and the faith.

Thus, all nationalists remarked upon the economic underdevelopment of Quebec. Moreover, they virulently denounced the economic dictatorship of foreign monopolies and the absence of francophones from those decision-making centres where the life of the community is determined. But they ruled out the use of effective measures to correct the structural imbalances they identified. These nationalists relied on strategies of economic reconquest based upon national solidarity. These strategies linked the economic future of the French Canadians to the purchase of provincially produced goods, the co-operative movement, and the formation of a competent business class.

Even though economic considerations began to appear during this period, these still reflected the dominance of the Church's social thought. This thinking did not acknowledge the positive character of state action, and indeed held that the state must not become an autonomous centre of authority. Except in the fields of agriculture and natural resources, the state should confine itself to the maintenance of order.

While the state was mistrusted in Quebec, on the federal scene one witnessed the development of the socio-economic functions of the state in response to the Depression and the exigencies of an increasingly monopolistic economy. Centralization and growth in the powers of the federal state altered the federal/provincial balance of power and tended to diminish the authority of the provinces. This process initiated the constitutional crisis of the present day. In this respect, it should be noted that the Second World War saw an increase in the federal invasion of provincial jurisdictions, thereby threatening the principle of provincial autonomy. The spending power, residual powers and the general interest clause of the *BNA Act* were the means used by the federal government for unwarranted interference in provincial affairs. The federal government instituted old-age pensions in 1927, followed by unemployment insurance in 1941, family allowances in 1944, and finally (with the collaboration of the Godbout government in Quebec) came to monopolize the power of direct taxation. This centralist conception of federalism was confirmed by the Rowell-Sirois Commission (1937), which was instructed to inquire into federal/provincial relations. On this matter, the Canadian bourgeoisie favoured the development of the federal state apparatus in order to attenuate the contradictions of capitalism. Likewise, the Judicial Committee of the Privy Council (JCPC) in London, until 1949 the final court of appeal in the interpretation of the Canadian constitution, legitimized this centralist orientation in relying upon the so-called emergency powers doctrine whereby the federal Parliament could, during exceptional circumstances such as war or other crisis, legislate in areas of provincial jurisdiction.

The growth of the federal state apparatus can be illustrated by developments in public expenditures and the size of the federal public service. Whereas total expenditures of the federal state amounted to $385 million at the end of the Depression (1939), in 1949 they reached $1987 million. In terms of employment, the federal public service increased from 43 000 persons in 1929, to 46 000 in 1939, and 124 000 in 1949.[4] From 1913 to 1960, the rate of increase in the federal public service (excluding the military) was four times as great as that for the population as a whole. The year 1939 marked the turning point in this regard. The Second World War and its after-effects led to an increase of 40 per cent in military personnel, while the new socio-economic functions of the federal state were responsible for a 20 per cent increase in the public service. These data demonstrate clearly the transformation in the role of the federal government. Expansion in the functions of the central state rendered the constitution out-of-date, and the provincial states increasingly dependent. This constituted a threat to the very survival of Quebec. In response, the nationalist movement turned towards the past and opposition through the courts in defence of provincial autonomy, instead of trying to develop the political powers of Quebec.

If the nationalism of this period was built upon the rejection of the state, this was because the Church constituted a state within the state and, at least, acted as a cohesive social influence at the heart of Quebec society. This type of nationalism established borders along cultural lines (language and religion) rather than political lines. The nation was French Canada, and the Church was the centre for organization and representation of that nation.

> The thinking which has been characterized as autonomist did not express in general a demand for additional power for the Quebec state. Rather, it expressed a rejection of any external intervention that could have endangered the internal organization of control, i.e., the respective roles of the Church and the Quebecois state in their specific articulation.[5]

Hence, for more than a century after the defeated Rebellion of 1837-8 the dominant ideology in French Canada expressed the internalized effects of colonization. The ideology of collaboration prevailed in elite circles. Nationalism assumed the complexion of the early defeat and concealed a social vision shaped by the interests of the clerical elite. These nationalists defended Confederation since it provided French-Canadian professionals with access to well remunerated positions and, at the same time, enabled the Church to make use of provincial authority to carry out its plans for a theocratic society. Thus, religion and culture occupied the foreground of the ideological stage while the Canadian economy was entering its industrial phase. The ideology subscribed to by French Canada's dominant class ran against the trends of an industrial world in rejecting industrialization, urbanization, and an active role for the state in economic development. Instead, this ideology took refuge in such conservative values as messianism, spiritualism and life on the land. This ideology was cut off from reality. Moreover, it was incapable of directing the development of society since it corresponded to the interests of an undynamic social group which was excluded from the real centres of decision-making. This group used nationalism to protect its status as intermediary, and to justify its collaboration with the economically dominant class. In brief, this century was characterized by a powerless and submissive nationalism which conceived of Quebec as a rural and clerical society.

Nationalism in the Monopoly Phase of Capitalism

After the Second World War the industrial structure of Quebec was modernized through the massive influx of American capital. The process of capital concentration produced two major consequences: i) modification in the composition of the social structure; and ii) development of the functions of the provincial state. This accelerated adaptation by Quebec society is referred to as the Quiet Revolution. Modernization of the political and ideological superstructure began with the coming to power of the Liberal party (1960) and the replacement of the traditional petite bourgeoisie by a new educated urban-based petite bourgeoisie as the dominant social group.

During this period the economic development of Quebec took place along outwardly oriented and dependent lines. This state of dependence expressed itself empirically through the domination of foreign monopoly capital, the export of staple commodities, the importation of capital and finished products, the weakness of secondary industry, and the lack of diversification in international trade which flowed mainly between Quebec and the United States. Quebec was a social formation integrated within an advanced capitalist society, but with features resembling those of Third World countries. The concentration of capital was very high (particularly in the banking sector), finance capital dominated, and pre-capitalist modes of production were almost totally eliminated. Finally, Quebec had another peculiarity in that it constituted a social formation with a truncated state. This state was possessed of only weak powers on the fiscal and monetary levels, and was incapable of influencing the direction of investment and employment.

The class structure was dominated by American imperialism and its indigenous ally, the English-Canadian bourgeoisie. This latter group was joined by certain francophone elements which formed neither a distinct class nor an autonomous fraction. French Canadians, who constituted 80 per cent of the total population, controlled only 4 to 5 per cent of industrial enterprises with assets in excess of $50 million, and owned only a third of all small and medium-sized firms.

The economic condition of francophones in Quebec in comparison to anglophones was described by the Royal Commission on Bilingualism and Biculturalism during the 1960s. Overall, this study demonstrated that with respect to income and occupation francophones in Quebec were always at the bottom of the ladder. In terms of income, French Canadians ranked twelfth among ethnic groups in Canada. This gap was confirmed by a study made in 1971, and more recently by an investigation which found that the income gap between anglophones and francophones, measured in constant dollars, remained on the order of $2000 between 1971 and 1978. In 1971, anglophones earned an average of 23.8 per cent more than francophones. Even in the case of bilingual francophones, average income is less than for unilingual anglophones.

On the subject of occupations, the Commission demonstrated clearly the under-representation of francophones in well-paid and prestigious occupational strata. From the *Directory of Directors* it was found that only 9.5 per cent of the 12 741 names registered in 1971 were French. A large proportion of these were lawyers and former politicians, so that the directorship was not due to the ownership of capital.

Nationalism during this contemporary period cannot be reduced to the level of an ideological or psychological phenomenon. This is because national oppression has consequences for economic relationships and, in fact, created the concrete conditions for an alliance between the new petite bourgeoisie and the working class.

Linguistic discrimination is one of the most obvious aspects of national oppression. It makes tangible and directly perceptible the social contradictions which flow from the political subordination of one nation to another. The nationalist movement of this period is therefore the expression of a class struggle with an ethnic dimension. The distribution of the population according to ethnic origin provides a good illustration of the effect of subordination and inequality created by the cultural division of labour within the framework of national oppression.

TABLE 1: Distribution of linguistic groups by occupation: Quebec, 1970[6]

	Anglophones	*Francophones*
Percentage of the total population	14	86
Administration/management	31	69
Clerical/office worker	21	79
Sales	19	81
Manual worker	10	90

Thus, anglophones are over-represented in job categories associated with intellectual work while francophones are over-represented in the manual labour category. This difference can only be explained by structural causes, namely, socio-economic imbalances which go all the way back to British colonization.

The national movement is also a social movement. As such it is based upon an alliance of classes which have similar interests in the struggle against national oppression. In fact, the working class is subject to the effects of national oppression and, in this sense, its interests converge with those of the new petite bourgeoisie. This is because language is a crucial medium in a society's system of economic and cultural relationships. Language constitutes an important part of working conditions, and when the language in use is not that of the majority of the population this leads to more or less serious consequences for the workers of the dominated nation (who comprise the vast majority of the working class). In this regard, Marcel Pépin, President of the Confédération des Syndicats Nationales, said the following:

> How many thousands of Quebec workers have been refused work in Quebec because they did not know English, or didn't know it well enough? How many workers...have been denied promotions, even below the managerial level, for lack of sufficient knowledge of English, or under the pretext that they lack sufficient knowledge? How many thousands of Quebecois have lost out on opportunities in their professional life, for lack of having had time or the means of providing themselves with double qualifications: technical competence and competence in English in addition to their own language? How many could very easily have acquired a technical knowledge if they had not had to know another language than their own in order to learn it? Just asking these questions one senses that the damage done up until now has been enormous.[7]

Thus, francophones in Quebec are under-represented in positions of responsibility and power and are over-represented in the agricultural, primary production and unskilled labour sectors. True, after 1945 francophones did move up the ladder of industrial occupations, but this advance did not mean access to the command posts of the economy. Modernization of the Quebec economy has not closed the economic disparity between Quebec, Ontario, and the rest of Canada. Since 1926, per capita income in Quebec has remained equal to about 73 per cent of that in Ontario. The level of inequality has managed to persist over time.

Industrial modernization and the development of the socio-economic functions of the state (necessary for the maintenance of economic growth) compelled the creation of a more highly qualified work force and the emergence of new social categories. The new management elite which these developments called forth was highly educated and aspired to upward social mobility.

Since young francophones were unable to use their competence to advance in the anglophone-controlled private sector, they concentrated on circles of power which they were able to control: i.e., the Quebec state.

The new elite which assumed the political direction of Quebec society in 1960 was not homogeneous. It included a fraction linked to the interests of English and American capitalism. This group supported the process of modernization but wished to control development within the framework of federal political structures. Accordingly, the Quebecois state required strengthening, but not to the point where it would be powerful enough to threaten the Canadian political system.

But above all it was time to make up for lost ground *(ratrapper)* in all areas by replacing the Church with the state as the principal institution in society. From this perspective, the Quiet Revolution democratized political institutions, modernized the public sector, and created numerous state corporations such as the Société générale de financement, Sidbec, Soquem, the Régie des rentes du Québec, the Caisse de dépôt et placement, and so on. It brought about the nationalization of electricity, the reform of the educational system, and the secularization of social services. This revaluation of the social and economic functions of the state is well illustrated by the evolution of public spending, which amounted to $91.1 million in 1945 and reached $13 billion in 1980. This dynamic of change, associated with the new functions of the state, served to reinforce the social position of the technocratic fraction of the petite bourgeoisie. This group has wanted to use the state apparatus to provide access to positions of responsibility and to strengthen its economic power.

The highly educated technocratic fraction is composed of intellectuals, engineers, economists, sociologists, and union leaders. At the end of the 1960s it broke off its alliance with the capitalist fraction represented by the Liberal party. This rupture was caused by the fact that the latter group has restrained the dynamic of change in order to protect the interests of the Canadian bourgeoisie. For its part, the new technocratic fraction desires to transform its knowledge, its principal asset, into power. It sees the state as an instrument for collective promotion and, consequently, the promotion of its own class interests. This new elite therefore is based on planning and a more interventionist use of the state in the economic sphere. It displays a greater intransigence towards the federal state. Moreover, it wishes in some way to bring the Quiet Revolution to a close and transform Quebec into a complete society, capable of political self-determination. In order to bring this about, it has developed a new type of nationalism.

One can therefore state that the revaluation of the state's role which took place after 1960 revived national self-awareness through rejection of the nationalism of conservation and survival, and its replacement with Quebecois nationalism. The juridical, cultural and defensive aspects of traditional nationalism were replaced by a political nationalism. The national question became a question of political power, with political sovereignty for Quebec the ultimate objective. The exercise of new powers by the Quebec state required expansion of its ability to tax and legislate. Thus, the division of responsibilities within the framework of the federal system was called into question. Quebec needed complete control over the levers of political power in order to guarantee its existence as a nation and ensure economic development. At the same time, this control guarantees access to channels of upward social mobility for the new technocratic elite. By breaking free from federal power Quebec can recover the powers of a normal state. Such is the content of the new nationist ideology which has resulted from changes in the functions of politics during the monopoly phase of capitalism.

The Quiet Revolution created self-awareness of a new national identity. This identity is based upon control over our destiny through the conjuncture of the state and the nation. One no longer speaks of the province, but rather the state of Quebec: a state which asserts the power of Quebecois.

This revival of a nationalism of liberation has been manifested through the creation of several independentist movements, of which the most important are the *Rassemblement pour l'Indépendance Nationale* (RIN) and the *Parti Québécois* (PQ).

The ideology of the RIN assumed the necessity of independence. Its argument went as follows. We are foreigners in our own land. Our economy and our natural wealth are developed to serve foreign interests, and not those of the Quebecois. This economic dependence has repercussions at the cultural level, and leads inevitably to assimilation and to permanent minority status for francophones. Within Confederation Quebec is a dominated society that is deprived of the powers which would enable it to take charge of its own destiny. Until we win our political independence, economic independence and Quebec culture will remain myths.

Nationalism of liberation is distinguished from traditional nationalism by the fact that it eliminates the religious dimension from its definition of the nation. It rejects linguistic and cultural homogeneity. On the positive side, it supports a design for social change which insists on the need for economic planning, an interventionist role for the state, a more egalitarian distribution of income, the secularization of society, and the nationalization of natural resources and those sectors of the economy characterized by monopoly power.

During the eight years of its existence the RIN served as catalyst for the national question. Through its propaganda and its work in political education, the movement played an active role in the Quiet Revolution by forcing the traditional political parties to clarify their constitutional positions. With the founding of the Parti Québécois in 1968, the RIN dissolved in order to further the unity of the independence movement.

The PQ took up the torch of the independence project, and attempted to enlarge its electoral basis by toning down the issue of separation from Canada. The reforms proposed by the PQ were premised upon independence. Indeed, without independence Quebec society cannot determine its own economic, social and cultural priorities. In this respect, the Canadian constitution is seen as a straightjacket which impedes the collective development *(épanouissement)* of the Quebecois. For Quebec to exist as a nation therefore requires full command over the levers of politics. However, the PQ added to the idea of political sovereignty an explicit plan for economic association with the rest of Canada—sovereignty-association.

In summary, the rise of independence movements and the development of a new dominant ideology occurred as unforeseen effects of the modernization of the industrial structure. Modernization required a more qualified labour force, it caused the growth of the service sector and, finally, it necessitated the development of the functions of the state given the role this latter had to play in supplementing and guaranteeing economic growth. Thus, the state became the basis for the upward rise of a new social stratum, the technocratic petite bourgeoisie. This class is indispensable to the operation of monopoly capitalism, and desires to use the Quebec state to consolidate its hegemony and strengthen its position in the private sector. Due to the fact that it experiences more directly the effects of national oppression within the relations of production, this social stratum constitutes a major element in the social basis of the nationalist movement.

This new ideology attempts to mobilize a large social basis of support in order to redefine, through the medium of political power, the economic relationships between national groups. It counts on the state to act as the central agent of collective development. In addition to the cultural and linguistic *épanouissement* of the francophone population, one of the issues raised by the national question involves the control and utilization of public resources to further the economic development of Quebec.

The new nationalism redefines the means for the survival and development of the francophone community. This redefinition is based on awareness of the special requirements of advanced capitalist societies, in which control over political power is necessary for a collectivity that wishes to develop *(s'épanouir)*. Quebecois nationalists no longer agree to live within a political framework in which they are doomed to eternal minority status, and consequently are incapable of directing decisions according to the priorities which they judge essential.

Conclusion

Through this review of the currents of nationalism in Quebec we have observed that the content of nationalist ideology has varied over time, but also that there is a line of continuity which runs through these various forms of nationalism. Since the English Conquest, the Quebecois have used different means and strategies in putting up fierce resistance to assimilation. They have carried on a relentless struggle to reconquer the political power that was lost with the military defeat of 1760. The sovereignty-association project extends this continuity through adaption to the new conditions of the modern world. In this changed world a people that wishes to survive, develop, and make a positive contribution to humanity must be independent and control the centres of political decision-making.

Nationalism in Quebec is not a passing and superficial current of thought. It is a constant in the collective life of the Quebecois, deeply rooted in the circumstances of our political subordination. Every generation has been absorbed in building that nationalism. And as long as the national problem goes unresolved, and we do not have a political framework which permits self-determination in that which concerns us, future generations will be faced with the same task.

NOTES

[1] Marcel Rioux, *La question du Québec* (Montréal, Parti Pris 1976), p. 78.

[2] Cited by Mason Wade, *Les Canadiens français de 1760 à nos jours* (Montréal, Cercle des livres de France, 1966), p. 554.

[3] Marcel Rioux, op. cit., p. 89.

[4] See Richard M. Bird, *The Growth of Government Spending in Canada* (Toronto, Canadian Tax Foundation, 1970), pp. 239 and 299.

[5] Nicole Laurin-Frenette, *Production de l'État et formes de la nation* (Montréal, Nouvelle Optique, 1978), p. 100.

[6] See J. Mascotto and P.-Y. Soucy, *Sociologie politique de la question nationale* (Montréal, Éditions coopératives A. St.-Martin, 1979), p. 80. This data is taken from F. Vaillancourt, *La situation des francophones sur le marché du travail québecois* (Montréal, 1977).

[7] M. Pépin, "Le français au travail, une lutte ouvrière et nationale," *L'Action Nationale*, LXIII (April/May 1974), pp. 633-4.

The Role of Intellectuals in Modern Quebec: The Drive for Social Hegemony

ALAIN G. GAGNON

I would like to thank Guy Beaulieu for his assistance in compiling the material used in the preparation of this essay, and for his useful insights from which I have benefited greatly. This research has been made possible through a grant from the Advisory Research Committee at Queen's University.

The translations of quotes derived from French-language works are our own, and we bear responsibility for them.

Introduction

This essay involves an analysis of the evolution of the role, discourse, and modes of social involvement *("engagement")* of Quebec intellectuals, especially in the social sciences, from 1960 to 1980. At the same time, our intention is to acquaint the English-speaking reader with the literature on this subject produced by the French-speaking *Québécois* social scientists. Consequently, the analysis conducted here will consist more of a new synthesis of previous works than of a critical survey of the literature. Moreoever, to a certain extent this study will reflect the debates and ambiguities found in both the attempts of Quebecois social scientists to construct Quebec society as an object of analysis, and in their social involvement to move this society along lines consistent with the characterizations developed through their researches.

This analysis will be divided into two main sections. In the first section, we will examine the roles and class position of intellectuals in general and in the social sciences in particular. The concept of role as used in this part of the essay should be understood both in its strict sense and in the sense of social function, in that, under this heading, we will integrate practice and social effect. This analysis will be of a general and abstract nature and will focus on questions such as hegemony and legitimization, the production and reproduction of intellectual capital, the reproduction of class positions and the pursuit of class interests. Thus, we will inquire into the social significance of intellectual practice.

From a sociological perspective, it is impossible to examine the roles and social functions of social groups without situating them in the social structure. Thus, the study of the class positions of the intellectuals is an analytical necessity. We will in this section follow closely the evolution of thought found in the Quebecois works on this subject. This approach is justified both for reasons of elegance, inasmuch as this topic would require an essay in itself, and for reasons of relevance, in that the class position of intellectuals has been the central issue addressed by Quebec social scientists since the coming to power of the Parti Québécois in 1976. While there were class analyses previous to 1976, either of a general nature or specifically on the class position of intellectuals, and we will present them, it can be said that this type of study has been largely a function of the introduction of Marxist studies in the early 1970s. Thus, class analysis will also reflect, to a certain extent, the evolution of theoretical instruments in the social sciences in Quebec. This section, then, will furnish us with a structural grounding for the analysis of the role, discourse and social involvement of Quebecois social science intellectuals.

The second section of the essay will examine concrete manifestations of social involvement in Quebec intellectuals, and the evolution of thought regarding the characterization of this involvement. There will thus be a direct link between the two sections of this study, inasmuch as the first will have presented the theoretical context of analysis of the intellectuals' social involvement. This also means that the second section will concentrate on the period 1960-80, and on the social movements and organizations where this involvement occurred. The study will be on the concrete manifestations of this involvement. The main areas to be considered in this section will be technocratic planning, the trade-union movement, citizens' group movements and extra-academic intellectual networks such as the journal *Parti pris* or the Centre de formation populaire.

In the conclusion to this essay, we will be able to reaggregate the analyses and descriptions presented in these two sections. This will permit us to situate the development of Quebec's social science intellectuals in the context of social evolution and, thus, in the reproduction and reorganization of social classes in Quebec. It will further permit us to analyze the relative autonomy of the social sciences from a societal perspective and, finally, to present, if only in a hypothetical manner, the issues and problems confronting Quebec's social science intellectuals and society.

Part I: The Class Position of Intellectuals

The issue of the class position of the intellectuals in Quebec has been addressed both directly and in the context of larger analysis of Quebec society as a whole or of the class nature of the Parti Québécois and of the tactics of the left towards the Referendum and the social vision articulated by the PQ. The theoretical frameworks used in such analyses have changed over time. This presentation will aggregate different interpretations on the basis of their theoretical approach, respecting the chronology within them but not necessarily between them. Furthermore, it should be noted that, since this presentation has a functional purpose in this essay, we will not enter into all the subtleties and debates that have arisen on this question.

The first approach to be considered was inspired by stratification and elite theory, and its articulation occurred essentially during the 1960s. The work of Dofny and Rioux[1] constitutes our point of departure, especially as it was a seminal work both for what it expressed and for the critiques that arose from it. The basic thesis presented by the authors was that the specificity of the French-Canadian stratification structure and the existence of an ethnic consciousness necessitated the definition of the actors of the global Quebec society as an ethnic class. The concept of class was defined as "large real groups, appearing in societies where economic structures predominate and determine the play of incompatibilities towards the other systems of activity, groups whose differentiation is mainly based on economic inequality."[2] Thus, it was the global economic inferiority of French Canadians relative to English Canadians, both in terms of positions and incomes, which permitted one to consider French Canadians as a class relative to English Canadians. But, for these authors, this would not have been sufficient. The further confirming element was that this class also possessed an ethnic consciousness, a "we-feeling." It must be noted, and the authors were conscious of this, that this concept of ethnic class constituted a conjunctural interpretation, in that it translated in theoretical terms the then-renewed prevalence of the national question over the social question. The issue of the class position of intellectuals was not addressed directly, apart from some remarks on the traditional (ecclesiastic) intellectuals. While these were characterized as petit bourgeois, this was more a journalistic or common language characterization than a theoretically grounded one.

The analysis of Falardeau on the traditional and the new elites addressed directly the class position of intellectuals.[3] The concept of elites is defined as "dominant or directing social categories."[4] The social science intellectuals of the 1950s are characterized as a clandestine elite which will attain its full power, influence and prestige in the 1960s as social technicians, especially in the field of planning. "This is a new elite."[5] But, at the same time, Falardeau sees the appearance of an economic elite, in competition with this technocratic one. Thus, politics will constitute largely a forum for the struggle between these two elites over control of the state.

Related to Falardeau's analysis, and complementing it, is that of Brazeau on the new middle classes.[6] He defines the middle classes by their intermediary functions, i.e., the middle strata in public administration, the service sector and private enterprises. In this context, intellectuals would be defined as members of the elite or of the middle classes depending on the institutional positions occupied or of the prestige and influence attained. Thus, the academic intellectuals constituted an elite in the 1950s but would be considered as members of the middle classes in the 1960s, with the exception of those socially consecrated as opinion or scientific leaders.

The second approach to be considered is that inspired by Marxism. We will here consider the three main interpretations of the class structure of Quebec. The first characterization[7] denies or belittles the existence of a Quebecois bourgeoisie as a distinct fraction of the Canadian bourgeoisie or as a distinct fraction as such, i.e., as a different type of bourgeoisie. It thus sees the social dominance/dependence of francophones as centred on the ideological and political levels, based on the exclusion of francophones from the economic level. Thus, within this ethnic or national context, the dominant but not ruling class is the new urban petite bourgeoisie whose main resource is intellectual capital. The expansion of the state and of the educational network is seen as a policy of expansion and reorganization of this class, allied with popular forces against the previous alliance of the traditional petite bourgeoisie with Canadian and foreign capital. Thus, the pursuit of the class interests of this new petite bourgeoisie involves the establishment of its hegemony. As with Falardeau's two elites, this petite bourgeoisie is also seen as divided into two main fractions, the one economic and the other technocratic. This division is further explained in terms of the ambivalence of this class arising from its position between the bourgeoisie and the working class. Intellectuals are seen as part of the new petite bourgeoisie, holding hegemonic positions through their technocratic-political (partisan) roles, and as organic intellectuals of their own class. In this interpretation, politics in Quebec since the Quiet Revolution would have to be seen as the politics of petit bourgeois hegemony, confronting the distribution of powers in the federal context as an obstacle to its expansion.

The second characterization,[8] on the contrary and in reaction to the first one, grounds its analysis on the existence of a Quebecois bourgeoisie, characterized by the fact that it is situated in a process of accumulation. It is either a specific bourgeoisie or a fraction of the Canadian bourgeoisie. Considered as a specific bourgeoisie, its distinctive feature is the fact that, contrary to the Canadian bourgeoisie, the Quebecois bourgeoisie is a non-monopolistic one. Because of this, some of its fractions will favour a nationalistic and statist policy as a strengthening factor in its competition against the monopolistic Canadian (and foreign) bourgeoisie. But, by the same token, other fractions will either attempt to ally themselves to this Canadian bourgeoisie or will see the federal government as the locus of power that can support them (for example, through trade policy). Thus, we find here again a fractioning of the dominant, and to a certain extent, ruling class, but this is linked more closely here to the sectors of economic activity and the hierarchical ordering of this bourgeoisie. In this interpretation, the intellectuals are either part of the bourgeoisie, particularly those who occupy controlling positions in the state enterprise sector, or they constitute a "classical" stratum of organic intellectuals as petit bourgeois supporters of the bourgeoisie. Hence, the expansion of the state in Quebec is seen as a partial catching up to the mainstream of North American monopoly capitalism, characterized by greater socialization of the costs of production and reproduction and, for some class fractions, as a strengthening of their competitive position. That this also brings about an expansion and increased importance, both socially and financially, of the petite bourgeoisie is in this context both incidental and functional (functional in that it tightens the bonds or social integration and further obfuscates the locus of real power).

The third characterization,[9] which is still being elaborated at this time, is related to the issue of *autogestion* and the disaffection with the statist emphasis of the first two approaches. It is also a part of the attempts to transcend Marxism by introducing into it new perspectives and concepts, especially as regards the analysis of the state and of ideology, and the concept of class. For Nicole Laurin-Frenette the question of the class position of intellectuals must be situated in the process of the extensive reproduction of capital. This process necessitates the articulation of agents, apparatus and means. Thus, the concept of class cannot be limited to the agents. Intellectuals, in this interpretation, will be members, or more exactly sub-segments, of the dominant or dominated classes depending on their position relative to the ownership and control of production. It follows that the concepts of bourgeoisie or petite bourgeoisie are rejected as reductionist ones and that the class position of intellectuals cannot be established outside of the functional effect of their activity relative to the regulation of social control and reproduction. In the case of Renaud,[10] the concept of petite bourgeoisie is rejected as antiquated and is replaced by that of middle class in the sense of white-collar workers. In other respects his analysis replicates the first characterization in seeing this class, whose main resource is intellectual capital, striving for hegemony, expanding the state sector to create more opportunities, and developing a nationalist and statist ideology to justify this expansion (an expansion necessitated, however, by the development of North American monopoly capitalism).

Summary

While the issue of the class position of intellectuals (and the larger question of the class structure of Quebec society) is not yet resolved and may yet rebound in unsuspected directions, the characterizations presented above indicate the types of linkages that can be established between their class position, once defined, and their roles and functions.

If we consider the intellectuals in the social sciences as members of a new petite bourgeoisie, we must then consider the institutionalization of the social sciences as also a process of reorganization/transformation of the traditional petite bourgeoise. We can also link the intellectuals' three basic roles to their fundamental character as holders of intellectual capital. These three roles could then be re-interpretated as the production (researcher), reproduction (teacher) and circulation (expert) of intellectual capital. If we consider also that the petite bourgeoisie, through the occupation of positions in the political, ideological and state economic field, is a dominant if not ruling class in Quebec society, we would have to interpret such events in Quebec society as the rise of the social sciences and the social involvement of Quebec's intellectuals as a process of valorization and of the setting up of the conditions for the extensive reproduction of intellectual capital.

Such an interpretation would still leave the issue of the relationship between the petite bourgeoisie and the Canadian and foreign bourgeoisie. This would have to be considered in terms of the historic position of the petite bourgeoisie, whether traditional or new, in relation to either the bourgeoisie or the working class. In that sense, the fractioning of the petite bourgeoisie would have to be studied in terms of class alliances in the pursuit of hegemony, on the one hand, and in terms of the functional character of the extension of the state and the socialization of costs in modern capitalism, on the other (i.e., in objective terms as an antagonistic complicity).

If, however, we accept the second characterization and thus the existence of a Quebecois non-monopolist bourgeoisie, the intellectuals in the social sciences would still be considered as members of a petite bourgeoisie, with the exception of the holders of positions of control in the state or the private sector. Thus, the teacher and the researcher, and to some extent the expert, would be seen in the same way as in the previous characterization in regard to self-reproduction and valorization. But this would constitute an incidental effect to their primary functions of maintenance of order and of general ideological legitimization, i.e., they would constitute a stratum of organic intellectuals. Their fractionization would then have to be considered, in theory at least, primarily along the social axis. This reflects once again their socially ambivalent position inasmuch as, along the national axis, they would tend to reflect the division of either the bourgeoisie or the working class. However, and especially relative to the working class until it produces its own intellectuals, the fact of reflection does not imply the absence of autonomy. Intellectuals, as definers of society and articulators of hegemony, translate social facts to a certain extent according to their own class logic. Furthermore, the efficient performance of their class functions requires that these functions be obfuscated and, thus, that intellectuals at least appear autonomous.

As to the third characterization, it conceives of the intellectuals as either members of the dominant or dominated class, depending on their position relative to the ownership/control of production and the question of the sale of labour power for a wage. As members of the dominant class they would constitute a sub-group occupying "intermediary positions in the regulation of control and reproduction, corresponding to the administration of the apparatus which corresponds, at different levels, to the new requirements of the capitalist processes."[11] They would thus be organic intellectuals of the dominant class. While less clear in the case of the dominated classes, intellectuals would occupy similar positions in the organizations of these classes, such as the trade unions.

We may thus conclude this section by noting that the role-function of intellectuals in general, and in the social sciences in particular, reflect and concretely articulate their class positions in society, however defined. It should also be stressed that these ambiguities constitute a further indication of the relationship between their scientific discourse and their involvement (even when only academic) in the transformation and politics of Quebec society.

Part II: The Social Involvement of Social Science Intellectuals

This section will examine concrete manifestations of social involvement by social science intellectuals, focusing on the period 1960-80. Let us note that this involvement represented a continuation of a tradition of involvement by intellectuals in Quebec, whether as journalists, politicians or ecclesiastics. To remind the reader of the different modalities of the involvement before 1960 of the social science intellectuals, we provide this quote from J.L. Roy:

> This duty of presence, this involvement, Falardeau takes an impressive schematic stock of it: the rebirth of the cooperative movement, the impetus to popular education, the creation of social services, the diffusion of knowledge through the Centre de culture populaire, the collaboration with Canadian, American and European universities, with numerous organizations and as-

> sociations, in particular, with the workers' movement and, among others, with the Confédération des Travailleurs Catholiques du Canada which needed economists and counsellors.[12]

It is thus appropriate to characterize the intellectuals of the late 1940s and 1950s as an intellectual vanguard of the anti-Duplessis social movement.

However, the process of maturation in the social sciences necessitated the evacuation of this involvement from the university and the separation of the academic role from the social one, with the exception of expertise as an institutionalized and, thus, legitimate form. This section will examine this new pattern of involvement and will focus on its extra-academic modalities. We will study more specifically the questions of technocratic planning and *"animation sociale,"* the role of the intellectuals in the trade-union movement, and extra-academic intellectual networks such as the journal *Parti pris* and the Centre de formation populaire.

Technocratic Planning and Animation Sociale

In this context the fundamental development, which set the stage for others and established the parameters of debate, was the Bureau d'Aménagement de l'Est du Québec (BAEQ), created in 1963. Its object was to promote the economic and social development of the East of Quebec through the integrated instruments of planning and participation. Gabriel Gagnon notes the importance of the BAEQ for sociologists (and, by extension, for other social scientists):

> On the one hand, [BAEQ] constituted in Quebec one of the first forms of applied research on a large scale, involving, in one way or another, a large segment of the *Québécois* sociologists of that time and, on the other hand, in attempting, through *animation sociale*, to establish links with the population, it was trying in its way to detect the potential social movements and to contribute to their emergence.[13]

It should be noted immediately that this quote tends to overemphasize somewhat the attention given to the population, as we will see below.

The two elements of planning and participation constituted the abstract project, the instruments and, to a large extent, the ideology of the BAEQ and of its agents. The basic themes related to the planning aspect were: 1) the functional and productive integration of resources, population and socio-economic organization; 2) the transformation of the local traditional and rural mentalities into urban industrial ones through *animation sociale*; and 3) the acculturation of the population to the framework of planning through the establishment of administrative and territorial structures.[14] As to participation, we find the following themes: 1) education through participation as an apprenticeship to the functioning of the structures established under the plan; 2) *animation sociale*, to favour the emergence of the new mentalities and of new local leaders; 3) consultation and information; and 4) regionalization, i.e., the setting-up of an intermediary administrative structure between the central (provincial) and the local levels.[15] These different themes indicate, first, the close connection between technocratic planning and *animation sociale*, and the general ideology of the Quiet Revolution. Secondly, they constitute the ideology and practice of the struggle between the traditional local elites (local, provincial and federal politicians, the clergy, and the small and medium businessmen) or petite bourgeoisie and the new technocratic elite, which has been discussed in Section I. Gagnon[16] made this quite clear on the basis of his analysis and data, and subsequent events demonstrated it. Furthermore, it should be noted that the BAEQ's actions, as can be perceived from these themes, were essentially of an integrative and, in the final analysis, directive nature. Thus participation and *animation sociale* became a double-edged sword inasmuch as its objective of making the local population receptive to the plans elaborated by the central bureaucracy could and did rebound into a call for real participation.

Of these events, the *Opérations Dignité*[17] of the 1970s and the policies pursued by the Parti Québécois should be noted. The first consisted of a grass-roots protest, under the initial leadership of local traditional leaders, especially the parish priests, against the closing of marginal parishes and, more fundamentally, as "an effort of appropriation of the diverse tools of development through a popular mobilization''.[18] This is to be linked also with the emergence of worker- or popular-controlled enterprises, i.e., the appropriation of forms of property, and popular-controlled media.[19] These developments joined the resistance of both popular and traditional forces against the bureaucratization of power and technocratically imposed decisions, and also evinced the divisions among the new intellectuals between the statist and grass-roots tendencies and fractions (i.e., the division between the bureaucrat and the activist).

While the BAEQ and the other institutions of regional development were directed towards the rural areas, we must also consider the *animation sociale* occurring in the cities and oriented towards community development. We find as objectives of these actions the physical and social improvement of the environment, the coordination of resources, the development of new resources, and the creation of a new leadership.[21] In the 1970s the service functions of this *animation sociale* were coopted by the state, as *Centres locaux de services communautaires*. Thus, the animators were confronted with the choice of finding new areas of intervention or becoming integrated into the state sector. These new areas would be those of education and information, consumer cooperatives, or political action groups. There occurred also a radicalization of the animation process and a shift of the more activist to action towards the working class at the factory level. We will discuss this last development in the study of the Centre de formation populaire.

The basic problems encountered within this general context of urban *animation sociale* were: 1) the issue of resources, i.e., the choice between government funding and the possible lack of sufficient means to carry out objectives; 2) the diversity of popular groups both on a functional and an ideological basis, and the resulting difficulties in establishing common fronts leading to the emergence of a social movement—the failure of the Front d'Action Politique (a Montreal municipal political party opposing Mayor Jean Drapeau) and the difficulties of the Ralliement Citoyens de Montréal on the municipal scene are examples of this; and 3) the role of the animators and activists in the popular groups as agents of either integration, transformation or politization and radical change.

This development of technocratic planning and *animation sociale* can be understood in the context of the general valorization of the state as an engine of development and a modality for the transformation/reorganization of the petite bourgeoisie on the basis of the expansion of state-bureaucratic positions. Thus, the BAEQ and similar experiences insured the legitimacy and social value of the intellectual in the social sciences as an expert and as a researcher, and constituted an instrument of struggle to disqualify the traditional intellectuals in the rural setting. But the attempt by the new petite bourgeoisie to impose its dominant technocratic ideology, and the lack of sufficiently speedy favourable results from such as policy (it was rather the contrary), undermined any possibility that might have existed of an alliance with popular rural forces. The retreats and the shifts in alliances that occurred are evidence of this. In the urban setting, the highly localized character of interventions in poor areas produced similar problems of efficiency in terms of results and integration. Added to this, more rapid politicization of the issues involved, reflecting the greater competition between intellectuals for the positions available, contributed to controversy over both the role of the animator in these groups and his relations, administrative or ideological, to the state (and, thus, to the dominant classes). Thus, the politicization and radicalization of part of the intellectual class reflected the problems arising from the economic crisis of the 1970s and the ensuing "crisis of growth" of the new petite bourgeoise.[22]

The Trade-Union Movement

Involvement in the trade-union movement had been part of the general process of social involvement of the Laval social science intellectuals. Moreover, the labour movement had constituted one of the fundamental elements of the anti-Duplessis social movement. In 1960, the CTCC abandoned its confessional character and became the Confédération des Syndicats Nationales. The CSN benefited from good relations between the Liberal government and its leaders, and its membership expanded rapidly with the expansion of positions in the public sector. It can be said that the CSN participated in the general ideology of the Quiet Revolution and profited from it. This constituted an element of the alliance between the new petite bourgeoisie and popular forces against the traditional petite bourgeoisie. Furthermore, the elimination of Church influences also meant that of the traditional intellectuals, even though their influence had declined steadily during the 1950s. The Fédération des Travailleurs du Québec did not profit as much during the early 1960s because of its international character and its more pan-Canadian positions. Also, it had tended to recruit its membership in the industrial sector and, thus, was not ready to benefit from the expansion of the state sector.

The mid-1960s saw a convergence of the positions of the two unions and their adoption of a more critical stance towards the government. This has to be linked to the growing disillusionment with the slowing pace of reform and the fractioning of the new petite bourgeoisie on the national and social issues. The CSN valorized the concept of the working class, proceeded to a globalist critique of society and of the anarchic nature of capitalism, and advocated a really democratic order grounded on participation at all levels.

> This participation can be realized through decentralization and the control of decision-making by members of the union, by union action and participation in decision-making at the level of the business enterprise, through cooperation and the organization of consumers at the level of the economy, and through political action.[23]

The CSN's position also presented a class ideology that associated workers with the popular classes and considered employers as class adversaries. This new ideological stance of the CSN, articulated with Marxist concepts, defined itself as reformist in methods and as anti-dogmatic under the banner of internal democracy. As Tremblay notes on this last point, the stress on internal democracy freed the union from the previous dominance of the new intellectuals, as demonstrated by the working-class origin and internal succession of CSN leaders.[24] Meanwhile, the FTQ, while maintaining a more economist position, also advocated working-class and popular solidarity. This position must be understood in the context of the unionization of public sector employees, the resulting confrontations with the state as the legislator of labour law and as employer, and worsening economic conditions in Quebec.

This last factor tended to increase inter-union competition in most sectors, except for the public and para-public one where the confrontations between the state and the union common front (CSN/FTQ/Corporation des Enseignants du Québec) assumed great proportions. At the same time, the politicization of the unions, through their manifestos and the political education of their members, brought about a schism in the CSN and the founding of the Centrale des Syndicats Démocratiques under a more neutralist banner. The election of the Parti Québécois government in 1976 did lessen state-union tensions until after the Referendum. This was a result of the social-democratic stance of the party and of its policy of garnering popular support for its constitutional position. In this case, the FTQ took positions closer to the government's, while the CSN adopted that of the "critical yes." Need we add that this relative honeymoon did not survive the government's defeat at the Referendum?

The events and positions summarized above can, to a large extent and especially for the CSN, be considered as a process of institutionalization of that union, in an analogical sense with reference to the same process in the field of the social sciences. In this case, the attainment of relative autonomy was a double process in that the CSN had to free itself from the dominance of the Church in the first place, and in that the two unions had also to free themselves from the dominance of the new intellectuals in the second place. This second aspect can be seen by the greater autonomy of the union discourse relative to the dominant ideological discourse of *rattrapage* (literally, "catching up") and technocratic planning and participation, and in the production through the ranks of its organization leadership. In an ideological sense, it can be said that relative autonomy was only partially attained in the middle 1960s, inasmuch as this discourse demanded a fuller implementation of planning and participation rather than presenting an original social project. We can thus see a similarity with the contestation between technocratic planning and *animation social* described previously. Yet this homegrown leadership occupied administrative and intellectual positions in the unions. While they may have a working-class origin, their positions would define them as a populist petite bourgeoisie. Thus, the removal of outside intellectuals would have to be considered as a process of succession, as in the case of traditional intellectuals and new intellectuals, rather than a process of the constitution of worker or proletarian organic intellectuals.

Yet, if the new intellectuals were removed from the leadership positions in more than a formal manner, and the remarks above indicate our doubts as to this, they did not disappear from the unions but rather reappeared as organizers and activists and in their educational and research branches. We thus find analyses and manifestos couched in a Marxist conceptual framework, and internal debates inside the unions on the issues of the degree of political or partisan involvement and on the existence and role of political groups within them. Thus, while the overt dominance of the intellectuals has probably diminished, as indicated, their actual hegemony as definers of the role and social project of the unions would seem to have been maintained in new forms. This, we would argue, is all the more evident from the fact that the unions have not yet been able to elaborate a social project that is not dependent, in one way or the other, on the state, which constitutes the privileged area of the petite bourgeoisie as a class and of the intellectuals as a social category.

The Journal Parti pris

Parti pris, founded in 1963, was the main organ of the nationalist left until the journal folded in 1968, largely because of dissension among its editors and main contributors.

> The journal, from its inception, is recognized for the radicalism of its positions in favour of socialism and of the political independence of Quebec and by its proclaimed breach with the generations of intellectuals whose position of "objectivity" and of

> "impartiality" have left them as "spectators of reality" rather than combatants in its transformation.[25]

It thus adopted a Marxist understanding of philosophy and science, a position confirmed by the objectives of *Parti pris*.

> In relation to this objective of a free, secular and socialist Quebec state, the journal claims for itself the double function of "demystifying" the alienating structures and to express by reflecting and criticizing it, "the revolution becoming conscious of itself as it proceeds".[26]

Analysis of Quebec was from a class perspective, with the Quiet Revolution defined in terms of the political and social success of a new industrial and progressive (compared to the previous one) bourgeoisie attached to the state. Hence, the political position taken by the journal, inspired by this analysis and by the literature of decolonization, was one of tactical support of this new dominant class, especially as the trade-union movement was then seen as an obstacle to working-class consciousness due to its economism and of its support of *rattrapage*. Thus, the *Parti pris* manifesto of 1964-5 could declare: "We are in spite of ourselves the objective allies of the national bourgeoisie in this first phase of the struggle; and we must sustain it and push it forward in its reformist enterprise".[27] We find here an *étapist* strategy, based on the prerequisite of independence before the building of socialism. The transition period between national independence and socialist revolution would then be characterized by the creation of political cells and by popular education and mobilization.

With the slowing of the reforms of the Quiet Revolution, in addition to growing labour unrest and the perceived and actual repression by the government of demonstrations, *Parti pris* had to modify its position on the progressive character of the new national bourgeoisie. It should be noted also that it founded the Mouvement Parti pris, autonomous from the journal, with the objective of developing activists for an eventual party of the nationalist left. This movement became the Mouvement de libération populaire (MLP) in 1965, with the rediscovery of the working class. *Parti pris'* second manifesto (1965-6) presented as its main thesis and strategy, "the national democratic revolution under the impulse of the labouring classes".[28] It should be noted that this constituted a radicalization of the previous thesis, in that the operative word was "impulse". The second manifesto identified the labouring classes as the only ones with an interest in the struggle for independence and socialism. This new thesis involved an amplification of the vanguard role of the left intellectuals, through the MLP, and called for the regrouping of leftist forces and, especially, left activists, through the project of a revolutionary party.

From 1966 to its demise in 1968, *Parti pris* encountered the problems and tribulations of the left in Quebec, centred not so much on the issue of the social project but on the question of the most efficient strategy to attain this project in pragmatic terms without losing it through compromise and dilution. Divisions among contributors, after the failure of the Parti Socialiste du Québec (PSQ), can be seen by the three options defended in the journal: 1) a workers' party based on a common struggle with the trade unions; 2) a return to *étapisme* through the support of the Rassemblement pour l'Indépendence Nationale as the party of the progressive technocratic fraction of the petite bourgeoisie; and 3) entry into the RIN to radicalize it and transform it into a workers' party. These divisions were also demonstrated in the journal's emphasis on a more theoretical perspective, and the adoption of a neutral position relative to the different perspectives of the nationalist left. As with many other nationalist organizations, the founding of the Parti Québécois was the final blow and *Parti pris* gave up the ghost, figuratively and literally, in late 1968.

The case of *Parti pris* constitutes a perfect example of the process of intellectual succession and of the ideological-theoretical struggle attendant upon it. In the same way that the social science intellectuals of the late 1940s and 1950s had to repudiate their predecessors in the academic, political and social fields, those of the 1960s and 1970s sought to repudiate their own predecessors through the use of new analytical frameworks and via social involvement. In this sense, the vanguardism of the *Parti pris* intellectuals cannot be dissociated from the traditional role of the Quebec intellectuals, nor from the actions and tactics of the new technocratic intellectuals in positions of power. One can also note that the internal division of *Parti pris* replicated, in a different language and in somewhat different circumstances, the division of the new petite bourgeoisie and intellectuals into private and state-technocratic groups.

The Centre de formation populaire (CFP)

The CFP was created in 1971. It is part of "the movement of *animation sociale* which Quebec has known in the last ten years and which has mobilized many young intellectuals who have studied in the faculties of social sciences".[29] Its objectives have been described as follows: 1) "To become a crossroad for exchanges, debates, and better understanding of the diverse experiences of struggle"; and 2) "To furnish, while maintaining its autonomy, instruments and programs for the development of activists in the workers' movement (trade unions, popular groups defending the interests of the workers, etc.)".[30] While the CFP is in the same line as *Parti pris*, it diverges from it in that the CFP also comprises popular organizations and the trade unions, and not just individual activists. Thus, it constitutes more of a collective *animation sociale*, as a locus of reflection and research, than an attempted ideological vanguard. Its positions also reflect developments within these member organizations, with the criticism of trade-union economism, of business cooperatism and of bourgeois or petit bourgeois nationalism and the advocacy of socialist independence and radical trade unionism. Furthermore, the CFP has acted as a support group for the trade unions, especially the CSN and the CEQ, through its contribution to the setting up of union research structures, social action committees, and through the preparation and diffusion of the unions' analyses and manifestos.

The CFP has furnished a statement of principles. In this statement, *formation* is defined,

> as a collective research activity permitting groups of workers to develop an understanding improving the appropriateness and ef-

> ficiency of their struggles. In this sense, formation must necessarily be closely linked to past, present and future struggles and must enable the activist to better act in the area of his involvement (work place, neighbourhood, etc.).

From 1974 to 1976, the CFP encountered the proverbial divisions of the left. First, its legitimacy was placed in doubt by worker-intellectuals, i.e., intellectuals working in factories, who denied the CFP's relevance as an organization of non-worker intellectuals and of economist trade unions. Second, with the opening-up of its structures, the CFP had to combat the attempt of the dogmatic left to take it over as an instrument of political class struggle. Since 1976, it has been able to return to its 1973 manifesto and practice, i.e., the position of maintaining close links with worker organizations while remaining an autonomous entity. It was thus in a position to reflect the ambivalence of the CSN and the CEQ—the FTQ adopted a Yes position—on the issue of the Referendum. It characterized the Parti Québécois as a dualist party, embracing both a neo-liberal tendency associated with the petite bourgeoisie and a social-democratic one, associated with the petite bourgeoisie and a segment of the evolving state bourgeoisie. We find here a parallel with the division which brought about the demise of *Parti pris* but, and this is a fundamental difference, this division has been reflected in the CFP's characterization of the class character of the Parti Québécois. This can be interpreted as an indication of the greater sophistication of the CFP and, more important, of greater autonomy in that analysis defines the events rather than events defining the analysis and, as a result, the fate of the organization.

Summary

In this section, we have briefly presented concrete manifestations of extra-academic social involvement. We have stressed the ideological aspect and messages to be found in these instances, for it is the possession of an intellectual capital that defines intellectuals as a relevant social category. We have also furnished indications as to the class character and strategies attendant upon these concrete cases. To summarize, we should note a certain number of points.

First, these cases of involvement apply particularly well to the social science intellectuals and they must be seen, in a larger historical view, as a continuation of the tradition of involvement as a necessary requirement of social relevance and valorization. They must also be considered in the light of events of the Quiet Revolution, whose main characteristic at the ideological level is the establishment of a comparatively more open form of hegemony. Thus, these cases constitute illustrations of Gérard Pelletier's order of the day: "Deceased unanimity".[32]

Second, these cases illustrate the concrete complexity of the reorganization/transformation of a class and/or of a social category. This has been shown in the presentation on technocratic planning and *animation sociale*, in that the taking of power, in the sense of the occupation of the places of power and the establishment of a hegemonic ideology, does not necessarily eliminate other loci of power. This, we would argue, is even more the case when such a shift occurs in the same class or social category and when the object and mode of struggle are of an ideological nature.

Third and finally, we have seen a change in the nature of the intellectuals in the social organizations presented in this section. Over time, it would seem that they assumed, or were forced to assume, a more supportive rather than directive role-function. This would indicate the paradox of the intellectuals' social involvement under the banner of democratization and liberation, in that their success in that function means the downgrading or elimination of their role. This might also indicate, but only in a tentative way, the start of a process involving the production of organic popular or worker intellectuals of the popular or working-class forces. This is evidenced to some extent by the emerging emphasis on grass-roots groups and organizations and on a socialism based on worker and popular management in contradistinction to the earlier state-control approach.

General Conclusions

In this essay, we have argued that a proper understanding of the class position of Quebec's social science intellectuals between

1960 and 1980 requires the study of: 1) their class position in the evolving class structure of Quebec, and of their roles and functions; and 2) their continued social involvement. We have looked at each of these elements separately, both for purposes of clarity and because each perspective throws a different light on the class position of this group. Furthermore, because of the second purpose of this essay, introducing the English-speaking reader to the French-language literature on this subject, we have had to give considerable attention to the ambiguities and debates found both in this literature and in practice. We are now in a position to synthesize these different perspectives and identify stages in the changing significance of social science intellectuals in Quebec society.

The period from 1945 to 1960 can be characterized as *the struggle for legitimacy* of the social science intellectuals, and for the institutionalization of the field. This process was the result of the interaction of many factors. First, the regime in power and the dominant ideology could not mask their increasingly evident inability to cope with the times and, thus, could not stop the erosion of their hegemony. While intellectuals in the social sciences played a vanguard role in this process of undermining the domination of the Union Nationale, support for change cut across society as a whole. It is in this sense that the anti-Duplessis forces have been defined as a social movement. Furthermore, intellectuals had an undeniable self-interest in a global reform of Quebec society, especially as they defined it, which does not deny that other social groups and classes shared this interest in change or that the involvement of these other groups was not also motivated by social (normative) concerns. This self-interest was to be found in the crisis of reproduction of the traditional petite bourgeoisie, in that the number of positions available in its usual fields of activity (i.e., the liberal professions, the clergy, and small business) were insufficient.

Thus, the process of institutionalization of the social sciences constituted an expansion of positions in the context of the reorganization/transformation of the traditional petite bourgeoisie into a new petite bourgeoisie. This is demonstrated by the fact that the new social science intellectuals at Laval University had acquired their expertise and their ideology of reform outside of Quebec, and by repudiation of the non-specialized teaching staff as a fundamental element in the institutionalization of the field. With the achievement of institutionalization it became necessary to separate academic activity and social involvement so as not to endanger the former by overextension or the loss of autonomy resulting from an official identification with particular social groups or organizations. Furthermore, institutionalization in the social sciences also meant the establishment of self-regulated production and reproduction of intellectual goods and agents, i.e., the social sciences as an internally regulated system and the process of maturation of this field.

The second period (1960-9) can be characterized as *legitimacy on the march*. With the Quiet Revolution, the social reforms advocated by the social services, the establishment of state enterprises, and the adoption of technocratic planning and *animation sociale* under the banner of the ideology of *rattrapage* met real social needs. Yet, at the same time, these reforms opened a new array of positions for the intellectuals of the new petite bourgeoisie, even though it must be noted that they were obviously not alone in benefiting from these reforms. But this expansion also transcended the academe while increasing its social importance, in that the need for trained managers expanded correspondingly. Intellectuals in the social sciences followed two main paths. First, within the scientific field they proceeded along the path of maturation and further legitimization by the nationalization of the field through the construction of Quebec society as a global object of analysis, and by the creation of intellectual networks. This practice cannot be dissociated from the nationalization of society as a whole, occurring with the valorization of the provincial state as an engine of development and as the proper locus of problem-solving. Second, within society at large, social science intellectuals occupied positions in the state structure and in the field of social engineering.

The Quiet Revolution thus saw the establishment of the hegemony of the new petite bourgeoisie, which, by definition and as we have seen, does not imply the total eliminaton of the traditional intellectuals. Developments during this period also contributed to the creation of at least a state bourgeoisie (if we define a bourgeoisie on the basis of control of capital rather than ownership) and possibly provided support to the national bourgeoisie in the private sector, if one accepts the existence of this class. The state expansion of the Quiet Revolution also benefited the Canadian and foreign bourgeoisies in Quebec through the socialization of costs and the integration of Quebec into the North American model of development. Thus, the early emphasis on planning and on *animation sociale* was an attempt at deepening this hegemony through education and developmental benefits.

However, this hegemonic ideology also contained the seeds of contradiction, as all ideologies do, simply because they constitute a definition of society in terms of either an ideal state or a social project. At the academic level, these contradictions were reflected in the introduction of Marxism in the curriculum and the founding of the Université du Québec, the radical non-Marxist critique of the North American way of life and dominant theoretical frameworks and assumptions, and the competition for academic positions. At the social level, the protests against technocratic participation and rationalization, against the state as an employer, and against directive and integrative *animation sociale*, demonstrated clearly the divisions within the new petite bourgeoisie and the intellectuals who expressed the new dominant ideology. The problems and dissensions encountered by the *Parti pris* group provide clear evidence of this division, especially the manner of the journal's disbandment over the renewal of its *étapist* strategy and support for the Parti Québécois.

The third period (1970-80) can be characterized as *legitimacy in crisis*. This period saw a continued politicization of popular groups during a time of deteriorating economic conditions. Thus, support for the Parti Québécois gradually declined after the PQ's election in 1976, as its Referendum strategy forced the PQ to dilute its independence project and face the realities of holding power. The great ambivalence of the CSN, the CEQ, and leftist independentist groups expressed in their "critical Yes" indicated the difficulties encountered by the new petite bourgeoisie in its attempts to build class alliances and to maintain a positive hegemony, i.e., something more than a sullen acceptance of its rule either as a lesser evil or in the absence of an alternative. Need it be added that the private sector-oriented fraction of this class, usually represented by the Liberal party, did not then appear as a favourable alternative?

The period covered by this study was one which saw the downfall of a particular hegemony and its replacement by another that was better adapted to the prevalent continental conditions. In this sense, it cannot be denied that the social science intellectuals performed a historical service for Quebec society. At the same time it must be affirmed that they were among the foremost beneficiaries of this transformation. Yet, by integrating Quebec society into the North American mainstream they also confronted that society with new problems and debates, translated into *Québécois* terms.

NOTES

[1] J. Dofny and M. Rioux, "Les classes sociales au Canada français," *Revue française de sociologie*, III, No. 3 (1962), pp. 290-300.

[2] Ibid., p. 290.

[3] J.-C. Falardeau, "Antécédents, débuts et croissance de la sociologie au Québec," *Recherches sociographiques*, XV, No. 2-3 (1974), pp. 131-45.

[4] Ibid., p. 131.

[5] Ibid., p. 141.

[6] J. Brazeau, "Quebec's emerging middle class," in M. Rioux and Y. Martin (eds.), *French Canadian Society* (Toronto, McClelland and Stewart, 1964), pp. 317-27.

[7] See also Denis Monière's chapter in this book, as well as Monière, *Ideologies in Quebec: The Historical Development* (Toronto, University of Toronto Press, 1981); M. Fournier, "Sciences sociales, idéologie et pouvoir," *Possibles*, and R. Mayer, *Les mobilisations populaires urbaines* (Montréal, Nouvelle Optique, 1982).

[8] See also D. Brunelle, "La structure occupationnelle de la main d'oeuvre Québécoise: 1951-1971," *Sociologie et Sociétés*, VII, No. 2 (1975), pp. 67-88.

[9] Refer to M. Renaud, "Quebec's New Middle Class in Search of Social Hegemony: Causes and Political Consequences," *International Review of Community Development*, No. 39-49 (1978), pp. 1-37; and Nicole Laurin-Frenette, *Production de l'État et formes de la nation* (Montréal, Nouvelle Optique, 1978).

[10] M. Renaud, op. cit.

[11] Laurin-Frenette, op. cit., pp. 125-6.

[12] J.-L. Roy, *La Marche des Québécois—le temps des ruptures (1945-1960)* (Montréal, Leméac, 1976), pp. 285-6, referring to J.-C. Falardeau, "Lettre à mes étudiants à l'occasion des vingt ans de la Faculté des Sciences sociales de Québec," *Cité libre*, 10, No. 23 (1959).

[13] G. Gagnon, "Sociologie, mouvements sociaux, conduites de rupture: le cas Québécois," *Sociologie et Sociétés*, X, No. 2 (1978), p. 117.

[14] See J.-J. Simard, *La Longue marche des technocrates* (Laval, Éditions coopératives Albert Saint-Martin, 1979), pp. 54-62.

[15] Ibid., pp. 62-71.

[16] A.G. Gagnon, "Le développement regional, l'État et le rôle des groupes populaires" (Ph.D. dissertation, Political Science, Carleton University, 1983).

[17] A.G. Gagnon (dir), *Les Opérations Dignité: Naissance d'un mouvement social dans l'Est du Québec* (Ottawa, Carleton University, 1981).

[18] H. Dionne, "Introduction: animation sociale et développement régional du BAEQ à nos jours," in B. Lévesque (ed.), *Animation sociale, entreprises communautaires et coopératives* (Laval, Éditions coopératives Albert Saint-Martin, 1978), p. 51.

[19] Ibid., p. 52.

[20] For more details on this interpretation see A.G. Gagnon, "The Evolution of Political Forces in Quebec: The Struggle for Supremacy," in *Quebec: State and Society in Crisis* (Toronto, Methuen, 1984).

[21] M. Corbeil, "Historique de l'animation sociale au Québec," *Relations*, No. 349 (1970), p. 142.

[22] Mayer, op. cit., pp. 260-1.

[23] L.M. Tremblay, *Le Syndicalisme québécois—idéologies de la C.S.N. et de la F.T.Q. (1940-1970)*, (Montréal, PUM, 1972), p. 43.

[24] Ibid., p. 45, referring to S. Perlman, *A Theory of the Labour Movement* (New York, Augustus M. Kelley, 1966).

[25] R. Denis, *Luttes de classe et question nationale du Québec: 1948-1968* (Montréal-Paris, Presses socialistes internationales, 1979), p. 360.

[26] Ibid., p. 363.

[27] Ibid., p. 381, quoting from "Manifeste 1964-65," *Parti pris*, 2, No. 1 (1964), p. 14.

[28] Ibid., p. 472, quoting from "Manifeste 1965-66," *Parti pris*, 3, No. 1-2 (1965), p. 24.

[29] M. Fournier, "Le CFP et le mouvement ouvrier: une expérience de formation," *Possibles*, 3, No. 2 (1979), p. 41.

[30] Ibid., p. 40, quoting from CFP, "Le CFP et le mouvement ouvrier," *Bulletin du liaison du CFP*, 1, No. 4 (Montréal 1978), pp. 2-3.

[31] Ibid., p. 48.

[32] F. Desoer, "Intelligentsia et medias: de l'éducation populaire au pouvoir," *Politique*, 1, No. 2 (1982), p. 116.

Historical Evidence and Contemporary Insights

Western Political Consciousness

BARRY COOPER

Regional identity is at the heart of Western political consciousness. For many Westerners, as for many francophone Quebecers, the significant public realm is not Canada but the region or province. Canada for them is, first and perhaps last, a legal structure that performs certain administrative functions. It is not first of all a collective political reality, nor an important source of meaning or pride, save under exceptional circumstances. In contrast, the region, the West, carries a constant and positive emotional valence: it is here and us. In this essay[1] I would like to discuss some of the factors that constitute Western political consciousness. But first a few distinctions will be made.

Unity and Identity

In the preface to his collection of writings on Canadian culture, *The Bush Garden*, Northrop Frye distinguished between national unity and regional identity. The question of Canadian identity, Frye argued, is badly posed. Identity, he said, is local, regional, cultural and imaginative; unity is national and political. Frye is a skilful interpreter of cultural matters, especially of literature; his understanding of the tension between unity and identity illumines a central political issue. According to him, "the essential element in the national sense of unity is the east-west feeling...expressed in the national motto, *a mari usque ad mare*". If the tension between unity and identity dissolves into either of its poles the result is either "the empty gestures of cultural nationalism" or "the kind of provincial isolation which is now called separatism." The east-west feeling, he said, has developed historically along the axis of the St. Lawrence drainage system. The provincial isolation called separatism referred to Quebec.

Later in the book, in a chapter that originally appeared as the Conclusion to the first edition of the *Literary History of Canada*, Frye summarized his impression of the way that the *Canadian* imagination has developed in its literature as being characterized by "what we may provisionally call a garrison mentality." The earliest maps of the country showed only forts. Simcoe had read his Tacitus and established outposts along the Niagara frontier to keep the barbarians at bay until they swore allegiance and became *socii*. The cultural maps of a later time also showed only forts, according to Frye. Now, a garrison is a closely knit, because beleaguered, society, held intact by unquestionable morals and authority. Motives count for nothing. One is either a fighter or a deserter. As Margaret Atwood, one of Frye's most gifted pupils, put it: "The central symbol for Canada—and this is based on numerous instances of its occurrence in both English and French Canadian literature—is undoubtedly Survival, *la Survivance*."[2] The point of garrison life, evidently, is to survive. Garrisons are also sites of military and administrative rule.

When the discourse of sensitive and intelligent minds contains elementary contradictions, these are not necessarily errors, that is, accounts that are not adequate to reality. Assumptions may not have been sufficiently clarified, of course, but more to the point, Frye's account is interested. I do not mean by this that Frye did not intend to tell the truth nor that he did not tell the truth, but that truth is never disinterested. It is always limited, always deployed against another truth and so never independent of power, never not at the service of a particular interest.

In the present example Frye maintained *both* that identity is regional and local and imaginative, which is why the literature of one's own country can provide the cultivated reader with "an understanding of that country which nothing else can give him",[3] *and* that there is a Canadian mentality expressed imaginatively in a Canadian literature. If one holds to the first insight, by implication Frye becomes something of a emptily gesturing cultural nationalist. That is, the survival of the garrison, which is by all arguments the symbolization of an identity of some kind, has become an expression of a national identity. In the quotation given above, the "country" is identified with the abstract political unit and not with the concrete and etymological sense of land lying opposite an observer, which is to say, a local meaning. Now, Frye has said that the national sense of political unity is an east-west feeling centred upon the St. Lawrence. This, let us say flatly, is nonsense. There is no Laurentian feeling in British Columbia. The dim memories of such a feeling on the prairies are mostly hostile.

In sum: Frye made a useful distinction between unity and identity, which he then surrendered with his evocation of a national identity expressed in a national literature that makes articulate the garrison mentality. A plausible account of why this occurred, which is to say, an exposition of Frye's interestedness, is contained in the discourse of a third literary critic, Dennis Duffy. In the concluding remarks to his fine study of Upper Canadian/Ontario literature[4], he declared that the book he wrote was not what he intended to produce. He planned to write "another CanLit theme book" similar in that regard to Atwood's "thematic guide". The evidence, however, restricted his focus. The works considered made imaginatively articulate not Canada and not even the contemporary political unit of Ontario, but the heartland of Upper Canadian Loyalism, the wedge of land between the Ottawa River and Lake Huron. In that place the myth of exile (from the American colonies), covenant (loyalty to the Crown), and return to a garden (the transformed wilderness) fully expressed the regional identity of "Canada". To be more precise: "Canada", as a symbol of identity, is centred in the Loyalist heartland, is full of garrisons concerned about survival, and is indeed moved by feelings of a meaningful east-west axis.

This "Canada", which is imaginatively real, is, however, imaginatively unconnected with even the Loyalist Maritimes, as Duffy pointed out.

It is even less connected with the West. Duffy sensed this. The "ampler Canada that Loyalism and its successors envisaged", the "noblest product Ontario had to offer to the rest of Canada", namely the east-west feeling centred on the St. Lawrence and expressed in the national motto, was "sectionalized, misappropriated, its rhetoric employed to justify the smashing of the alternative Canada that had sprung from the Metis experience".[5] Duffy did not enlarge on what the Metis-inspired alternative might have been. He did, however, connect the alternative with the West, which showed that he sensed that an ampler Canada that did not betray itself was somehow linked to the export of the noblest product of Ontario. He did not dwell on what made that "vision of nationhood" noble nor did he say what he meant by nation.

Nevertheless, Duffy has clarified some of the unanalyzed assumptions of Frye and Atwood: Canada the imaginative reality belongs to the experience of the Loyalist heartland. Like all such experiences it is local. Canada the political reality, the noblest product of Ontario, was generated by the acts of sectionalization, misappropriation, and the use of rhetoric, national rhetoric, to smash an alternative that Duffy identified in an unclear way with the Metis. To put the matter bluntly: Canada, the imaginative reality centred in the Loyalist heartland, became Canada the political reality. By so doing it betrayed its own regional identity and destroyed the possibility of an alternative political reality that might have grown from the Metis experience and in any event was located in the West. The contradictory statements of Frye, therefore, may be understood as reflecting the ambiguity of the term Canada. In Frye's terminology, there is indeed a Canadian identity, but it is restricted to the Loyalist heartland. There is a Canadian political unit as well, and it was created at the expense of what Duffy called Metis experience. It was also created at the expense of a genuine Canadian (i.e., Ontario Loyalist) identity.

Duffy described himself at the close of his book, as standing at the corner where Mythology runs into Politics. His own activity in writing the book was likened to a dash into an intersection in the hope of slowing traffic long enough to glimpse its flow. So far we have approached the intersection by way of the discourses of literary critics, along the street named Mythology; now let us consider the avenue of Politics.

Politically speaking, national unity is a matter of will. The greatest theorist of national unity was Rousseau; the greatest practitioner, Robespierre. "Il faut, une volunté UNE.... Il faut qu'elle soit républicaine ou royaliste," said Robespierre the Incorruptible. National unity inspired by a single will does not mean stability. Like the will of an individual, it can change direction and preference without losing unity. Accordingly, under most circumstances, it is a formula for instability "puisqu'il est absurde que la volunté se donne des chaines pour l'avenir".[6] There is, however, a significant and exceptional circumstance: the many become one when confronting an external and threatening other. Historically this condition has arisen spontaneously under the circumstances of war, but never in post-Confederation Canada. One need only observe that the conscription crises were crises. Nor has the threat of United States economic control, which is a danger (if it is a danger) that falls far short of war, caused a unity of will in response. Nor, it hardly needs to be said, has unemployment, inflation or any other element of domestic incompetence. In short, only in the presence of an enemy can such a thing as *la nation une et indivisible* exist. And Canada, the peaceable kingdom, has never experienced the requisite enmity.

Why, then, the persistent calls for national unity? One explanation lies in the writings of Rousseau. Not only opposition to a threat can unify he said, but also "l'accord de tous les interêts se forme par opposition à celui de chacun".[7] That is, Rousseau tacitly identified will and interest, with the asumption that will is a spontaneous or automatic interest. Thus, the *volonté générale* is, according to him, the interest of the people or the nation: it *is* national unity. Accordingly, its generality must be opposed to each individual interest or will. The enemy of the *volonté générale*, that is, lies within the breast of each individual, each particularity. This has the convenient consequence that the doctrine of national unity can be broadcast in the absence of any threat, real or apprehended. The reason for this is because the image of national unity is sentimental, and like all sentiments it is boundless. Thus it can be enjoyed independent of any political realities. In Canada the sentiment is expressed, with nauseating regularity, by whining phrases such as: if only Canada were united, then....Then all things would be possible. The century would be ours.

Furthermore, since will, and by Rousseau's reasoning, interest too must be made concrete and institutionally actual, it can be concentrated in a small body of men, and even in the soul of one man. The danger of tyranny in such a view has been explored by Rousseau's critics and is also apparent to practical men who understood and opposed those political events in modern history that bear the mark of Rousseau's reasoning.

These remarks on Rousseau's political thinking help clarify the matter of unity and identity. Canadian identity, we say, is confined to the part of present-day Ontario I called the Loyalist heartland. Loyalism was forged by two crucial experiences: by the successful rebellion of the Thirteen Colonies and the consequences, the foundation of the United States and the explusion of the Loyalists. The second crucial event was the War of 1812. In it the covenant made with the royal authority was confirmed and Canada survived, a genuine garrison facing a genuine enemy, united in fact, until 1837; united in aspiration still. The conclusion I would draw from this is the following: national unity is a symbol expressing "Canadian" identity, the identity of the Loyalist heartland. It was formed under the strenuous circumstances of exile, maintained by strength of character, by a patient allegiance to the Crown, and justified at last by military endurance.

Western Regional Experience

Identity

A sense of identity, we learned from Frye, is imaginative and is expressed in literature. Accordingly, Western regional identity, to the extent that it is distinct from "Canadian" identity, refers to distinct experiences expressed by way of distinct symbols and themes. Literary critics who have turned their attention to Western literature nearly all emphasize the importance of the landscape. "All discussion of the literature produced in the Canadian west," Henry Kreisel announced, "must of necessity begin with the impact of the landscape upon the mind."[8] Donald Stephens made a more explicit contrast: "The 'garrison mentality' so obvious in the writing of Eastern Canada (in the Maritimes, Quebec, and Ontario) is not prominent in that of Western Canada (the Prairies and British Columbia)." The reason, he said, is because "the prairie is a landscape that makes them [the inhabitants] greater than [garrison] life; it is an environment that brings out the best, and the worst, in man."[9] Finally, the land is not, as it apparently is according to Frye and Atwood, chiefly a threat. "Prairie man," wrote Ricou, "may feel insignificant or immensely self-confident; he may feel free or inescapably trapped; he may be deeply religious or a rebel against all authority; his imagination may be stifled or stimulated. In each case, however, his nature or outlook will be linked to his curiously abrupt position in a vast and uninterrupted landscape."[10] There is plenty of additional critical and imaginative evidence that could be cited. The point, I think, is plain: the West is not a transplanted imaginative Ontario garrison.[11]

The imaginative prairie landscape has both a spatial and a temporal dimension. Spatially it extends, as David Carpenter said, "from the dryland to the Promised Land," that is, from Manitoba and Saskatchewan to Alberta.[12] Imaginatively, Alberta is the quintessential West, the far West, McCourt called it in his classic study, and British Columbia is the near East.[13] However that may be, changes over time are more important for our purposes than changes over space.

The historical theme of Western identity consists in variations in the response of European groups and individuals to a non-European landscape. The new land did not have an impact on an empty head but on a conscious one filled with the old culture. Right from the beginning British words such as meadow and snow proved inadequate to the reality experienced. Only recently have cultural geographers and historians devoted much attention to the problem of how the Western landscape was articulated by the pre-settlement explorers.[14] After the early explorers, who were more interested in markets than landscape anyhow, descriptions turn technical or fictional; from about the mid-nineteenth century, economics and calculative reason parted company with imagination and emotion. Explorers were supplanted by expeditions, hastily scribbled journals by official reports, by scientific accounts and scientific speculations about rainfall, flora, and isotherms. Maps were drawn on grids. From the start, then, the West has felt the impact of the most advanced technology of the day. Unlike the great technologies of central Canada, Western ones were concerned directly with resource extraction not industrial manufacturing. At the same time, however, they were subordinated to central Canadian technologies. Consider, for example, the prairie town. The "hugeness of simple forms" that Wallace Stegner evoked congealed in towns into the mass production of identical elevators, banks, and railway stations, a main street called Main Street, and a dirt road beside the tracks called Railway Avenue. It was as if the CPR had one blueprint and people had to fit it.

Not until recently has the balance between landscape and technology shifted decisively in favour of the latter. Eventually, in our own day, technological activity has transformed the prairie space into an imaginative void, at least for the most sensitive minds.[15] Even today, however, it may be doubted that the poetic sensibilities that discover a sense of nothingness in the existence of a high-tech multi-section Saskatchewan wheat farm are shared by the person who operates it. In any event, Western identity, such as it is, has been made articulate in the past by imaginative writers who found meaning, not its absence.

The earlier settlers, from Britain and Ontario, and the earliest writers clung to the cultural forms they left behind. Consequently they made inappropriate responses to the new environment. The settlement experience was in many respects a frontier experience, though it was not seen that way by the literary imagination. On the contrary, the West was part of an imperial civilization whose most idyllic fictional characters, the policeman, the preacher, and the teacher, were its agents. When, during the

1920s, the work of Grove and later, of Ross, began to displace the romantic pastorals of Connor, a new awareness of Western experience had achieved articulate form. The chaste, sunlit and superficial garden myth was rejected along with the spirit of empire. Constriction and isolation, the dark effects of conquering rather than cultivating the land, became major themes of Western literature. The closest the West ever came to creating a garrison mentality was in the "prairie realism" of the 1930s, most notably in Sinclair Ross' *As For Me and My House*.[16] Contemporary Western literature, the comedy of W.O. Mitchell or Robert Kroetsch, for example, offers less a rejection of sentimental romance, as did Ross and Grove, than a self-conscious new beginning. "The habit of beginnings, of starting again," wrote Dick Harrison, "is deeply ingrained in the western consciousness, and comedy is its necessary expression."[17] At the very least, such a view accords well with common-sense experience.

Let me bring this rapid *tour d'horizon* to a close. The conclusions I would draw are these: the West is not imaginatively part of "Canada". There is scant evidence of a garrison mentality; survival is not the dominant theme save under extreme and adverse conditions, which soon give way to the spirit of new beginnings.

Early Historiography

Poets and historiographers, according to Aristotle, can be compared because their common subject is praxis and lexis, action and speech. Both translate their remembrance into a poesis, a fabrication, that eventually gets written down and lasts *(Poetics*, 1450a 16-22; 1451b1 *et seq.*). As a constituent of human life, stories antedate literacy; poetically understood, however, the origin comes in the *Odyssey*, Book VIII. There the Phaiakian harper sings of Odysseus' life and the hero weeps to behold his own story, an object outside his life. From the other side, Herodotus, whom Cicero called *pater historiae*, said he wished to say what is, to fabricate a memory of the futile and perishable and thereby disclose through words what owes its existence to men, lest it be obliterated by time. Stories, including the systematic stories we call history, reveal meanings, local and particular ones first of all, and through them general and universal ones. History, too, is a source of identity; historical literature also shows who we are and where is here because it recounts what was done and said. The shift in this section, then, is from the imaginative to the narrative mode.

With the closing of the settlement frontier in Canada West during the 1850s, ambitious and expansionist men turned their thoughts towards the lands north and west of the Lakes. The railway to Collingwood, completed in 1855, gave Toronto access to the upper Lakes; the work of the Geological Survey provided knowledge of the Shield. The Hind and Palliser expeditions, both of which began in 1857, were concerned with the potential of the Northwest as an agricultural area not its actuality as a habitat for fur-bearing animals. North of what was thought of as the Canadian extension of the Great American Desert, they discovered the ''fertile belt'', a huge arc of land that began at Red River, swept up the valley of the North Saskatchewan and down the foothills to the United States border. This deployment of knowledge ended the indigenous self-understanding of the Selkirk settlement: Red River acquired a destiny. It ceased to be a link between the wilderness and the maritime civilization of Europe, as Alexander Ross had declared as late as 1856, and became an outpost with a future tied, in the eyes of the eastern expansionists, to Canada.

The confrontation between Riel and McDougall over annexation of the Northwest revealed as much about the designs of the Canadians as it did about the Metis. The Canadians believed that the inhabitants of Red River were united in their desire for annexation; they equated opposition to the Hudson's Bay Company with affection for Canada; they thought the fervent annexationists on the *Nor'Wester* spoke for the entire population. Consequently they expected the inhabitants to be grateful for the end of Company rule. Annexation would bring civilization and progress. In the eyes of the Canadians these were unambiguously good things. Accordingly, the resistance was incomprehensible. True to its garrison mentality, Ontario saw itself as patriotic and dissent as treason. When the expedition led by Ottawa's lieutenant governor-designate, William McDougall, did not go as planned, sabotage by the untrustworthy French and Catholic Minister of Militia, Cartier, must be the reason. The Metis ceased to be Indian savages in order to become French, which in turn enhanced the English, Protestant, and regional nature of Canadian expansion. When the expeditionary force entered Fort Garry in August 1870 it made annexation to Canada a reality. The great contrast with the American West was thereby established. Oregon, Texas and California had supplied the pressure for annexation; Red River had resisted it.

The expansionists' account of the Northwest celebrated its future and told a peculiar tale of its past. Before the amalgamation of the two fur-trading companies in 1821, the Northwest Company and its predecessors alone, and not the Hudson's Bay Company, explored the land and claimed it for the Empire. The year 1821, then, marked the betrayal of Canadian interests. Darkness descended until the expeditions of the 1850s and the British parliamentary inquiry of 1857; dawn arrived fully in 1870. This simple drama of Canadian expansion and Company intransigence had to revise two awkward facts: Selkirk settled Red River without Canadian involvement or Company opposition; Selkirk's settlers were violently opposed by the Northwest Company, leading to the Seven Oaks massacre in 1816. No problem: Selkirk was turned into an agent of the Hudson's Bay Company, not a genuine colonist. As for Seven Oaks, the colonists fired first. Other revisions followed. Before 1870, the Metis were evidence for a Canadian claim to the Northwest; after 1870 they ceased to be part of the heroic tradition of the Northwest Company and symbolized wild lawlessness. "According to the expansionist view of history," Doug Owram observed,

> western development began not in 1811 but when Canada moved to open the region....And if the real development of civilization in the region was the result of Canadian intervention, it then followed that western society and the western identity had its real roots in the East which had provided the manpower, money, and direction for this development.[18]

The writing of Western history also reflected the expansionist view. For example, W.H. Withrow's *History of Canada* (1886) took over five hundred pages to tell the tale of British North America on the eastern part of the continent between the years 1763 and 1867; the history of western British North America, which arguably antedated even the Hudson's Bay Company charter of 1670, took under eight pages to recount. Western historiography and Western development alike, it seemed, might pass into eastern hands.

As early as 1871 there was resistance: J.J. Hargrave's *Red River* (1871) proved about as effective as Riel's *Declaration* of 1869. In 1879 the Historical and Scientific Society of Manitoba was formed, whose purpose, Charles N. Bell declared ten years later, was "to rescue from oblivion the memory of early missionaries, fur traders and settlers" in the Northwest.[19] The destruction of Fort Garry in 1882, the passing of the buffalo from the plains about the same time, the completion of the CPR in 1885, steamboats on the Saskatchewan, all were events charged with meaning: an era was ending. In 1882 George Bryce, an Ontario immigrant, began in earnest the work of rescuing memory from oblivion with *Manitoba: Its Infancy, Growth and Present Position*. Five years later he wrote a historiographic curiosity, *A Short History of the Canadian People*, that aimed, he said, at writing from a "'Dominion' viewpoint". This meant putting everything in chronological order. Thus 1811 (Selkirk Settlement) was followed by 1812 (War with the United States), an event with which it was completely unconnected. Apparently a disjointed narrative was a small price to pay in order to counteract eastern developmental bias. The next rearrangement of chronology followed not a high-altitude "Dominion" perspective but the pattern of Western events.

The year 1811 grew in importance over 1821, the date of amalgamation of the fur-trading companies. The next thirty-five years were no longer an oblivion of darkness, the reputation of the Northwest Company and of Canada was not pristine and philanthropic. In particular the primary intention of Selkirk, to relieve the miseries of Highland crofters, and not his tactical involvement with the Hudson's Bay Company, received emphasis. Equally, the lawlessness of the Northwest Company and their use of violence and intimidation in the West was emphasized. By 1900, Bryce was confident enough to praise the Hudson's Bay Company as an integral part of Western history, an edifying contrast with the "eastern" Nor'Westers.[20] In a more popular mode, life at Red River before the Canadians arrived was recalled by old-timers as a pastoral utopia: people were happy; the sun shone and no one locked their doors. The very title of his 1909 work, *The Romantic Settlement of Lord Selkirk's Colonists*, expressed George Bryce's mature views: the chapter dealing with the Canadian annexation was entitled "Eden Invaded". The significance of this early historiography is that it testifies to the experience of a real distinction: the history of the West was not the same as the history of eastern involvement in the West. Politically speaking, 1811 was to the West what 1812 was to Ontario; the myth of Red River served the same purposes in the West as the myth of Loyalism did in Ontario. Even for immigrants from Canada the Loyalist myth proved unsatisfactory since it corresponded not at all to their Western experience. The myth of Red River, in contrast, could be adopted by all settlers.[21]

W.L. Morton: Western Historian

In recent years the bright colours of historiographic controversy have been muted, but the underlying conflict remains. Consider, for example, one or two aspects of the work of W.L. Morton, perhaps the greatest of recent Western historians.

Prior to Confederation, the "neo-archaic" economy of the prairies was integrated not with Canada and not even with the continent, "but rather by sea with the British Isles—a reminder the prairies were, to a degree are still, a maritime rather than a continental hinterland".[22] Continental integration began seriously in 1844, when the railroad reached St. Paul, Minnesota. The first HBC outfit to the Canadian Northwest travelled via St. Paul in 1858; in 1878 Winnipeg and St. Paul were linked by rail, and four years later the CPR arrived, putting an end to the old water route up and down the North Saskatchewan. Meanwhile, out West, regular traffic still moved along the cart road between Fort Benton and Fort Edmonton. The neo-archaic economy, then, had begun its process of disintegration when Riel was hanged, separating Indians and Metis from the modern settlers and ending forever the neo-archaic polity. It changed, as well, the character of Red River, the emporium of the British plains. For over two generations the Red River settlers had outrun the Industrial Revolution. They could escape it no longer.[23] The United States, moreover, was less a threat to Red River than an economic partner. Until the Canadian government provided an alternative transportation system and an artificial barrier to trade in the form of the tariff, lengthening cart brigades and steamboats on the only major and navigable river that crosses the border told of strong ties to the commercial capital of the region, St. Paul.

As for the modern newcomers, Morton said, their experience may be summarily described as a mixture of European civilization and pioneer life. "Europe is not, as in the East, re-created. Civilization in the West endures only in virtue of challenge—the physical challenge of wind and drought, blizzard and piercing frost—daily taken up."[24] Old farming techniques, the time-honoured methods of European and eastern woodcraft, had to be abandoned owing to scanty rainfall west of the 96th or 98th meridian. New American plainscraft, the chilled steel mould-board, summer fallow, "barbwire," and the windmill took their place. Advanced agricultural technology was firmly established when the Brandon Experimental Station was opened in 1886. In short, Western history must be examined "in terms of conscious adaptation at the margin of a living culture to an environment not to be denied, but with which terms may be made".[25] Considering only the environment, one finds mono-techniques—beaver, wheat, oil and gas—and high risks. In the past much has been made of these economic/technological facts as if they somehow explained Western politics. But in addition Morton insisted upon culture, *living* culture, and *conscious* adaptation. The Americans had political ideas as well as barbed wire; so did the Icelandic communities, the Ukrainians, and even the British. And none of them arrived with the expectation that they would be assimilated to Canadian, that is, Ontario, colonial life and institutions.

Yet, "it was the fate of the West to become the colony of a colony, which brought to its new imperial role neither imagination, liberality, nor magnanimity".[26] Responsible government and Confederation dissolved many of the imperial controls in Canada; in the West the old controls were replaced by those granted the Dominion under Sections 90 and 91 of the *BNA Act*, 1867. "Before the old restraints had been forgotten, before communal and local rancours had been dissipated, there were new bonds to chafe at, a new claim to allegiance to stifle the simple loyalties of religion, race, and region."[27] The Dominion Land Survey is perhaps the best symbolic expression of the homogenizing intentions of the annexation by Canada. The survey was indifferent to natural terrain and social customs; land was nothing more than a commodity, "to be cut and sold like broadcloth on a counter. It was emphatically not an expression of social community, much less the cradle of a race. The square survey was rather the sieve through which people would be shaken into mixed and diverse settlement."[28] The consequences of this and of other co-ordinated policies were not, however, what the Dominion authorities anticipated. It is true that the West was partially "Ontarioized", but in the process Ontario became what it had not been before, namely one pillar of the duality of central Canada.[29]

The effects of distinct historical experience have been felt in recent Canadian historiography as well. In a 1973 review that considered two collections of essays, one written to honour Donald Creighton, the other to honour Frank Underhill, Morton noted that, whatever their differences, both historians "saw Canada as being, for good or ill, an extension of Ontario....Neither had a sense of the vigour of regional sentiment in the various parts of Canada, including their own province." Neither had a firm grasp of Canadian pluralism. In general, the "Laurentian" thesis, of which Creighton was the most powerful exponent,

> fails to take account of regional experience and history and makes coherent Canadian history seem an "imperialist creed", an imposition on Maritime, French-Canadian, Western and British Columbian history of an interpretation which distorted local history and confirmed the feeling that union with Canada had been carried out against local sentiment and local interest.[30]

Morton was more emphatic about the unfortunate consequences of the Laurentian interpretation in a piece written twenty-five years earlier. Such a reading of Canadian history told nothing more than a story of commercial exploitation and imperialist methods of domination "aiming not at political justice but at commercial profits". Accordingly, "Confederation was brought about to realize the commercial potentialities of the St. Lawrence. Where self-government existed it was recognized; where the people of territory annnexed resisted, it was granted but starved of the means to live; where they had an alternative and were too distant to be intimidated, it was granted in full."[31] Morton's point, of course, is not that Donald Creighton was insensitive to matters of political justice nor that he over-valued commercial profits. Rather it was that an emphasis on commercial development brought about by imperial Dominion rule, with its attendant cultural uniformity, inevitably has led to a split between political allegiance and local identity. That split appeared, and still appears, as a sense of sectional or regional injustice.

Morton characterized some of the political consequences in a remarkable essay, "The Bias of Prairie Politics." The distinctiveness of Western politics is obvious enough, he said; the explanation of it is historical and not merely economic or sociological.

> The difference between prairie and other Canadian politics is the result of an initial bias, which, by cumulative historical process—the process which takes account of sequence, conjuncture, and will, as well as logic, category, and necessity—has resulted in traditions and attitudes even more distinctive than the original bias.[32]

The first element, the original bias, was found in the political subordination of the West following annexation in 1870; after 1878 the National Policy made visible the most prominent aspect of political subordination, economic exploitation. A second element, which built on the first, focused upon prairie agriculture. The railways, especially the CPR, the banks, the elevator and grain companies, exploited their temporary monopolies and were opposed by the Farmers' Unions, the Patrons of Industry, and the grain growers' associations. The tariff and party political organizations came under attack as well. A third element, occasioned by the Depression but also conditioned by the prior agrarian discontent and quasi-colonial political status of the West, was identified by Morton as "utopian". Evangelical protestantism, prohibition, women's suffrage, direct legislation and what Lipset somewhat misleadingly called agrarian socialism were added. Perhaps one could add a fourth element in the post-Leduc era: rapid province-building paid for by large economic rents extracted from the development of mineral resources, petroleum, potash, coal, and uranium.

Considered together, the elements that constitute the bias of prairie politics amount to a sort of nationalism, "a nationalism neither racial like the French nor dominant—a 'garrison' nationality—like that of Ontario, but environmental and, because of the diversity of its people, composite".[33] According to Morton, then, the West is both a creation of the Dominion and an emancipated colony of the old Canada. Unlike the Maritimes or British Columbia, which have always had genuine options to incorporation within Canada, the West has never existed outside its subordinate position. The reciprocal is also true: Canada could exist without the Maritimes or British Columbia, but not without the West.

Significance

The first section of this essay explored the distinction between identity and unity. In the second section evidence of Western regional consciousness, insofar as it appears in literature and historiography, was presented. In this concluding section, I would like to suggest the pragmatic and theoretical significance of it all.

It is a measure of regional diversity or of regional misunderstanding that what is called "Western alienation" should stir the hearts of Canadians so deeply. The term itself is significant. It derives from a Latin verb meaning to make something another's. What is alien belongs to another. To the extent it makes sense to speak of Western alienation, then, the central experience is political. The simple loyalties of which Morton spoke, loyalties that express a sense of place and of time, of here and now and us, have their legitimacy attacked when they cannot be expressed politically. That is, when the public realm belongs to another and what is to count as legitimate discourse within that realm is determined by another, then it makes sense to speak of political alienation. There is, therefore, nothing psychological, economic, or sociological about Western alienation properly speaking. It is a political phenomenon whose basis can be found in the initial bias that Morton detected, political subordination. Doug Owram recently made a similar point: "The West has never felt in control of its own destiny. None of the wealth of recent years has eased this feeling. In fact, the tremendous wealth of the region merely sharpens the contrast with the political powerlessness that exists on the national level."[34] Under such conditions the actual content of policies implemented by the Dominion government may be less important than that the Dominion's citizens in the West were not consulted regarding their formation.[35]

A second general area of practical significance concerns "political culture", or more precisely, the political consequences of regional identity. To begin with, dualism is not the political issue in the West that it is in central Canada. Moreover, multiculturalism does not mean the same thing to a third or fourth generation non-French, non-British Westerner as it does to someone from the Azores or Calabria living on College Street in Toronto. As David Smith said, "the label 'ethnic' has ceased to carry either stigma or benefit" in the West.[36] Second, the institutional or structural subordination of the West has often led Westerners to view the Dominion government as a threat to their interests.

This is why Western political strategies have shifted, historically, from attempting to influence the dominant party, to third-party persuasion of the dominant party, to third-party balance-of-power tactics, to support for the chief opposition party. At the same time as pursuing this flexible strategy at the Dominion level, Westerners have pursued complementary goals provincially. The "quasi-party system" of Alberta is the most famous example, though the interpretation generally made of this party system seems to me to be more than a little misleading. Howard and Tamara Palmer are closer to the mark: "The political movements which have served as the channels for these regional grievances [the United Farmers of Alberta and Social Credit] have also, for many Albertans, provided a sense of identity."[37] Accordingly, glib chatter from Marxian and Eastern intellectuals about funny-money and fascism is but a mildly irksome insult.

A third aspect of "political culture" is found in the local strategy of deliberate adaptation to the environment. In Morton's words, "agricultural techniques and political administration have been purposively reduced to complete co-operation by scientific research and instruction and by an unusually wide and deep diffusion of political power in Western society".[38] There is no mystery about Western populism; certainly it has nothing to do with industrial socialism. Private property and individual entrepreneurship were a consequence of frontier necessities and established legal institutions, not psychological traits of rugged individualism. Even though co-ops have meant a compromise with the right of an individual to dispose of his or her own resources, this has not conflicted with a commitment to private property. The reason is a consequence of Western political consciousness: co-ops were understood to be

> a collective strategic response to the pressures and constraints imposed on the Prairie producer by the organizations of the national and international market: the grain companies, the railroads, the banks. In short it was a response to exploitation, or rather, to the inadequacies of individual entrepreneurship in the face of exploitation by outsiders.[39]

Western political consciousness, then, may be characterized as one of pragmatic flexibility in defending local and regional interests in a comparatively hostile environment that historically has encompassed frost, grasshoppers, uncertain markets and the predatory political and economic institutions of the central garrison.

In the course of discussing the topics of unity and identity, of western literacy and historiographic efforts, substantive political matters have naturally enough been raised. As a final but necessarily tentative point, I would like to translate the foregoing remarks into the less immediate but more articulate language of political theory.

The theoretical significance of Western political consciousness, I believe, needs to be understood in the context of the Canadian founding, which in turn was a consequence of the American Revolution. The intention of the rebellious colonists to the south was not to establish a new regime but to recover the rights of freeborn Englishmen. In that aim there was nothing new and certainly nothing revolutionary: there was no question but that the government must be limited by laws. But more turned out to be involved than the rebellious restoration of ancient liberties in the face of an alleged tyrannical usurption. Had the rebellion against tyranny not been followed by a new founding it would have been useless and futile.

The chief problem faced by the rebellious colonists, then, was how to establish a new government when, following the Declaration of Independence, allegiance to the Crown had been forsworn and the authority of Parliament had been abolished. The "solution" to this "problem" emerged from the experience of political action itself, from the actualization of political power for the purpose of establishing a new regime, namely the constitution of, in the sense of founding, a government. (I am referring here to the activities and reflections of the members of the assemblies who met in the several colonies with the purpose of drafting a constitution, to their returning to the town halls to debate and approve the Articles of Confederacy, and to the later experiences of the state congresses debating and approving the articles of the Constitution.) The establishment of new centres of power, of a new government, and of a new body politic, was by no means the same as reconfirming safeguards for British civil liberties.

The great authority on the topic of power and one to whom the colonists regularly turned was Montesquieu. "Pour qu'on ne puisse abuser du pouvoir," he wrote, "il faut que, par la disposition des choses, le pouvoir arrête le pouvoir."[40] That is, power can be checked, kept in existence, and not be destroyed, only by power. Accordingly, Montesquieu's famous separation of powers is more than a guarantee against monopolization by one part of government. It is a kind of regulator in the midst of government that constantly generates power within limits that are not so much established by law (since power can change law) as maintained by other power. Separation, opposition, balance among the branches of the central government as well as between it and the constituent states was a means of generating power, not abolishing it. And power (more emphatically expressed in Montesquieu's French) is the ability to act, to say not "I will" but "I can".[41]

From the start of the rebellion, and certainly as it continued, the recovery of the rights of Englishmen proceeded in harness with the constitution of power and authority that had been lost with separation from the Crown. Power was constituted initially in the several conventions of the rebellious colonies, and subsequently in the balance and separation of the parts of government. Because of the generation of power from the people assembled in townships, counties and districts, the several conventions and congresses commanded sufficient authority to create the new law. Authority, considered by itself, was concentrated in the Constitution, in a written thought-thing, an objective worldly document, more tangible, more stable, more durable than either will or power. The rapid elevation of the Constitution into an object of quasi-religious veneration was not the consequence of some eighteenth-century enlightenment idolatry but was a response to a genuine and pressing necessity, the necessity for an external source, a "higher" law to bestow legality on legislative acts. The Constitution, in effect, created a new political world, a new public realm within which power appeared.

One may summarize the American achievement as follows: a new authority was constituted from duly authorized subordinate political bodies; this constitutional authority confirmed and preserved unimpaired the power of those bodies; by so doing it confirmed and preserved its own authority as well. Unlike European theories, this dialectic of power and authority was independent of the national state and of state sovereignty. That is, authority in the United States was derived from below, not from a fictional absolute such as the Crown but from the people organized into several bodies politic whose power, whose ability to act, was exercised in accordance with the laws and was limited by them. A single past, a single ethnic origin, language or religion, which was the decisive social characteristic of the European national state, was made unnecessary because of the joint initiative of founding.

The contrast with the founding of Canada is striking, though not, obviously, as concerns the rights of freeborn Englishmen.[42] There was no question of founding a new authority and consequently the question of founding a new power also did not arise. The institutions of both power and authority were largely inherited, but in an imperial age the "image and transcript of the British constitution" (Simcoe) naturally emphasized the importance of authority and the legitimacy of rule in general. At the same time, lacking the equality that comes from an act of founding, it was necessary to emphasize factors such as French or British ethnicity as a source of continuity with the "higher" law of tradition, religion, and antiquity. Where the Americans idolized the Constitution, the Loyalists, like the British, endowed the monarch "with the strength of religion" (Bagehot). Where the Americans created a new political world, the Loyalists preserved intact as much of the old one as possible. And they did so, as Frye rightly observed, within an imaginative garrison.

An equivalent though not identical contrast exists between Canada and the West. In 1869 there *was* a question of the foundation of authority; Riel and Dugas brought it up in their *Declaration*.[43] There was, moreover, the existence of an organized society, a power, to be dealt with: the settlement at Red River existed, neo-archaic though it was. The Metis were organized around the buffalo hunt. Both were eclipsed not by the constitution of supplementary powers but by the violence of an imperial authority. In the twentieth century the contrasts were less bloody: co-ops, temperance unions, Social Credit study groups, even the scientific and technical agricultural extension programs constituted an articulate social power facing a remote and antagonistic political authority. Politically speaking, the division between unity and identity is a divergence between power and authority. Western power, in the shape of an indigenous neo-archaic society, of co-ops, unions, and more recently of provincially coordinated governments has faced the authority of the Dominion and the command of violence and of bureaucratic and legal rule that Ottawa enjoys. Regional identity in the West, then, has had a political as well as an imaginative dimension. The myth of Red River was not just the story of a faithful and beleaguered garrison but a story of comic expansiveness as well.

For contemporary Westerners national unity is distrusted because it appears as the manifestation of the garrison will, not simply the will of the Loyalist heartland, but of the entire east-west axis, the St. Lawrence valley. This present-day Eastern garrison is not beleaguered, though it is filled with moral certainty; it is a garrison whose chief aspect is that it is an instrument of domination. Politically speaking, will is sheer authority; and authority without power, that is, without the deliberate and deliberative generation of support, is simply administrative rule. Rule without power may well be obeyed since violence can always compel, but it is obeyed reluctantly and with resentment because it is seen to be unjust. In contrast, Western regional identity is the manifestation of both power and interest. Interest, inter-est, is what is between us, namely the web of relations that distinguishes us as an "us" and not "them". It does so by stories where we see and understand ourselves and discover our identity. That is why regional identity is at the heart of Western political consciousness.

NOTES

[1] An essay, as distinct from a memoir, thesis, treatise, summa, critique or meditation, is undertaken in a mood of speculative confidence, and with a minimum of qualifi-

cation, caution, or scholarly scaffolding. It is an interpretative rather than disquisitive or expositive exercise. Soon enough I hope to publish a longer, more complete version, bristling with references to "original" sources. This sketch uses a broad brush.

[2] Frye, *The Bush Garden* (Toronto, Anansi, 1971), pp. i-iii, 225-6; Atwood, *Survival* (Toronto, Anansi, 1972), p. 32. In 1976 Frye wrote of "National Consciousness in Canadian Culture". Here the identification of imaginative Canada with the political unit is even more pronounced. The essay is reprinted in James Polk (ed.), *Divisions on a Ground: Essays on Canadian Culture* (Toronto, Anansi, 1982), pp. 41-56.

[3] Frye, *Bush Garden*, p. 163.

[4] Denis Duffy, *Gardens, Covenants, Exiles: Loyalism in the Literature of Upper Canada/Ontario* (Toronto, University of Toronto Press, 1982).

[5] Ibid., pp. 131-2.

[6] Jean Jacques Rousseau, *Du contrat social*, livre II, ch. 1.

[7] Ibid., p. 3, fn.

[8] Henry Kreisel, "The Prairie: A State of Mind," *Transactions of the Royal Society of Canada*, Series IV, Vol. VI (1968), p. 1973. Consider the opening sentence of W.O. Mitchell's *Who Has Seen the Wind*: "Here was the least common denominator of nature, the skeleton requirements simply, of land and sky—Saskatchewan prairie."

[9] Donald G. Stephens, Introduction to Stephens (ed.), *Writers of the Prairies* (Vancouver, University of British Columbia Press, 1973), p. 2

[10] Laurence Ricou, *Vertical Man/Horizontal World: Man and Landscape in Canadian Prairie Fiction* (Vancouver, University of British Columbia, 1973), p. 173.

[11] Greg Thomas and Ian Clarke in "The Garrison Mentality in the Canadian West," *Prairie Forum*, 4:1 (1979), pp. 83-104, discussed the Hudson's Bay Company forts and the tree-planting pallisades of prairie homesteads. They said nothing, however, of the "many tender ties" that joined the men of the HBC and the women of the country; pallisade trees, which also acted as windbreaks, were in any case characteristic only of Ontario settlers' homesteads.

[12] David C. Carpenter, "Alberta in Fiction: The Emergence of a Provincial consciousness," *Journal of Canadian Studies*, 10:4 (1974), p. 17.

[13] Edward A. McCourt, *The Canadian West in Fiction* (Toronto, Ryerson, 1949), p. vi.

[14] A selection of these early writings is in John Warkentin (ed.), *The Western Interior of Canada: A Record of Geographical Discovery, 1612-1917* (McClelland and Stewart, 1964). Discussion of the writers excerpted by Warkentin may be found in: D.W. Moodie, "Early Images of Rupert's Land" in Richard Allen (ed.), *Man and Nature on the Prairies*, Canadian Plains Studies, 6 (Regina, Canadian Plains Research Center, 1976), pp. 1-20; B. Kaye and D.W. Moodie, "Geographic Perspectives on the Canadian Plains," in Richard Allen (ed.), *A Region of the Mind: Interpreting the Western Canadian Plains*, Canadian Plains Studies, 1 (Regina, Canadian Plains Research Center, 1973), pp. 17-46; G.S. Dumbar, "Isotherms and Politics: Perception of the Northwest in the 1850s" in A.W. Rasperich and H.C. Classen (eds.), *Prairie Perspectives*, 2 (Toronto, Holt, Rinehart and Co., 1973), pp 80-101; R. Douglas Francis, "Changing Images of the West," *Journal of Canadian Studies*, 17:3 (1982), pp. 5-17.

[15] Laurence R. Ricou, "Circumference of Absence: Land and Space in the Poetry of the Canadian Plains," in Richard Allen (ed.), *Man and Nature on the Prairies*, p. 72.

[16] At the same time two things ought to be borne in mind. In 1941, when Ross' book was published, it sold only a few hundred copies. And second, those who have certified Ross' novel as a "prairie classic" were critics for whom garrison literature was most familiar, that is, Easterners. Certification was as much a political as an artistic judgment.

[17] Dick Harrison, *Unnamed Country: The Struggle for a Canadian Prairie Fiction* (Edmonton, University of Alberta Press, 1977), p. 179. See also Laurence Ricou, "Field

Notes and Notes in a Field: Forms of the West in Robert Kroetsch and Tom Robbins," *JCS*, 17:3 (1982), pp. 117-23, and Robert Lecker, "Bordering On: Robert Kroetsch's Aesthetic," ibid., pp. 124-33.

[18] Doug Owram, *Promise of Eden: The Canadian Expansionist Movement and the Idea of the West, 1856-1900* (Toronto, University of Toronto Press, 1980), p. 197.

[19] "Inaugural Address," *Historical and Scientific Society of Manitoba*, 34 (28 Feb. 1889), p. 1.

[20] George Bryce, *The Remarkable History of the Hudson's Bay Company* (London, Sampson, 1902).

[21] In addition to Owram, *Promise of Eden*, see L.G. Thomas, "Historiography of the Fur Trade Area" in Allen (ed.), *A Region of the Mind*, pp. 73-85; T.D. Regehr, "Historiography of the Canadian Plains after 1870," in ibid., pp. 87-101; Lewis G. Thomas, "The Writing of History in Western Canada," in David Jay Bercuson, Philip A. Buckner (eds.), *Eastern and Western Perspectives: Papers from the Joint Atlantic Canada/Western Canada Studies Conference* (Toronto, University of Toronto Press, 1981), pp. 69-84.

[22] Morton, "A Century of Plain and Parkland," in Allen (ed.), *A Region of the Mind*, p. 167. Once in Papeete, Tahiti, I was entertained by the skipper of a blue-water ketch out of Edmonton. He had not sailed her down the North Saskatchewan; Edmonton, however, is still a Canadian port so the ketch could be registered as being from there.

[23] Morton, "Agriculture in the Red River Colony" in A.B. McKillop (ed.), *Contexts of Canada's Past: Selected Essays of W.L. Morton* (Toronto, Macmillan, 1980), p. 71.

[24] Morton, "Marginal" in *Contexts*, p. 41.

[25] Ibid., p. 44.

[26] Morton, "Clio in Canada: The Interpretation of Canadian History," in *Contexts*, p. 109.

[27] Ibid., p. 105.

[28] Morton, "The West and the Nation, 1870-1970" in Rasporich and Classen (eds.), *Prairie Perspectives 2*, p. 16. Similar things could be said of other "neutral" aspects of Dominion power such as the North West Mounted Police or the Department of the Interior.

[29] As early as the Manitoba Schools Question (1890-7), it was clear that in the West French Canadians were immigrants like everyone else; as late as the Official Languages Act (1969) the extension of central Canadian duality has been resisted. The West, since 1870, has not been bilingual and bicultural; it has been monolingual and multicultural.

[30] Morton, "Canadian History and Historians," in *Contexts*, pp. 32-4.

[31] Morton, "Clio in Canada," in *Contexts*, p. 107.

[32] "The Bias of Prairie Politics," in *Contexts*, p. 149. This formulation amounts to a commonsensical version of the "fragment theory" of Louis Hartz.

[33] "Clio in Canada," in *Contexts*, p. 110.

[34] Owram, "Reluctant Hinterland," in Larry Pratt and Garth Stevenson (eds.), *Western Separatism: The Myths, Realities, and Dangers* (Edmonton, Hurtig, 1981), p. 61.

[35] The institutional consequences, which in turn perpetuate the conditions to which they respond, are the several "systems" of Canadian politics; the federal system, the party system, the electoral system, the cabinet system, and so forth. See, for example: Edwin R. Black and Alan C. Cairns, "A Different Perspective on Canadian Federalism," *CPA*, IX:I (1966), pp. 27-44; Alan C. Cairns, "The Electoral System and the Party System in Canada, 1921-1965," *CJPS*, 1 (1968), pp. 55-80; Richard Simeon, "Regionalism and Canadian Political Institutions," *Queen's Quarterly*, 82 (1975), pp. 499-511; Donald V. Smiley, "Territorialism and Canadian Political Institutions,"

Canadian Public Policy, III (1977), pp. 449-57; Roger Gibbins, "American Influences on Western Separatism" in Pratt and Stevenson (eds.), *Western Separatism*, pp. 193-201.

[36] David E. Smith, "Political Culture in the West," in Burcuson and Buckner (eds.), *Eastern and Western Perspectives*, p. 174. Perhaps one should be more cautious and say that the label does not carry *as much* meaning as it does in the large cities of central Canada.

[37] "The Alberta Experience," *Journal of Canadian Studies*, 17:3 (1982), p. 23.

[38] Morton, "A Century of Plain and Parkland," in Allen (ed.), *A Region of the Mind*, p. 179.

[39] John W. Bennett and Seena B. Kohl, "Characterological, Strategic, and Institutional Interpretations of Prairie Settlement," in Anthony W. Rasporich (ed.), *Western Canada: Past and Present* (Calgary, McClelland and Stewart West, 1975), p. 25.

[40] Montesquieu, *Espirit des Lois*, XI, p. 4

[41] In this respect consider Madison's remarks in *Federalist*, 14 and 43.

[42] The degree of Lockean liberalism that the Loyalists imported in their heads has been hotly debated by Professors McRae, Horowitz, Christian, Bell and Preece, to mention only the more prominent political scientists; several historians have also added their views. My point, however, is that, whatever their differences, the idiom of civil rights was common to both the Loyalists and Republicans of the generation that experienced the rebellion. By 1812 I believe it is fair to say that John Beverley Robinson and Bishop Strachan would have had difficulty engaging in civil discussion with Andrew Jackson.

[43] See Thomas Flanagan, "Political Theory of the Red River Resistance: The Declaration of December 8, 1869," *Canadian Journal of Political Science*, XI (1978), pp 153-64.

*Liberalism and Assimilation: Lord Durham Reconsidered**

JANET AJZENSTAT

*Many of the ideas in this paper were first developed in conversation with Samuel Ajzenstat.

We should always be suspicious when we find the arguments of thoughtful men of the past treated as mere "history", that is, as the simple result of the failure of benighted ages to grasp truths obvious to us. To refuse to make earlier observers a party to current debates is to lose the opportunity to consider insights that they had, and we may have forgotten, or—even where we judge them wrong—to illuminate the ground of our own thought by trying to understand theirs.

In this essay I shall take a more open approach to Lord Durham's recommendation for the assimilation of the French Canadians than is usual among commentators. For although in Durham's case, too, the assumption of our superiority to the past is unhelpful, it is the prevailing attitude.

Thus one commentator argues of the assimilation proposal that,

> ...Lord Durham could not know as clearly in 1839 what we know today, that it is fool-hardy and naive to speak of breaking down the customs of a well-established and organized ethnic and cultural community....[1]

Another suggests that "knowledge concerning cultural differences was still primative" in Durham's period, and another would have us believe that prejudice was "natural" to men of Durham's class.[2] "From the perspective of our own times," argues Gerald Craig, editor of the most widely used edition of the *Report*, the assimilation proposal seems "the one great blot in an otherwise admirable and enlightened analysis".[3] According to Chester New, author of the standard biography, it was a "striking failure"; according to R. MacGregor Dawson, in *The Government of Canada*, "a startling miscalculation". Mason Wade, in *The French Canadians*, and Kenneth McNaught, in *The Pelican History of Canada*, see the measure as an expression of "racism", while Peter Burroughs, in *The Canadian Crisis and British Colonial Policy*, speaks of Durham's "cultural chauvinism".[4]

As William Ormsby puts it in the first sentence of his essay, "Lord Durham and the Assimilation of French Canada,"

> Lord Durham's *Report* is generally regarded as one of the most perceptive and significant documents in Canadian history, but at the same time his recommendation that the French should be assimilated is deplored as a regrettable blind spot.[5]

In the essay, and in his book on the period, Ormsby gives his own reasons for reaching the same conclusion.[6]

So well entrenched is this approach to the *Report*, so often repeated in textbooks and in the classroom, that to call it in question must seem at first like sacrilege. It has become one of our national teachings, a part of our Canadian political culture. That it has rendered us unable to do Durham justice, and more than this, has deprived us of an important means by which to develop our own theory of liberalism and nationality, I hope to show in what follows.

I shall argue that the proposal for assimilation did not in fact spring from a prejudice or ignorance on Durham's part. It followed logically from his liberal convictions and his understanding of the conditions necessary for liberal justice. At the heart of his argument we shall find, not an assessment of the strength or value of the French-Canadian culture, but the supposition that a people hived off, by deeply entrenched customs and separate laws, from the economic and political life of the larger nation will surely be vulnerable to exploitation. And in that supposition, I believe, lies a hard core of truth—as relevant now as ever.

In what way is it relevant I suggest in the last section of the essay. Durham's views are compared briefly with those of recent liberal theorists who advocate a revision of liberal doctrine to accommodate the idea of multiculturalist policies and collective rights. I argue there as well that it was above all the confrontation of French and English in Canada that gave British liberals occasion to bring out the teaching on nationality implicit in seventeenth-century liberal teaching, and that what we have in the Canadian documentary record generally as a result is a series of observations and reflections on this issue that are by no means all prejudiced or "primitive". Other thinkers from the past have been treated in much the same fashion as Durham.

In the first and second parts of the essay I outline Durham's argument and the views of English- and French-Canadian commentators. French-Canadian opinions of the *Report*, as we shall see, cast a revealing light on the standard English-Canadian approach, and point toward the more comprehensive interpretation of Durham's thought that I assume in the last section.

I

"I entertain no doubts as to the national character which must be given to Lower Canada," wrote Durham, "it must be that of the British Empire; that of the majority of the population of British America; that of the great race which must, in the lapse of no long period of time, be predominant over the whole of the North American Continent."[7] To this end he proposed that the imperial Parliament pass a bill uniting the colonies of Upper and Lower Canada. Once the French-speaking people of Lower Canada were subjected to the "vigorous rule of an English majority", he argued, they would forever abandon their "vain endeavour to preserve a French Canadian nationality".[8]

"From the perspective of our own times," argues Craig, the proposal for assimilation seems "the one great blot in an otherwise admirable and enlightened analysis".[9] It is said to be the "great error", or "defect", a "first-rate blunder".[10] Some historians, as I have noted, refer to the policy as "racist".[11] Others suggest that Durham was simply ignorant of the strength of French-Canadian feelings. "It is obvious that Durham greatly underestimated the depth and vitality of the French-Canadian culture and nationality," argues Ormsby.[12] Such sentiments are repeated by one writer after another.

What these authors admire in the *Report* is the famous recommendation for "responsible government", a measure by which the colonies were to acquire, in nearly full measure, the parliamentary form of government typical of the home country.[13] This aspect of the *Report* is said to be "far-sighted", "humane", and liberal, where the proposal for assimilation is "insular", intolerant and illiberal.[14] According to Nicholas Mansergh, for example, Durham was "a radical in politics", but "conservative and insular in respect of culture".[15]

Even in the most recent books and articles this picture holds true. Historians today are less inclined to praise the document in the extravagant terms used by the authors of twenty or thirty years ago. But they perpetuate the analysis of the earlier commentators by treating "responsible government" as liberal, and the proposal for assimilation as illiberal. They see less to admire than their predecessors in the political proposals, but are quite as ready to condemn the analysis of French Canada.[16]

The fact is, however, that this approach does not sit well with the most common assumptions in modern social and political thought. Underlying Durham's argument is the idea that particular traditions must fade as individuals come to participate in the rights and freedoms of modern nations, and that the differences between the nations themselves will become less as modern doctrines are disseminated—and this is not an exceptional idea, nor peculiar to Durham and his era. Rather it is characteristic of modern thinkers in many fields from the time of Hobbes and Locke. More important, it does not spring from prejudice against cultural minorities, or ignorance of "cultural differences among nations, but is grounded on the liberal view of modern society and justice. The presence of deep-seated cultural cleavages in a modern or modernizing nation was held to be simply incompatible with political and economic justice.

So Durham believed that the presence of sharply felt ethnic differences in Lower Canada—the high feeling about "race" characteristic of the period—was evidence that the British had followed an unjust policy of prejudice and exclusion in the past.[17] He was convinced too that if the French retained their distinctive way of life conditions would worsen and that they would become ever more vulnerable to economic and political exploitation.[18]

Justice demanded then that French Canadians be allowed to compete in business and politics. He favoured the encouragement of French business enterprise, and he argued for the union of the Canadas because he believed that only in the larger community of the two provinces would the French at last be enabled to attain high government office and political rewards.[19] And from this he went on to suggest that as French and English engaged in common endeavours, the French would inevitably become as aggressive and self-seeking as the English; they would inevitably see the advantages of giving up the laws, habits and customs that set them apart. They would become—English.

How typical Durham's views are may be seen by comparing them with those sketched in the following passage:

> Among most...analysts there appears to be an agreement that a modern society is one that has a sufficient cultural homogeneity and public acceptance of common legal and social norms that rights and public policies can be made universal and produce similar consequences for all individuals in society without differential adjustment based on ascriptive categories or socio-cultural groupings.[20]

The statement perfectly depicts Durham's position. He argues for universality as against particularism, and for policies recognizing achievement, as against ascription, because he believes the former just and the latter unjust. His ideas are in every way in keeping with what might be called "mainstream" liberalism.[21] What Durham's commentators have seen as the expression of prejudice and ignorance is an argument that lies at the very heart of modern liberal thought.

It may well be true that Durham, and "mainstream" liberals generally, did not give enough place in their thought to the strength of human loyalties and the desire to be associated with a collectivity. This is a supposition to which I shall return in the third part of the essay. But central to the "mainstream" argument is the suggestion that deep cultural cleavages are incompatible with the full realization of liberal rights, and it is this understanding, that we must assess before praising or condemning the view.

The proposal for assimilation then, is an integral part of Durham's liberal position. It is based on the same idea of good government and the same view of human nature as the proposal for "responsible government". The historians, condemning the one measure and praising the other, have not addressed the *Report* as a coherent statement, and for this reason have not given us the critical response needed to illuminate Durham's views—or indeed their own position. Nothing so easy to dismiss as prejudice or ignorance lies behind Durham's belief that the French Canadians would and should adopt the way of life prevailing on the continent.

The peculiar deficiencies of the typical English habits of thought about the *Report* will emerge from a comparison of the French- and English-Canadian commentators.

II

That Durham greatly underestimated the vitality of the French-Canadian nationality is, as I have suggested, perhaps the most common theme among English-Canadian commentators. It is often argued in this connection that he was surprisingly naive to suppose that such a simple measure as the union of the Canadas would suffice to erase the French Canadian nationality. According to one writer it was "ridiculous" for Durham to maintain that the danger of political threat from French Canada "could be counteracted simply by an English-speaking majority in the united assembly".[22] According to another, "The Canadian problem had long been virtually insoluble to the British because the solution which they desired, that the French Canadians should cease to be disaffected, and preferably cease to be French, was beyond the reach of legislative fiat...."[23] Durham's assumption that the English-speaking members would act as a bloc was "incredible", according to one author.[26] Much the same idea was put forward in a recent series of articles on nineteenth-century Canadian history in *The Globe and Mail*, under the heading, "Lord Durham wanted to see the end of French Canada's nationality. But a resolute group of reformers hatched a bold scheme to frustrate his design."[27]

No one supposes the story ended in the 1840s; other "bold schemes" and other "resolute reformers" were required. As one historian notes, "French Canada evolved and it has continued to evolve". Indeed, he goes on, the French Canadians have adopted "social and moral values similar to those held by the Anglo-American majority in North America". French Canada has "adjusted", it has been "transformed", but it has not been assimilated.[28] That French-Canadian "survivance" is a triumphant fact today is an article of faith among English-Canadian commentators. As two students of contemporary Quebec suggest, in typical fashion, "The arguments as to why French Canada survived continue, but there is no denying the fact of survival."[29]

According to the accepted view of Durham then, he failed to see on the one hand that ethnic groups might possess a stubborn vitality and ability to resist law and institutions, and on the other, that liberal society could and should develop institutions to accommodate that vitality. In any event, it is suggested, history has proved Durham wrong. The proposal for assimilation was impractical and ineffective—perhaps ill-intentioned, even malevolent—certainly "naive", "ridiculous", "incredible".

A quite different picture emerges when we turn to French-Canadian commentators. It would be highly incorrect to suggest that the French approve of the *Report* or the proposal for assimilation. But they do not see the measure as impractical or ridiculous. On the contrary, they condemn it precisely because they believe it is the kind of recommendation only too likely to be effective. And from this perspective, I would argue, they give a far more convincing account of Durham's position.

One of the best descriptions of what Durham was about is found in the Introduction by Denis Bertrand and André Lavallée to Bertrand and Desbien's translation of the *Report*:

> Après avoir analysé les principaux arguments qui militent contre ou en faveur du maintien d'une collectivité canadienne-française, Durham rejette catégoriquement toute méthode de contrainte, pour appuyer une politique de lente assimilation, par la force naturelle des choses, grâce à la mise en minorité et aux autres moyens d'intégration déjà en usage en Louisiane, par le camouflage de l'égalité des droits, le mythe de l'autonomie locale, le guêpier de la législature mixte et du bilinguisme, les querelles de partis et l'émulation. L'immigration massive, la force normale d'attraction de la scène fédérale et les contraintes de l'économie auront tôt fait, ajoutet-il, de vaincre une résistance autant désuète qu'inutile.[30]

It is tempting to argue that Bertrand and Lavallée have simply heaped at Durham's door all the forces and events in Canadian history that in their view have endangered the French-Canadian nationality. But underlying their account is the perception that assimilation results from modern liberal practices and liberal justice, and in this sense their charge against Durham is faithful to his position. What prompts assimilation according to the "mainstream" liberal philosophers and social scientists is exactly "la force naturelle des choses", in a system based on equality of rights, with institutions promoting the cooperation of peoples of every origin and background.[31]

Durham's prescription, in the argument of Bertrand and Lavallée, "laissait déjà entrevoir la Confédération et fixait, dans ses grandes lignes, la stratégie du dialogue et de la collaboration qu'allaient suivre pendant plus d'un siècle les principaux chefs du Canada anglais".[32] In similar fashion Marcel-Pierre Hamel argues in the Introduction to his 1948 translation of the *Report* that the centralizing trend of Canadian politics in the 1940s had come close to bringing about Durham's scheme for a legislative union of the English and French provinces, thus nearly realizing Durham's cherished project. But, he adds, "nous ne serons jamais les assimilés de la Louisiane. Demain tout recommence."[33] Like Bertrand and Lavallée, Hamel is hostile but far from seeing Durham's proposal as "foolhardy", or "ridiculous".

But the most crucial commentator from our point of view was Durham's contemporary, Étienne Parent, editor of *Le Canadien*, who published a series of articles on the *Report* immediately after it appeared. What was most striking about Parent's reaction was that in response to the argument he found in the *Report* he at first endorsed the idea of assimilation. He had always been an ardent supporter of liberal principles of government, and he accepted outright the idea that to adopt liberal principles would mean abandoning nationality.[34] (Hamel complained, "Étienne Parent, lui assui, eut un terrible moment de faiblesse".)[35]

Almost immediately Parent set out to try to reconcile the insight he had taken from the *Report* with his own hopes for the survival of the French-Canadian nationality, and the great interest of his work lies in this endeavour. But we cannot suppose that his acceptance of assimilation was due simply to a failure of will or intelligence. That would make nonsense of everything he wrote on the subject of nationality, for he himself claimed that his initial acceptance of the proposal was based on his previous understanding of the nature of liberal political institutions, while his later articles must be seen as attempts to resolve this understanding with his desire to see pride in nationality remain to the French Canadians. He argued in the end that the French nationality might be preserved in a federal union of all the British North American colonies, but the character of his debate with himself on this subject shows that he never turned his back on the fundamental idea he derived from the *Report* or found confirmed there—to put it simply, that there is something problematic about the supposition that nationalism and liberalism may be easily reconciled.

The best known of Durham's French-speaking commentators today is Michel Brunet. Ramsay Cook notes,

> Durham's views, which infuriate most French Canadians, exercise a peculiar magnetism on Brunet, who once called the English lord, "the best historian in Canada." Brunet seems torn between suspicion that Durham was accurate in his analysis of the 1837 affair, and, therefore, right in his prescription of assimilation on the one hand, and his nationalist commitment to *la survivance* on the other. Brunet the social scientist attempts to use Durham's analysis without reaching the conclusions that are repugnant to Brunet the nationalist....[36]

Cooks' own writings do not follow the received tradition in the matter of the Durham *Report*, while Brunet's treatment of the proposal for assimilation on the level of theory, that is, as a problem or challenge rather than a "deplorable error" or "startling miscalculation" is far indeed from the usual textbook picture.

Behind the arguments of Parent, who settles for federalism, and Brunet, who hopes for independence, lies the same insight, I suggest. Both know there is much to be valued in the liberal regime—above all, the famous liberal guarantees of equality, rights and freedoms. But both know as well that it is the exercise of these principles that wears away particular national loyalties. It is just this understanding that enables them to interpret Durham so well. They have recognized the liberal character and the weight of Durham's position on nationality as the English-speaking commentators have not.

English-Canadian commentators then believe that only ignorance and prejudice stands in the way of a thorough-going dualism or multiculturalism—that good will and "knowledge concerning cultural differences" will win the day. But the French are far more sceptical. From their more philosophical position the problem looks less tractable. And as for good will, tolerance and the mutual participation of French and English together in the affairs of the nation—why these, they suggest, are Durham's very remedies.

It is surprising that the English-speaking historians have so misread the *Report*. The mistake results largely from not putting

Durham in the context of British political philosophy and the modern social sciences. But it has been easier for them to pronounce judgement, I believe, because they have seen themselves as modeling their views on those of respected Englishmen of the turn of the century.

In the decade after 1900—the years of the South African crisis—attention focused sharply on the Durham *Report* once more.[37] Many observers wondered if Durham's famous proposal for assimilation would prove appropriate for the new Dutch subjects. However prominent historians of the time believed that plans to assimilate the Dutch were ill-founded. And they were quite as ready to argue that Durham had erred in proposing assimilation for the French.

These Edwardian views at first sight resemble those of the later writers. Indeed, as I have suggested, we can trace the clichés about Durham to this point. H. E. Egerton's observation, from the introduction to *Canadian Constitutional Documents*, is typical: "The time-spirit has dealt summarily with one of the main tenets of Durham's political belief—the view that it was necessary to absorb the French national character in a dominant Anglo-Saxon type."[38] A closer examination, however, reveals fundamental differences. The Canadian writers copy only the broad conclusion of their predecessors—that the French should retain their way of life—but they bring quite different arguments to support it.

They oppose the idea of assimilation because they wish to see the French in Canada remain French. The Edwardians, on the other hand, writing at the height of the Empire, had been chiefly concerned to see that the British remained purely British. They believed that the British had a "nationhood", that is, as Egerton explains, an imperial mission which set them apart.[39] Egerton's vision of empire has a multicultural dimension, it is true. He pictures the British Empire as a mosaic, for example, and no more than later Canadians who use the same image, does he wish to see the various components lose their distinctive characteristics. But he develops the metaphor as no later writer would. The Empire, he suggests, is

> ...an elaborate mosaic, wherein, side by side with the Empire of India—Dominion, Commonwealth, self-governing colony, Crown colony, chartered company, Protectorate, sphere of influence, adds each its lustre to the pavement which is ever being trod by fresh generations of our race as they pass to and fro.[40]

It is for the British then to rule. This is their "nationhood", a "nationhood" in which the subordinate peoples of the Empire are not to participate. The French, indeed, in this analysis, would remain distinctively French only so long as they refrained from participating with the British in the great affairs proper to the British "race".

The Edwardian argument in fact turns on the same observation as Durham's: participation assimilates. Durham favours assimilation because he has adopted the principle of equal opportunity for all. But no such idea hampers the Edwardian scholars; and if they reject assimilation it is because they believe some tasks of government and empire simply inappropriate for the French Canadians.

The English-Canadian historians have taken from their mentors an idea of pluralism. But they marry it to the doctrine of justice as equal opportunity. They wish to see the French Canadian nationality retain its lustre while ensuring French Canadians at the same time perfect political equality. The idea is sympathetic, as all must acknowledge. But insofar as the historians have not entertained the idea—central to Durham and the Edwardians as well—that equal opportunity and thoroughgoing pluralism are incompatible, it is far from well grounded.

III

In recent years the "mainstream" liberal position has been challenged from several quarters. Politicians, until recently, in keeping with the principles of the "mainstream", would typically represent the cause of minority peoples by arguing that the same rights were due to each and all in a modern nation. But today a different doctrine is in vogue, and politicians more often invoke the idea of collective rights and special status. They demand rights for their constituents not as citizens of the larger society, but as members of a caste, clan, tribe, ethnic or nationalist group.

On the basis of the older philosophy social scientists and political thinkers, as I have argued, suggested that the assimilation of minorities was both inevitable and good. They believed that differences of language, habit and custom would become matters of private life and private preference, within nations predominantly liberal and commercial in character. Now, however, they will as often argue that ethnic and nationalist differences are too vital and too deeply entrenched to be contained in private associations, and that continuing cultural diversity is the most salient and perhaps the most welcome feature of the modern world.

The "mainstream" of Western political thought, according to Kenneth McRae, "has shown little understanding or respect for the cultural diversity of mankind, and has made scant allowance for it as a possible concern of government." "Hobbes made politics a science," he argues, "but a science that suppresses or subordinates every major source of human variation."[41] "Liberals and their historic doctrine neglect collective entities," argues Vernon Van Dycke. "Since the time of Hobbes and Locke, liberal political theorists have made it their primary purpose to explore relationships between the individual and the state."[42]

McRae believes that, "We must acknowledge cultural pluralism" and build on it openly, "before the time for rational discussion runs out."[43] According to Van Dycke, "The requirements of logic and the long-term requirements of universal justice commend the idea of accepting communities as right-and-duty-bearing units."[44]

It is easy to forget how great and how striking this change in political and social thought has been.[45] To argue now that law and government should remain totally indifferent to community and collectivity, tribe and ethnic group, is taken as a mark of intolerance; it is not considered prudent, given the character of ethnic demands in modern nations, but more than that, it is not considered just. But according to the earlier theory it was exactly indifference to community and collectivity that was tolerant, prudent and just. Discrimination on the basis of race, origin, colour or creed—to use the famous liberal formulation—was regarded as the very definition of intolerance and injustice. This is not to say that discrimination was not practised in liberal societies in former days; far from it. But lack of discrimination was always recognized as the standard, and it is that standard that is now being challenged. To identify the individual in law with the community of his birth was formerly thought reprehensible and may not seem commendable.[46]

Writers like McRae and Van Dycke are far from ignorant of the "mainstream" argument. Indeed they write chiefly to refute it. But in many ways nevertheless their argument reproduces that of Durham's commentators. They focus on the apparent strength of ethnic and nationalist demands in modern nations, and no more than the historians do they centre directly on the old liberal supposition that policies promoting social heterogeneity may erode liberal rights and freedoms still valued in our society.

What we need today, I suggest, is not another statement of the case for cultural pluralism and collective rights, but more reflection on the old "mainstream" position. It is far from true to say that the "mainstream" has shown "little understanding of cultural diversity", or that liberals have "neglected cultural entities". The rejection of collectivity in liberalism was not a matter of "neglect", or lack of understanding. Rather it was the founding principle of liberal philosophy that there should be no prescription on the basis of collectivity.[47] Hobbes' "men are by nature equal", denies any individual, caste or collectivity natural right to prescribe for others. For nineteenth-century figures like Durham, as I have shown, it was clear indeed that to allow or foster a truly separate collective identity within the larger nation would so breech the principle of equality as to be intolerable.[48] To subject a minority to a position where they must be ruled and no doubt exploited, was an offensive as to allow a minority to rule and exploit.

I do not argue here that the "mainstream" position is simply superior, but I suggest that shying away from it will vitiate attempts to formulate a theory and prescription for the ethnic and nationalist demands of today. And to rediscover the "mainstream", I would argue, we could do worse than return to the Canadian documentary record. By discarding the habit of reading earlier materials on nationalism as statements of prejudice and ignorance, we may uncover a treasure-house.

I have suggested that it was the confrontation of French and English in Canada more than any other instance, that prompted British liberals to write concretely about nationality. As one student of political philosophy argues, North America was the provincing ground for the political thought of Hobbes and Locke.[49] In the social conditions of the United States and British North America, where the grip of old customs was looser than in Europe, and the poorest class affluent by European standards, the full consequences of Hobbes' equality principle first came to light. But only Canada exhibited the problem of nationality in full blown form.[50] The United States revealed no social cleavage comparable to that of the "two nations" in British North America. In the case of Lower Canada above all then, political observers had to consider equality and nationality together.

At bottom the issue had to do with exactly that central tenet of liberalism to which I have referred—the rejection of collectivity as the basis for authoritative prescription. There was no principle in the philosophy of Hobbes and Locke by which the English as a collectivity could assert title to rule. If the problem was always there for thoughtful individuals, it was no doubt usually ignored as the business of building an empire went on; rule by race or collectivity was justified in one fashion or another. The Edwardian historians are an example. Nevertheless, it remained true that according to the doctrine of the seventeenth-century philosophers, the conquered were as entitled to participate in government as the conquerors. If there was to be a legislative assembly or governing council in Quebec, the French were justified in demanding seats and positions on the same basis as the English. How then, were men differing in origin, language, religion and political education to learn to govern in concert?

A surprising proportion of Canadian historical documents record thoughts on this matter. What we shall find in this treasure-house, I suggest, are arguments that show us finer reasons to value collectivity than any that the recent advocates of dualism and pluralism can provide.

But we shall find there too, I am sure, arguments that will lead us to believe that in striving for collectivity, we will inevitably find ourselves relinquishing cherished liberal rights.

NOTES

[1] Gerald Craig (ed.), *Lord Durham's Report, An Abridgement of Report on the Affairs of British North America by Lord Durham* (Toronto, McClelland and Stewart, 1963), p. x.

[2] Peter Burroughs, *The Canadian Crisis and British Colonial Policy, 1828-1841* (Toronto, Macmillan, 1972), p. 5; Mason Wade, *The French Canadians, 1760-1967*, Vol. 1 (Toronto, Macmillan, 1968), p. 197.

[3] Craig, *Lord Durham's Report*, p. x.

[4] New, *Lord Durham, A Biography of John George Lambton First Earl of Durham* (Oxford, Clarendon Press, 1929), p. 497. Dawson, *The Government of Canada*, 4th ed., revised by Norman Ward (Toronto, University of Toronto Press, 1963), p. 10; Wade, *The French Canadians*, p. 197; McNaught, *The Pelican History of Canada* (Harmondsworth, Penguin Books, 1969), p. 94; Burroughs, *The Canadian Crisis*, pp. 1, 5, 103. Reviewing the 1968 edition of New's book, Burroughs said, "Although forty years have elapsed our view of Lord Durham corresponds very closely to the portrait drawn by Chester New in his celebrated biography." *Canadian Historical Review*, LII (June 1971).

[5] William Ormsby, "Lord Durham and the Assimilation of French Canada," in Norman Penlington (ed.), *On Canada, Essays in Honour of Frank H. Underhill* (Toronto, University of Toronto Press, 1971), p. 33.

[6] See Ormsby, *The Emergence of the Federal Concept in Canada, 1839-1845*, Chapter Two, "Lord Durham's Mission" (Toronto: University of Toronto Press, 1969). Other writers who rely on this approach will be mentioned in the course of my argument. Some not discussed can be noted: W.P.M. Kennedy, *The Constitution of Canada* (New York, Russell and Russell, 1922); R. G. Trotter, *The British Empire-Commonwealth, A Study in Political Evolution* (Toronto; Macmillan, 1932); Chester New, George Brown, Chester Martin and D. C. Harvey in articles in the issue of the *Canadian Historical Review*, XX (June 1939), celebrating the one hundredth anniversary of the publication of the *Report*; Alexander Brady, *Democracy in the Dominions* (Toronto, University of Toronto Press, 1947); George Woodcock, *Who Killed the British Empire? An Inquest* (London, Jonathan Cape, 1974).

[7] C. P. Lucas (ed.), *Lord Durham's Report on the Affairs of British North America*, Vol. 2 (Oxford, Clarendon Press, 1912), p. 288. All references to the *Report* are to the text in Volume Two of this edition, cited as *Report*.

[8] *Report*, pp. 307, 70.

[9] Craig, *Lord Durham's Report*, p. x.

[10] Wade, *The French Canadians*, pp. 207, 208. A. L. Burt, *The Evolution of The British Empire and Commonwealth from the American Revolution* (Boston, D.C. Heath, 1956), p. 261; Reginald Coupland, *The Durham Report, An Abridged Version* (Oxford: Clarendon Press, 1945), p. lxi.

[11] See above, Note 4; Kenneth McRoberts and Dale Posgate argue in their widely used text, *Quebec, Social Change and Political Crisis* (Toronto, McClelland and Stewart, 1980), that Durham's conclusions were shaped by his "racial and imperialist biases" (p. 31).

[12] Ormsby, "Lord Durham and the Assimilation of French Canada," p. 37.

[13] W. P. Morrell, continuing a long tradition, argued in *British Colonial Policy in the Mid-Victorian Age* (Oxford, Clarendon Press, 1963) that "Since Lord Durham's Report the main theme of British colonial policy has been the extension and deepening of his conception of responsible government" (p. 471).

[14] Wade, *The French Canadians*, p. 214; Burroughs, *The Canadian Crisis*, p. 1; Nicholas and Mansergh, *The Commonwealth Experience* (London, Weidenfield and Nicolson, 1949), p. 30.

[15] Mansergh, *The Commonwealth Experience*, p. 30.

[16] Morrell's view (see Note 13 above) has been sharply criticized recently. Durham is no longer seen as one of the great empire-makers. Burroughs sketches the reasons for the new perspective in *The Canadian Crisis*, pp. 1, 2. Recent English commentators have adopted an especially scornful stance. Ged Martin undertakes to deflate Durham's reputation generally and the importance of the proposal for "responsible government" in particular, in *The Durham Report and British Colonial Policy* (Cambridge, Cambridge University Press, 1972), but his underlying approach is in line with that of the former commentators. He provides no analysis of the text of the Report. William Thomas, in *The Philosophic Radicals: nine studies in theory and practice, 1917-1841* (Oxford, Clarendon Press, 1979), is even more anxious to reveal Durham as a figure of no account; he pays even less attention to the text. See his Chapter Eight, "Durham, the Radicals and the Canada Mission."

[17] *Report*, pp. 34-6, 38.

[18] *Report*, pp. 293, 294.

[19] That Durham intended by union to promote opportunities for the French in government and greater interaction between French and English generally is argued more fully in my article, "Liberalism and Nationality," *Canadian Journal of Political Science*, XIV:3 (September 1981). Durham discusses the salutary effects of business rivalry between French and English in Louisiana on p. 302. Cf. p. 42ff.

[20] Gordon Means, "Human Rights and the Rights of Ethnic Groups—A Commentary," *International Studies Notes*, 1 (1974), p. 12. Means refers to F. Toennies, F. X. Sutton, Talcott Parsons, Fred Riggs, David Apter and "a host of others." In the earlier edition (1976) of *Quebec, Social Change and Political Crisis*, Kenneth McRoberts and Dale Posgate argue that, using a model of social development from "tradition" to "modernity," one would have predicted "that social and economic development, by breaking down differences in values and goals between French and English Canadians, would have broken down the attachment of French Canadians to their Francophone collectivity" (p. 205). They cite S. M. Lipset, David Easton, Daniel Lerner and others as authorities for this model. See their notes on page 14.

[21] See Kenneth McRae on the "mainstream" below, p. 18.

[22] Ormsby, *The Emergence of the Federal Concept in Canada*, p. 33.

[23] Martin, *The Durham Report and British Policy*, pp. 51, 52.

[24] Craig, *Lord Durham's Report*, p. x.

[25] Ormsby, *Emergence of the Federal Concept*, p. 33.

[26] Ormsby, *Emergence of the Federal Concept*, pp. 33-4. See also Burroughs, *The Canadian Crisis*, p. 108; and Kenneth McRae, "Consociationalism and the Canadian Political System," in McRae (ed.), *Consociational Democracy, Political Accommodation in Segmented Societies* (Toronto, McClelland and Stewart, 1974): "Contrary to Dur-

ham's expectations, the French Canadians remained unassimilated, and the Union period produced perhaps the closest approach to institutionalized politics of accommodation to be found in Canadian history" (p. 255). Donald Smiley develops this in *Canada in Question: Federalism in the Eighties*, 3rd ed. (Toronto, McGraw-Hill Ryerson, 1980), pp. 215, 216. Many authors note that the "quasi-federal" features of the 1840s were not what Durham had had in mind when proposing union, but few in this context suggest that he might have had good reason to distrust such developments. Yet as some political scientists have pointed out, "consociationalism" or "elite accommodation" is easily transposed into a system of exploitation and repression. See for example, Reginald Whitaker, "The Quebec Cauldron," in Michael S. Whittington and Glen Williams (eds.), *Canadian Politics in the 1980's* (Toronto, Methuen, 1981).

[27] Jacques Monet, "French Canada: the Coming of Age," *The Globe and Mail* (Nov. 23, 1981), p. 10.

[28] Ormsby, "Lord Durham and the Assimilation of French Canada," p. 53.

[29] McRoberts and Posgate, *Quebec, Social Change and Political Crisis* (1980 edition), p. 23.

[30] Bertrand and Lavallée, in Denis Bertrand and Albert Desbiens (éds.), *Le Rapport Durham* (Montréal, Les Éditions Sainte-Marie, 1969), p. xlviii.

[31] Cf Report, p. 307; and see p. 71, where Durham speaks of influences that might have "brought the quarrel to its natural and necessary termination."

[32] Bertrand et Lavallée, p. li.

[33] Hamel (éd. et tr.), *Le Rapport de Durham* (Éditions du Québec, 1948), p. 51.

[34] For Parent on liberal principles of government, see his argument for "responsible government," in *Le Canadien* (June 19, 1833), reproduced in Jean-Charles Falardeau (ed.), *Étienne Parent, 1802-1874, Biographie, textes et bibliographie* (Montréal, Les Éditions La Presse, 1975), and also as an introduction to Hamel's edition of the Durham Report under the heading "Retrospective d'Étienne Parent." For Parent on the necessity of assimilation, see the article of October 23, 1840, reproduced in Falardeau: "...les Canadiens Français n'ont plus rien à attendre...pour leur nationalité. Que leur reste-t-il donc à faire dans leur propre intérêt et dans celui de leurs enfants, si ce n'est de travailler eux-mêmes de toutes leur forces à amener une assimilation qui brise la barrière qui les sépare des populations que les environment de toutes parts...." The article opens with a plea for "responsible government" as expounded by Lord Durham, M. Gowan and M. Howe, and ends with a picture of the great and powerful liberal nation that will rise on the banks of the St. Lawrence after the French have made the necessary sacrifice. But see H. D. Forbes, "Étienne Parent: Liberal and Nationalist," a paper prepared for the Canadian Political Science Association Annual Meeting, 1983. Forbes argues that such statements as I have quoted are not central to Parent's liberal point of view.

[35] Hamel, "Introduction," p. 51. See also Jean-Paul Bernard, *Les Rouges, Libéralisme, Nationalisme et Anticléricalisme au Mileux du XIXe Siècle* (Les Presses de l'Université du Québec, 1971), especially p. 22; and Jacques Monet, *The Last Cannon Shot, A Study of French-Canadian Nationalism, 1837-1850* (Toronto, University of Toronto Press, 1969), p. 27ff.

[36] Cook, *Canada and the French Canadian Question* (Toronto, Macmillan, 1966), pp. 138, 139. And see p. 131.

[37] The connection between the new interest in the *Report* and the South African crisis is discussed in Richard Garnett, "The Authorship of Lord Durham's Canada Report," *English Historical Review*, XVII (1902). Ged Martin's bibliography in *The Durham Report and British Policy* is a good guide to the English authors of this period.

[38] In the introduction to H. E. Egerton and W. L. Grant, *Canadian Constitutional Development shown by Selected Speeches and Despatches* (London, John Murray, 1907), p. vi.

[39] See, for example, Egerton, *A Short History of British Colonial Policy* (London, Methuen, 1897), pp. 525, 526: "There grows upon us, as we study history, the sense of an unseen superintending Providence controlling the development of the Anglo-Saxon race...the fulfilment of this destiny need not mean the loss of a single element of common nationhood...." But, *noblesse oblige*: as C. P. Lucas argues, in the introductory volume of the 1912 edition, Durham's proposal for assimilation ran counter to the "British instinct of fair play and generosity to the conquered, which after all is nearly the most valuable asset that a ruling race can possess." Lucas, *Lord Durham's Report*, Vol. 1, p. 280.

[40] Egerton, *The Origin and Growth of Greater Britain, An Introduction to Sir C. P. Lucas's Historical Geography* (Oxford, Clarendon Press, 1824; first published 1902), p. 179.

[41] McRae, "The Plural Society and the Western Political Tradition," *Canadian Journal of Political Science*, XII:4 (Dec. 1979). p. 682.

[42] Van Dycke, "Collective Entities and Moral Rights: Problems in Liberal Democratic Thought," *The Journal of Politics*, 44 (1982), p. 21; "The Individual, the State and Ethnic Communities in Politicial Theory," *World Politics*, XXIX:3 (April 1977), p. 343.

[43] McRae, "The Plural Society," p. 688.

[44] Van Dycke, "The Individual, the State and Ethnic Communities," p. 369. See also, for example, David Cameron, *Nationalism, Self-Determination and the Quebec Question* (Toronto, Macmillan, 1974), especially pp. 1-8; and Charles Taylor, "Why do Nations Have to Become States?" in Stanley French (ed.), *Philosophers Look at Confederation* (Montreal, The Canadian Philosophical Association, 1979), pp. 27-9.

[45] That this change is recent is suggested by Gordon Means in the 1974 article from *International Studies Notes* cited above. (See Note 20.) After pointing out that "most analysts" agree that cultural homogeneity is the condition of justice, he goes on to argue that the assumption now must appear unsupported; it would now seem, he says, that as modernization increases, aspects of tradition are intensified. Cf. Nathan Glazer and Daniel Moynihan, "Why Ethnicity," *Commentary*, 58:4 (Oct. 1974).

[46] See Howard Brotz, "Comments," *Canadian Public Policy*, VIII:4 (Autumn 1982), p. 613: "My...criticism of the multiculturalism policy in Canada is that it was one small step towards the politicization of ethnicity. By this I mean bringing into being a political situation in which the rights, privileges and disabilities of individuals are *legally* defined on the basis of their ethnic group membership. Apartheid in South Africa is a very good example...."

[47] For a fuller exposition of this point, see Rainer Knopff, "Liberal Democracy and the Challenge of Nationalism in Canadian Politics," *Canadian Review of Studies in Nationalism*, IX:1 (Spring 1982).

[48] For a discussion of the minor but pleasant differences that should persist in a free society, see Howard Brotz, "Multiculturalism in Canada: A Muddle," *Canadian Public Policy*, VI:1 (Winter 1980). Some nineteenth-century liberals held that differences of language were compatible with assimilation—among the minor but pleasant differences, as it were. See Durham on the bilingual policies of Louisiana, Report, pp. 299-302.

[49] Mathie, "Political Community and the Canadian Experience: Reflections on Nationalism, Federalism and Unity," *Canadian Journal of Political Science*, XII:1 (March 1979), p. 8.

[50] Cf. McRae, *Consociational Democracy*, p. 242; Vincent R. Harlow, *The Founding of the Second British Empire, 1763-1893*, Vol. II (London, Longmans, Green, 1964), p. 733ff. Marcel Rioux puts it this way: "French Canadians are without a doubt among the oldest colonized peoples in the world, if not *the* oldest." *Quebec in Question*; James Boake (trans.), (Toronto, James Lorimer, 1971), p. 3.

Instrastate Federalism and Confederation

JENNIFER SMITH

The Constitution Act, 1982, contains the most comprehsensive amendments ever made to Canada's constitution. Some even refer to it as the "new constitution", an incorrect designation that indicates the significance attributed to the document's contents. These include a Charter of Rights and Freedoms and a full set of amending procedures that dispenses with the old requirement of British consent for formal constitutional change. Thus the country's constitution is said to be "patriated", a "final vestige of its colonial past" removed. Change was accompanied by lengthy and at times bitter controversy and constitutional fatigue ought to have set in by now. Oddly it has not. One indication came in the fall of 1982 only a few months after proclamation of the *Constitution Act* when the federal government launched the Royal Commission on the Economic Union and Development Prospects for Canada. Although established primarily in response to deteriorating economic conditions, the Commission has terms of reference that reach beyond the economy into political life. As one of its brochures proclaims, it is concerned "about how we Canadians decide to do what we do", and that covers a lot of institutional territory. Certainly it includes Parliament and the electoral system, institutions that many observers classify under the heading of unfinished business. Most unfinished of all, it seems, is the Senate.

Many are eyeing the idea of Senate reform favourably, including some senators, and proposals abound. Those that seek simply to replace the existing method of appointment of members by Governor-in-Council with some form of election arise out of concern for the Senate's public reputation. Thus Senator Duff Roblin argues that the Senate lacks legitimacy and cannot carry out properly its primary role of representing regional interests. It lacks legitimacy because it is an appointed body and therefore "repugnant to modern perceptions of representative and parliamentary government".[1] Roblin wants to supply the Senate with a basis for the political authority it does not have and he knows that election is the strongest one available. His main concern is the integrity of an institution.

For others Senate reform, while important, is only part of a larger scheme. Their main concern is the validity of the central government's claim to be a *national* government. According to Roger Gibbins, "the national government is not perceived to be a truly national one". Thus his recommendations on Senate reform, which also include election, point beyond the Senate's reputation to that of the central government as a whole and are meant to enhance the national claims of both. The thinking that gives rise to recommendations of the second type takes the form of a critique of our central government institutions and issues in a set of proposals for redesigning them. I would like to examine this critique and then assess it in the light of Canada's constitutional past; I will do so with the following questions in mind. On what grounds did the Canadian founders defend the form of the central government adopted in 1867 and now in question? Did they consider anything like the alternative pressed by contemporary critics?

Alan Cairns distinguishes between two versions of the intrastate model of federalism. Both are aimed at increasing the central government's receptiveness to the regional character of the country but they involve very different results as far as federal-provincial relations are concerned. The provincial intrastate version recommends that provincial governments or their delegates be party to central government decisions. This would undoubtedly enhance the position of provincial governments. Centralist intrastate federalism recommends that central government institutions themselves be refashioned to reflect regionalism. Its proponents mean to enhance the central government at the expense of provincial governments.[2] Cairns observes that the intrastate model in its centralist guise was elaborated and applied to Canada initially by Donald Smiley in his 1971 article, "The Structural Problem of Canadian Federalism". There Smiley questions the old federal solution of divided powers (interstate federalism) to the problem of "territorial diversity" on two grounds: territorially based or regional conflicts have persisted, possibly worsened; the central government is weaker than it ought to be. In his view these things are undesirable and have come about because interests based on territorial diversity, denied an institutional home in the central government, have moved in with the provinces. To remedy this he recommends formal representation of the country's regions within central government institutions. The intention is to undermine both the provinces' monopoly on the role of regional representative and the utility of institutions like the federal-provincial conference which have arisen out of it, and to try to encourage resolution of regionally based conflicts within the central government itself. The desired effect overall, obviously, is to strengthen the central government.[3]

Smiley invokes both the past and the example of the American government in support of his position. Turning to the past, he suggests that the system of government established at Confederation did not rely wholly on the interstate mechanism of divided powers. By design and convention it exhibited some intrastate elements, for instance in the constitution of the Senate and in the conventions governing party and cabinet practices. Growing emphasis on jurisdictional questions combined with the atrophy of these representative elements are later developments. If this is true then Smiley's proposals are hardly foreign to the Canadian political tradition. The American government, on the other hand, is living proof of the effect of the centralist intrastate model. It discloses immense possibilities for representation of regional or local interests and the result is a "fragmented power system" that "allows geographical particularisms to play a more important role than is the case in Ottawa". In Smiley's view this has contributed much to the central government's undoubted dominance over the state governments.

Smiley concludes with a number of proposals. In the case of cabinet and Parliament they include free votes, restrictions on the prime minister's power to advise dissolution, and greater autonomy for parliamentary committees. The idea is to diminish the prime minister's ascendency over cabinet and caucus and the governing party's ascendency over Parliament. As a result individual members of Parliament, possessed of greater independence, might be expected to respond more to local influences in a manner not unlike that of their American counterparts. Proposals such as these leave the impression that centralist intrastate federalism is more consistent with congressional than parliamentary institutions. Smiley sees this and is troubled enough to insist that they constitute only a move in the direction of congressionalism, not abandonment of the parliamentary form. Parliamentary government is a "flexible instrument", flexible enough to accommodate his proposals and still emerge intact.[4] Roger Gibbins is not at all concerned on this score and thus manages to make the connection between intrastate federalism and congressionalism wonderfully clear. As in Smiley's case, there is no room to do justice to the fullness of Gibbins' argument and I propose to concentrate only on selected aspects of it, especially his use of the American example.

In 1971 Smiley thought Canada's "political federalism", as illustrated, for instance, by the federal-provincial conference, unable to resolve authoritatively persistent conflicts of a sectional or, as he prefers, territorial nature. In a later article he expressed it this way: "Canada cannot effectively be governed unless Ottawa is the focus of significant popular identifications and the political arena in which the interests of powerful groups are resolved."[5] Gibbins is more dramatic because he uses the political modernization model as backdrop and from its perspective Canada seems to suffer a case of arrested development. The modernization model contemplates favourably the eventual triumph of national over local loyalties, of national integration over localism, and associates it with such conditions as industrialization, urbanization and so on. In Gibbins' words, "as industrialization and urbanization occur, citizens are mobilized into the national political community". He argues that while the United States' development illustrates the model, Canada's defies it, and he seeks and finds an explanation for this in the two countries' respective political institutions.[6]

Turning first to the American founding Gibbins points to the many national elements of the new constitution, for example, the central government's power to act directly on the people, in order to demonstrate how it could become an agent of nationalization. He also points to the ways in which territorial or state interests were represented directly within the national government, for example, in the Senate and the selection of the president. Of course these two particular features, which James Madison and Alexander Hamilton cited as federal elements of a constitution they considered a hybrid or combination, have been altered. Senators are no longer chosen by state legislatures and the Electoral College is directed by the popular vote. In modern jargon, two provincialist intrastate features have been transformed into centralist ones, and presumably it is only in the latter guise that they have worked their nationalizing or centralizing magic. In the Canadian founding, by contrast, Gibbins naturally finds little in the way of intrastate federalism or even nationalizing inspiration and finds instead a heavy emphasis on interstate federalism, evidenced chiefly by the array of legislative powers awarded Parliament. Interestingly he thinks that the "Senate's powers and composition received far greater attention in the Confederation debates than did the division of powers between the provincial and national governments."[7] Smiley cites Peter Waite to this effect at length.[8] Most proponents of intrastate federalism like to think that the Fathers had their cause in mind. But the Fathers did not. The wrangle on the proposed Senate was over patronage.[9]

Gibbins pursues his comparison broadly, but I wish to concentrate on his analysis of the two country's representative bodies and the conclusions he draws from it. He describes how both the design of Congress and the comparatively weaker discipline of American political parties work to promote effective representation of local interests. This has deprived state governments of the monopoly they would naturally presume to have on that task and thereby enhanced the central government's position relative to them: "Effective territorial representation has been combined with, and indeed has helped to produce, a strong and relatively centralized national government."[10] By contrast of course he finds that the parliamentary system in Ottawa and its well-disciplined parties are not particularly well suited to the purpose of local representation and he does not choose to celebrate this difference. Indeed he considers it fatal. The central government is too brittle. The parliamentary form inclines towards majoritarianism, towards concentration of power, not the diffusion of power that permits representation and accommodation of local interests. The cacophony of local interests juggled within Washington's fold is replaced here by federal-provincial relations. Provincial governments are the chief representatives and defenders of local interests, not federal politicians from the various provinces, and this has deprived the central government of considerable authority, but not power. Indeed power is so concentrated in Ottawa, Gibbins argues, that provincial governments are among the few effective checks on it. This only enhances their reputation and tarnishes Ottawa's. Thus the Canadian marriage of federalism and parliamentary government that some have hailed as unique and exciting is in Gibbins' view a failure.[11] It is a failure because the parliamentary side dominates, preventing the federal side (at least the intrastate federalism he champions) from working the way it ought to, that is, the way it does in the United States.

In his concluding chapter Gibbins follows Smiley in advocating that the central government be rearranged to incorporate representatives of regional interests. His suggestions include an elected Senate designed to "break the premiers' monopolistic role as regional spokesmen in national politics" and changes in parliamentary practice that would enable legislators to break party ranks with impunity on issues of importance to their locale.[12] Both Smiley and Gibbins recall congressional practices and Gibbins is aware of Canadian prejudices on this score. He refers to the irony of looking to the American model for guidance in politics, the one area in which Canadians might be thought to have resisted successfully the giant's influence. But he counsels receptiveness: "Dogmatic resistance to American influence here may condemn Canadian politics to a future of territorial conflict and national disintegration."[13] There is another irony he fails to mention, namely, that of turning to the very form of government the Canadian Fathers affected to despise. Everyone knows the extent of their distaste for the states' rights tradition of American federalism. Their aversion to congressional government, or republicanism, to use their term, ought to be recalled as well.

Gibbins favours American republicanism because it is consistent with the intrastate federalism he values so much. The founders preferred parliamentary government, among other reasons precisely because it is not consistent with the politics of intrastate federalism. They did not take their preference for granted. W.L. Morton has demonstrated that the question of parliamentary versus republican government was not settled in pre-Confederation British North America, even though the adoption of responsible government by the colonies in 1848 marked an important step in the direction of the parliamentary model. Not until 1860, twelve years after responsible government was adopted, did the Nova Scotia Assembly permit the executive the initiative in introducing money bills, a practice well established in Britain. Moreover it was not clear that responsible, parliamentary government worked well in "small and fiercely democratic societies" containing few men of independent means. Morton cites the observation of Nova Scotia's Lieutenant Governor Mulgrave that intense partisanship, electoral corruption and greedy struggles for local benefits marked politics in that colony. Mulgrave sought a remedy in conditions more amenable to parliamentary virtue, namely, Maritime union. The larger political arena created by union, he thought, would diffuse the personal rivalries and selfish local sentiment inimical to the proper functioning of responsible government. According to Morton, the Lieutenant Governor's views anticipated one of Confederation's chief features, the "deliberate reinforcement" of the choice of British parliamentary institutions as the form of government for the new nation.[14]

There are also the elective upper houses to consider. Donald Creighton referred to the new elective second chamber in the Province of Canada in 1856 as the "last victory" for congressional enthusiasts and stressed the shift in opinion favouring parliamentary institutions that followed. But he conceded that it was popular among Macdonald's own Conservative colleagues as well as the Rouges and the Western Clear Grits.[15] Republican sympathies had always formed an important part of the views of the latter two groups. Frank Underhill drew attention to a series of editorials in the *Globe* in 1859 on the deteriorating political situation in the Province of Canada. The newspaper placed part of the blame on the "excessive influence" of the executive over the legislature, a feature prominently illustrated in the financing of railways and public works. It concluded that its favourite remedy for the Province's political ills, representation by population, was inadequate in the face of this problem and proposed instead a federation of the two Canadas bound together by a written constitution with explicit checks on executive spending power.[16]

Five years later at the Quebec Conference George Brown, *Globe* editor, was still concerned about the British cabinet system's tendency to undermine the independence of the legislature and to that end sought for Upper Canada a constitution based somewhat on the model of an American state government. Upper Canada, he maintained, did not want an "expensive" local government that took up "political matters". He urged instead a government of one chamber, headed by a lieutenant governor appointed by the central government. Its members would be elected on a fixed date every three years, and its executive officers, the number specified, would also serve three years. Hence "no power of dissolution", the convention critical to responsible government. George E. Cartier's response to these recommendations was to the point: "I entirely differ with Mr. Brown. It introduces in our local bodies republican institutions."[17]

The issue of parliamentary versus republican government was not settled before Confederation. It was settled by Confederation and, as indicated above, in the face of some sympathy for the republican alternative, a fact that undoubtedly contributed to the founders' preoccupation with the question. Not content simply to argue the merits of the parliamentary form, the Fathers vigorously attacked its republican rival. This amounted to an attack on American government, the greatest republican example at hand. In the Father's view the American government was defective in two major respects: it was democratic; and its executive was poorly designed. On the democratic point we find Cartier distinguishing the government of the Quebec Resolutions from its American counterpart. The American republic, he asserted, was a democracy. Indeed the Americans had founded their nation for the very purpose of "carrying out and perpetuating democracy on this continent". Democracy meant mob rule as opposed to the rule of legitimate authority, a phenomenon Cartier attributed to the impact of universal suffrage. According to him, even leading Americans were prepared to concede that universal suffrage had unduly extended governmental powers and subjected them to the demands of popular will. By contrast, the government of the Quebec scheme was designed to perpetuate the monarchical principle. In fact that principle was its "leading feature".[18]

D'Arcy McGee expanded upon this theme with a clarity even greater than that of contemporary observers of Canadian political authority like Edgar Z. Friedenberg.[19] McGee was alive to the "spirit of universal democracy", and especially America's assumption that its democratic principles would eventually overwhelm the whole of the North American continent. This alarmed him because he identified democracy with excessive liberty and insufficient authority. He supposed that the two great things men in free governments aim at are liberty and permanence. Permanence required authority, in particular, a "high central authority" and respect for the law for its own sake or the "virtue of civil obedience". In McGee's opinion there was more than enough liberty in British America, but insufficient authority. Thus he was not displeased that the proposed constitution "errs on the side of too great conservatism". Too much authority was hardly dangerous in light of the "downward tendency in political ideas which characterizes this democratic age".[20]

McGee favoured the full panoply in British parliamentary practices: royal authority, ministerial responsibility, a nominative upper house, full and free representation in the lower house and an independent judiciary. The monarchical principle he considered peculiarly essential to the maintenance of civil authority. It fostered particular virtues: "humility, self-denial, obedience, holy fear". But these were not nineteenth-century virtues; they were not "plants indigenous to the soil of the New World". The New World was characterized by the qualities of pride, self-assertion and pretension. In political life they encouraged a "good-as-you" feeling and supposed an "unreal equality" between youth and age, subject and magistrate, the vicious and the virtuous. By championing the older virtues the government of the proposed union snubbed the spirit of the age and its political science. But McGee was confident that political science was changing, that it was less impressed by the democratic prejudice than it had been in the days when Alexander Hamilton was abused for advocating a "solid and coercive union" with "complete sovereignty in Congress". Presumably the age likewise was changing.[21]

The Canadians preferred a form of government that limited popular influence. McGee spoke in abstractions, referring to what we would now call the "political culture dimension." Macdonald simply explained that the Quebec scheme eschewed universal suffrage and instead followed the principle that classes and property be represented as well as numbers.[22] This addressed the problem of mob rule, replacing the messy diffusion of power in the American model with a tighter, more ordered and confined practice. There remained the other half of Macdonald's mob rule and presidential despotism thesis. He subjected the office of the American chief executive to a peculiar attack by insisting on comparing it with that of the sovereign's representative in a parliamentary government rather than the office of prime minister. Hence the bizarre charge that the American president was not obliged constitutionally to consult his cabinet.[23] It is hard to believe that Macdonald did not understand how differently the two forms of government serve to check their respective executives. Other colonists did. In 1859 William Young, leader of the Reform party in Nova Scotia, in a letter to the British colonial Secretary, the Duke of Newcastle, attributed the colonies' rejection of the "written constitutions of the United States" to the hope that they, too, would enjoy the "vigorous Executives sustained by popular sentiment" characteristic of parliamentary government in Britain.[24]

It might be argued that Cartier and Macdonald were unaware of this potential for an efficacious and responsible executive at a time when the conventions of cabinet government were not wholly settled. Yet they and others had urged that one merit of the proposed union was its capacity to overcome the political deadlock in which the Province of Canada found itself. The strong government of cabinet rule permitted by legislative majorities, seemingly unattainable in the Province, was precisely what they hoped a larger union would provide. Their warning of the dangers of presidential despotism served effectively to draw attention away from this point, and also from the fact that the Americans demonstrated a much greater concern for the balance of power within governments than they did. As James Madison put it, while the government must be able to control the governed, it must also be designed to control itself. The key to this self-control is contained in *The Federalist's* exposition of the doctrine of the separation of powers.

In contrast to the Americans' abiding concern with the "interior structure" of government as a guard against usurpation of power, Macdonald advanced only one structural precaution to guard parliamentary government against it, namely, the accountability of ministers to Parliament. However, it is not clear that he considered this sufficient. He had observed that as part of the British Empire, the new nation would benefit from the example of Britain's free institutions, exemplary laws and administration, and able statesmen. This last in particular he described as "one great advantage" of the British connection, arguing that Canadian public men would be inspired by the same high principles guiding those in public life in the mother country.[25] It is tempting to relate this contention to a recognition that parliamentary government stands in greater need of good men. Certainly it differs markedly from the American effort to design a government that avoids the need for statesmen. Madison had related the substitution of structure for dependence on the appearance of good men to a rather dim view of human nature. Referring to the need to control the ambitious attempts of office-holders to extend their power, he remarked that the devices he had prescribed might reflect on men's natures. Yet what is government, he asked, if not the greatest reflection on human nature. Men are not angels and are not governed by angels and certain precautions in addition to election were needed to compensate for the "defect of better motives" among them.

The doctrine of separate powers, rightly understood, was such a precaution. Madison explained it so clearly: "The interest of the man must be connected with the constitutional rights of the place." By identifying the personal interest of the office-holder with the well-being of the office, and affording him powers sufficient to protect it, the system ensures that he will protect it. His self-regard is too dependent upon the office's integrity. The result is maintenance of the proper balance among the three great branches of government. They become "opposite and rival interests" confronting and checking one another in the course of their encounters. Thus Madison not only compensates for men's self-interestedness, he relies on it, judging it to be more dependable than political virtue. Left to themselves men can always be trusted to pursue their own self-interest. The trick is to use that pursuit to the advantage of the public interest.[26] Oblivious of this line of reasoning, parliamentary government concentrates the exercise of political power, as Madison himself observed: "The federal legislature of the proposed constitution will possess a part only of that supreme authority which is vested completely in the British Parliament; and which, with a few exceptions, was exercised by the colonial assemblies and the Irish legislature."[27] Parliaments offer the leading parliamentarians who control them some room for statesmanship.

The Canadians prized parliamentary government for its strength, order and authority. They repudiated its republican rival for lacking authority, for yielding to the "clamorous mob", for fragmenting power, in a word, for weakness. How, then, did they think to marry the "republican nature of a federation", as Morton puts it, to parliamentary institutions? His view is that they never really grasped the contradiction inherent in the idea of divided sovereignty. Be that as it may, it is useful to contemplate what they were combining, for Morton was surely correct to refer to a combination. The founders spoke about combining the principle of "unity of action" or the principle of legislative union and the federal principle. Thus the Quebec scheme was not a federal system simply but a mix of two opposing principles or elements. Unity of action subsisted in the central government, not only because of its array of legislative powers but because it was parliamentary. Alexander Galt made this point in his Sherbrooke speech when he contrasted the new central government with the defective government of the Province of Canada. The "inherent defect" of the latter was that it tried to combine *within itself* two contradictory principles, federalism and unity of action. In recognition of the federal principle, it gave the two sections equal representation in both houses of the legislature. At the same time, members from both sections were expected to deal "as one" with all matters, general and local, much as a parliament of a legislative union. In the event, the federal element proved overwhelming, paralyzing government. The Quebec scheme, he continued, remedied this by modifying the federal element of the new national government in such a way that it no longer seriously interfered with unity of action. The scheme introduced representation by population as the basis of the lower house and reverted to nomination for the upper house. Nomination subverted even the half-hearted federal mechanism of sectional representation in the second chamber.[28]

The central government was the new government and, for the Canadian delegates at least, it was the closest they had ever come to the British model. Macdonald insisted on the purest imitation possible, expecting to derive from it the "strength of a legislative and administrative union". Sectional representation in the Senate was the potential spoiler but, as indicated, nomination effectively neutralized that, and I suspect Macdonald shrewdly guessed it would. He certainly played the nomination versus election issue very nicely. Waite also thinks Macdonald not unhappily foresaw how weak the Senate would be but for another reason, namely, assumption of its alleged role as regional spokesman by the cabinet.[29] Either way it is not clear why Gibbins says that Macdonald "was a firm believer that territorial interests should and must be represented *within the institutions* of the national government rather than *to those institutions* by provincial governments'', citing Garth Stevenson as an authority.[30] The last thing the Canadian delegates wanted was the petty and paralyzing intrusion of local concerns in their proposed new national forum. They were looking for something close to a transformation of political discourse at the national level and that would have been impossible if national politicians were encouraged to define themselves as spokesmen for local interests. The Maritime delegates who were strong legislative unionists even dared to look to an end to partisanship.[31]

The hopes entertained for the style of politics at the national level were consistent with the place of the other element in the combination or ''happy medium'', the federal principle. Again the founders preference for something closer to interstate rather than intrastate federalism is clear. In Macdonald's mind, matters of general interest were quite separate from matters of ''private right and sectional interest'' and best dealt with separately. Experience in the Province of Canada proved that. Local matters in particular, it seemed, distracted men from proper consideration of general questions. The federal principle eliminated the distraction by permitting ''liberty of action for the different sections'' or ''sectional freedom''. Macdonald gave some idea of what this might mean by referring to each province's ''power and means of developing its own resources and aiding its own progress after its own fashion and in its own way''.[32] Brown spent considerably more time on the importance of the local level of government but his reasoning followed Macdonald's. He did stress the obvious advantages of returning the Province of Canada to its constituent parts. Beyond that, however, he argued that placing local matters under local control would raise the tone of national politics. When questions of local and national interest were lumped together, the former tended to overshadow the latter. Certainly in the past local questions had stirred the most ''hostile feelings'' and ''hot feuds'' among members of the Province's legislature. By removing such questions from the agenda of the new Parliament, the proposed scheme promised an end to petty discord and substitution of a more constructive atmosphere for deliberation in which representatives could turn their attention to the "great questions of national interest". It also freed them from persistent identification as sectional partisans. Local questions inevitably put a premium on loyalty to place. Members compelled to champion their own section in disputes over local matters invariably found themselves most unpopular elsewhere, and as a result denied national success in public life. Brown especially knew whereof he spoke. Separation of local from national questions remedied this by enabling politicians concerned with interests common to the country to appeal to electors everywhere. It enabled them to aspire to a national reputation.[33]

In these accounts the connection between the federal and the local is quite clear. Matters of "private right and sectional interest" were local matters and the federal principle meant local governments with the freedom to deal with them. It also meant confining local matters to this level. Galt made this clear when he explained that the Quebec scheme weakened the federal principle by giving effect to it at the local level only, and as much as possible removing it from the national sphere. In his words the scheme partook of the federal character in relation to local measures "as far as necessary" while preserving the union in relation to matters common to all. It relegated federalism to the parts.[34]

For the founders politics at the national level was to be a politics concerned with the "great questions", mostly economic, in which everyone had a stake. They conceived of a national political discourse liberated from local concerns, especially the dangerous kind having to do with nationality. Interstate federalism, a new name for the old fix on divided jurisdiction, supplied the key to this possibility. Cairns' reference to national government in the interstate model as "an instrument for expressing and fulfilling a set of national aspirations clearly differentiated from the more localized goals of the lesser communities and their governments" captures the older view. He observes that national government in the intrastate model, by contrast, is "an arena for the open clash of regional interests and their attempted harmonization within central institutions". Thus the substance of politics in the interstate and intrastate versions differs. This point becomes clearer in his "caution" when he warns that the intrastate model might serve to "inhibit national perspectives, country-wide definitions of issues, egalitarianism, and the sense that Canada is more than the sum of its parts".[35] Intrastate federalism, even the centralist version, risks an identifiable national discourse by promoting a self-consciously regional one. It unavoidably promotes while it accepts and placates regionalism, in which case the remedy exacerbates, not cures, the political ill.

There are differences of opinion on this point. Richard Simeon seems to share Cairns' concern that intrastate federalism could in fact inhibit national perspectives, although Simeon begins by reversing the notion of what national is generally taken to mean. In his "Regionalism and Canadian Political Institutions", Simeon states that the conventions of cabinet government and strict party discipline make it difficult for the federal government to "reflect within itself" the country's regional diversity. Of parliamentarians generally and cabinet ministers he writes: "For both, the system of incentives in Ottawa leads them to concern themselves with national matters, to stress issues in federal jurisdiction, and to stress their loyalty to the party—all in contradistinction to a view of themselves as spokesmen of a region, or of a province or provincial government." The founders' response was that release from the burden of being regional spokesmen, release from sectional partisanship, is precisely the condition of national politics. Otherwise the distinction between local and national collapses.

Simeon begins to collapse this distinction between local and national. Organizing the central government around regional interests, he states, means incorporating them directly into national policy-making. Regional interests become the stuff of national politics, so to speak. Yet the defenders of these interests, because they are members of a national forum, will be capable of greater detachment than, say, provincial government spokesmen are now. The result is to tame regional considerations, and at the same time encourage coalitions of interests on non-regional issues; class issues perhaps. As Simeon acknowledges in his case for intrastate federalism, his argument recalls

John Porter's point about the restraining or distracting effect of federalism on the development of a national, class-based politics.[36] But then Simeon does not use the American example to make his case. Smiley and Gibbins do, and since American politics is not exactly class-based they hold out no expectations of this kind. Smiley does suggest that restoring the Canadian "balance" to the "intrastate alternative" will encourage political dispute on non-territorial as opposed to territorial issues. But non-territorial issues—conservationism, consumer policy, science policy and so on—are not necessarily class issues. Essentially Smiley and Gibbins hold out the model of American politics, that is, a national politics constituted by the "open clash of regional interests and their attempted harmonization within central institutions".

Examination of contemporary opinion on intrastate federalism in the light of the Confederation debate gives rise to two considerations. The first is that *the debate on interstate versus intrastate federalism is in part a debate on parliamentary versus republican government*. It is about the relative merits of two forms of government, not the extent of liberty available in large and small states. Both are popular forms of government, both are indirect democracies based on the principle of representation. These are essential likenesses. But their interior structures differ radically and give rise to different characteristics. The Canadian Fathers described parliamentary government in the following manner: undemocratic yet popularly responsive; animated by the principle of unity of action; capable of great strength, vigour and speed; authoritative, possibly because of the monarchical element; majoritarian. To some, as we have seen, a central government on these lines spells insensitivity to regionalism and consequently invites rampant provincialism.

Critics of the parliamentary model recommend a move to the congressional system on the ground that it provides many more opportunities for regional representation. This it certainly does, in part simply because it is more extensively representative. More officials are elected and one of the legislative bodies is constituted on the basis of equal state representation. But congressionalism or republican government, as the Canadians were happy to point out, has other important features. It replaces the principle of unity with diffusion of power, its procedures are complex and cumbersome, it is more democratic and less authoritative. Congressional government suits the requirements of the centralist intrastate mode. Yet it is a particular form of government that was designed to resolve a number of political problems, not just regionalism. The American Senate, as noted above, is constituted by equal state representation. It stood service as a federal offering to the states. As Madison pointed out, however, it also serves the purpose of restraining the inherent aggressiveness of the legislative branch in popular governments. The House of Representatives and the Senate, differently constituted, cannot be expected to share the same interests and act as one. Thus the legislative branch is divided against itself and weakened.[37] Those who advocate an elected Senate here in response to regionalism ought to ponder this point. The Canadian founders' insistence on comparing the two rival forms of government should be recalled, so that we do not misunderstand what is at stake in proposals for reform of our central institutions.

The second consideration is a federal one. The Fathers combined the principle of legislative union at the centre with the federal principle in the parts. They combined the power of union and the freedom of federalism, that is, the greater liberty associated with popular governments in small states. The practical basis of the combination was the distinction they drew between "national" and "local". But we no longer mean what they meant by those terms. Under the category of national they appropriated all the great financial questions as well as such obvious matters as defence, in part because they supposed commerce one area where men could deliberate, untroubled by their diverse nationalities. Matters pertinent to nationality and the inner life of the community they were inclined to leave to the local level, to the extent that that was possible.

Today the level of national politics to which the Fathers were content to aspire is deemed unsatisfactory by many. Thus the old division between national and local is unsettled. Gibbins illustrates this when he explains his choice of the term "territorial". He rejects sectionalism as arcane and regionalism because it has both good and bad connotations. Hence his choice of "territorial politics", a "neutral" expression that he defines as the "intrusion of territorial cleavages into national politics".[38] His definition excludes items like class and ethnicity, two other possible bases for political organization. What this means for Quebec is not clear. However, Gibbins' definition certainly affects oddly the notion of national politics, since there can be few territorially based economic activities of real importance that are not somehow national matters. I suppose the neutrality of the term consists in the fact that it offers no clues as to the substance of national or regional politics.

Richard Simeon's analysis of the term "regionalism" indicates the myriad of conceptual difficulties associated with the concept.[39] It seems presumptious, therefore, to choose between interstate and intrastate federalism without first rethinking the distinction between the national and the local. This is obvious in the case of interstate federalism since it is based on a distribution of legislative jurisdictions. But it is equally so in the case of intrastate federalism. There is little point in talking about representing and accommodating regional interests within a newly designed central government if such interests are better dealt with at the local level to begin with. If the distincton offered by the Fathers is no longer appropriate, it is time to develop a new one.

NOTES

[1] Canada, *Senate Debates*, 24 February 1982, p. 3701.

[2] Alan Cairns, "From Interstate to Intrastate Federalism in Canada," Discussion Paper No. 5 (Kingston, Institute of Intergovernmental Relations, 1979), pp. 3-5.

[3] Donald Smiley, "The Structural Problem of Canadian Federalism," *Canadian Public Administration* (Fall 1971), pp. 328, 341-2.

[4] Ibid., p. 343.

[5] Donald Smiley, "Territorialism and Canadian Political Institutions," *Canadian Public Policy* (Autumn 1977), p. 456.

[6] Roger Gibbins, *Regionalism: Territorial Politics in Canada and the United States* (Toronto, Butterworths, 1982), pp. 1, 4.

[7] Ibid., pp. 59, 8-11.

[8] Smiley, "Territorialism and Canadian Political Institutions," p. 451.

[9] Joseph Pope, *Confederation: Being a Series of Hitherto Unpublished Documents Bearing on the British North America Act* (Toronto, The Carswell Co. Ltd., 1895), pp. 84-7.

[10] Gibbins, *Regionalism*, p. 77.

[11] See for example W.R. Lederman's "The British Parliamentary System and Canadian Federalism" in R.M. Burns (ed.), *One Country or Two?* (Montreal, McGill-Queen's, 1971).

[12] Gibbins, *Regionalism*, p. 194.

[13] Ibid., p. 196.

[14] W.L. Morton, *The Critical Years: The Union of British North America, 1857-1873* (Toronto, McClelland and Stewart, 1964), p. 82.

[15] Donald Creighton, *John A. Macdonald, The Young Politican* (Toronto, Macmillan, 1952), pp. 319-20.

[16] Frank Underhill, "Some Aspects of Upper Canadian Radical Opinion in the Decade before Confederation" in his *In Search of Canadian Liberalism* (Toronto, Macmillan, 1960), pp. 60-5.

[17] Joseph Pope, *Confederation*, pp. 74-5.

[18] *Parliamentary Debates on the Subject of the Confederation of the British North American Provinces* (Quebec, Parliamentary Printers, 1865), pp. 59, 62.

[19] Edgar Z. Friedenberg, *Deference to Authority* (White Plains, M.E. Sharpe, 1980).

[20] *Parliamentary Debates*, p. 143.

[21] D'Arcy McGee, "Speech at Cookshire, County of Compton, December 22, 1864" in his *Speeches and Addresses Chiefly on the Subject of British-American Union* (London, 1865), pp. 130-2.

[22] *Parliamentary Debates*, pp. 32, 35, 39.

[23] Ibid., p. 33.

[24] Morton, *The Critical Years*, p. 82.

[25] *Parliamentary Debates*, p. 44.

[26] James Madison, *The Federalist* (Modern Library Edition; New York, Random House, 1937), No. 51, pp. 335-7.

[27] Ibid., No. 52, p. 346.

[28] Alexander Galt, *Speech on the Proposed Union of the British North American Provinces* (Montreal, 1864), p. 4.

[29] Peter B. Waite, *The Life and Times of Confederation* (Toronto, University of Toronto Press, 1962), p. 116.

[30] Gibbins, *Regionalism*, p. 781.

[31] See for example Charles Tupper, *A Letter to the Right Honourable the Earl of Carnarvon, Principal Secretary of the State for the Colonies* (London, 1866), p. 38.

[32] *Parliamentary Debates*, p. 41.

[33] Ibid., pp. 94-6.

[34] Galt, *Sherbrooke Speech*, p. 4.

[35] Cairns, "From Interstate to Intrastate Federalism in Canada," p. 21.

[36] Richard Simeon, "Regionalism and Canadian Political Institutions" in R. Schultz, O.M. Kruhlak, J.C. Terry (eds.), *The Canadian Political Process*, 3rd ed. (Toronto, Holt, Rinehart & Winston, 1979), pp. 297-8.

[37] Madison, *The Federalist*, No. 48, No. 51 (p. 338).

[38] Gibbins, *Regionalism*, p. 5.

[39] Simeon, op. cit., pp. 293-6.